Ultimate Django for Web App Development Using Python

Build Modern, Reliable, and Scalable Production-Grade Web Applications with Django and Python

Leonardo Luis Lazzaro

www.orangeava.com

First published: January 2024

Published by: Orange Education Pvt Ltd, AVA™

Address: 9, Daryaganj, Delhi, 110002

ISBN: 978-81-96815-11-0

www.orangeava.com

About the Author

Born in Buenos Aires (la Ciudad de la Furia), Argentina, **Leonardo Luis Lazzaro** has always been fascinated by the idea of creating something out of nothing. His first contact with computers began at an early age, fueled by classic video games like Maniac Mansion and Monkey Island.

By the age of 12, Leonardo was already running his own Bulletin Board System (BBS) using ProBoardBBS Software, making him one of the youngest participants in online communities in Argentina. The BBS allowed him to meet other tech enthusiasts who introduced him to the programming world. His fascination with computer demos from the demoscene became a strong motivation for his continued discovery in programming.

Leonardo's academic path led him to study computer science at the prestigious Facultad de Ciencias Exactas, Universidad de Buenos Aires (UBA). He embarked on a Ph.D. in drug discovery, trying to apply computational skills to solve highly complex challenges on GPU simulations. However, his journey took a turn, leading him away from the academic world and becoming a Ph.D. dropout.

With 12 years of experience in Python, Leonardo has developed a profound expertise in this programming language. He is proficient in several Python frameworks, including Flask, Pyramid, Django, FastAPI, and others, showcasing his versatility and deep understanding of web development and application design.

About the Technical Reviewer

David Wobrock is a seasoned software engineer in the domains of backend web development, cybersecurity, and developer experience for multiple years. As an active contributor to Django, he plays a significant role in the Django Triage & Review team, showcasing his commitment to the advancement of the framework. Within Django, his primary focus revolves around contributions to the Django ORM and database migrations. Additionally, David is dedicated to maintaining open-source Python packages within the Django ecosystem.

He has worked for several startups, contributing not only to the growth of their technical stacks with reliable and secure software but also enhancing team efficiency by providing internal tools, guidelines, and best practices within the organizations. He believes that having the right tools, which make it easy for developers to do the right thing, is essential for building a great developer experience. Thus, when these tools are enablers for teams, they not only become more efficient but also build more reliable, scalable, and secure products.

Acknowledgements

Since childhood, I've always been fascinated by creating something from nothing. As a child, my imagination had intricate ideas, many of which magically took on lives of their own. This magical ability to turn thought into reality has stayed with me until now. This very power of creation has given life to this book.

This book is not a tribute to a single individual. Instead, it stands as a mark of respect and recognition for the open-source community. This work is a testament to the community's spirit of collaboration and shared knowledge.

To my readers, I offer this book as a guide into the world of Django. The book was crafted not from a place of ego but to contribute to our community's knowledge.

Special thanks to Nicolas Rebagliati for his review of Chapter 4. His insightful feedback and attention to detail have significantly enhanced the chapter, greatly contributing to the book's overall quality.

Preface

This book guides readers through building a comprehensive web application using Django and Python. Each chapter builds upon the last, from setting up a development environment to deploying a fully functional application running in a Kubernetes cluster.

Who this book is for

Beginners will find comprehensive coverage of foundational topics, while more experienced programmers will delve into advanced subjects, such as preventing double-form submissions and implementing offline pessimistic and optimistic locking techniques.

Download the code files

The complete code for this book is available on the GitHub repository at https://github.com/ava-orange-education/Ultimate-Django-for-Web-App-Development-Using-Python Each chapter's content is organized into separate branches, allowing you to practice alongside the book.

How to use the book

For beginners, a sequential reading of this book is recommended, as each chapter incrementally adds to the knowledge from the previous one. Experienced developers can directly jump to specific chapters or sections aligned with their interests or areas where they seek a more profound understanding.

As readers progress through the chapters of this book, the invitation is extended to share knowledge and contribute to the community. The hope is that this book enriches the reader's experience and is enjoyable to read, just as intended during the writing process.

What this book covers

This book guides readers through building a comprehensive web application using Django and Python. Each chapter builds upon the last, from setting up a development environment to deploying a fully functional application running in a Kubernetes cluster.

Chapter 1: Introduction to Django and Python

This chapter introduces Python and the Django framework, detailing Django's philosophy, the latest features in Django 4.2, and the compatibility of Python's syntax and semantics with Django.

Chapter 2: Setting Up Your Development Environment

This chapter guides you through establishing a reliable development environment, including Python installation, version management with pyenv, and creating isolated environments with poetry, equipping you for efficient Django development.

Chapter 3: Getting Started with Django Projects and Apps

This chapter introduces you to the initial steps of starting Django projects and apps. You'll learn about the Django project structure, the role of each component, Django's MVT architecture, configuring Django projects, and a brief introduction to Django's development server.

Chapter 4: Django Models and PostgreSQL

This chapter, focused on Django models and PostgreSQL integration, delves into creating models, Django's database API, ORM, queries, aggregations, and ensuring data integrity with model constraints.

Chapter 5: Django Views and URL Handling

This chapter explores the creation of views and management of URLs in Django, which are critical components in building the user interface of a Django application.

Chapter 6: Using the Django Template Engine

This chapter explores the Django Template Engine. Learn to create dynamic HTML content for Django apps, including static files, template inheritance, and custom template tags and filters.

Chapter 7: Forms in Django

This chapter covers handling and creating forms in Django, a crucial aspect of user interaction. It includes advanced form handling like ModelForms, Formsets, and techniques to prevent double form submission.

Chapter 8: User Authentication and Authorization in Django

This chapter provides a detailed look at Django's built-in tools for user authentication and authorization. It explains how to manage users and their access levels.

Chapter 9: Django Ninja and APIs

This chapter introduces Django Ninja, a modern framework for building APIs with Python and Django, focusing on creating efficient, robust, and scalable APIs.

Chapter 10: Testing with pytest

This chapter introduces pytest, guiding you through writing practical tests for Django apps. It covers testing views and forms, ensuring code reliability and maintainability.

Chapter 11: Deploying Django Applications with Gunicorn and Docker

This chapter discusses deploying Django applications using Gunicorn and Docker. It includes insights into creating Dockerfiles, configuring Kubernetes clusters, and adding liveness and readiness probes for application scaling.

Chapter 12: Final Thoughts and Future Directions

This concluding chapter reflects on building a Django task management app and looks ahead at Django's future. It discusses the Django ecosystem, additional tools, and staying updated with the community.

Get a Free eBook

We hope you are enjoying your recently purchased book! Your feedback is incredibly valuable to us, and to all other readers looking for great books.

If you found this book helpful or enjoyable, we would truly appreciate it, if you could take a moment to leave a short review with a 5 star rating on Amazon. It helps us grow, and lets other readers discover our books.

As a thank you, we would love to send you a free digital copy of this book, and a **30%** discount code on your next cart value on our official websites:

www.orangeava.com

www.orangeava.in (For Indian Subcontinent)

☑ **Here's how:**

Leave a review for the book on Amazon.

Take a screenshot of your review, and send an email to **info@orangeava.com** (it can be just the confirmation screen).

Once, we receive your screenshot, we will send you the digital file, within 24 hours.

Thank you so much for your support – it means a lot to us!

Downloading the code bundles and colored images

Please follow the links or scan the QR codes to download the **_Code Bundles and Images_** of the book:

https://github.com/ava-orange-education/Ultimate-Django-for-Web-App-Development-Using-Python

The code bundles and images of the book are also hosted on **_https://rebrand.ly/808c99_**

In case there's an update to the code, it will be updated on the existing GitHub repository.

Errata

We take immense pride in our work at **Orange Education Pvt Ltd,** and follow best practices to ensure the accuracy of our content to provide an indulging reading experience to our subscribers. Our readers are our mirrors, and we use their inputs to reflect and improve upon human errors, if any, that may have occurred during the publishing processes involved. To let us maintain the quality and help us reach out to any readers who might be having difficulties due to any unforeseen errors, please write to us at :

errata@orangeava.com

Your support, suggestions, and feedback are highly appreciated.

DID YOU KNOW

Did you know that Orange Education Pvt Ltd offers eBook versions of every book published, with PDF and ePub files available? You can upgrade to the eBook version at **www.orangeava.com** and as a print book customer, you are entitled to a discount on the eBook copy. Get in touch with us at: **info@orangeava.com** for more details.

At **www.orangeava.com**, you can also read a collection of free technical articles, sign up for a range of free newsletters, and receive exclusive discounts and offers on AVA™ Books and eBooks.

PIRACY

If you come across any illegal copies of our works in any form on the internet, we would be grateful if you would provide us with the location address or website name. Please contact us at **info@orangeava.com** with a link to the material.

ARE YOU INTERESTED IN AUTHORING WITH US?

If there is a topic that you have expertise in, and you are interested in either writing or contributing to a book, please write to us at **business@orangeava.com**. We are on a journey to help developers and tech professionals to gain insights on the present technological advancements and innovations happening across the globe and build a community that believes Knowledge is best acquired by sharing and learning with others. Please reach out to us to learn what our audience demands and how you can be part of this educational reform. We also welcome ideas from tech experts and help them build learning and development content for their domains.

REVIEWS

Please leave a review. Once you have read and used this book, why not leave a review on the site that you purchased it from? Potential readers can then see and use your unbiased opinion to make purchase decisions. We at Orange Education would love to know what you think about our products, and our authors can learn from your feedback. Thank you!

For more information about Orange Education, please visit **www.orangeava.com**.

Table of Contents

CHAPTER 1
Introduction to Django and Python

Introduction

Django has proven to be a robust and reliable framework, making it a popular and demanded tool in the Python ecosystem. Its high-quality standards and versatility enable the creation of unique web applications. In this chapter, we will dive into the core features of Python and explore how they interact with Django to promote effective web development. We will guide you through the philosophies of Django and explain why following them from the beginning is essential for a successful project. You will learn Python's language nature of dynamically and strongly typed language, which are fundamental to master. In addition, we will highlight the importance of Python's style guide, PEP 8, which guarantees the craft of clean, professional, and comprehensible code. As we conclude this chapter, a deeper understanding of the framework's features will increase your productivity.

Structure

In this chapter, we will cover the following topics:

- Introduction to Python

- Introduction to Django
- The Django Philosophy
- Notable features of Django 4.2
- Python Syntax and Semantics
- Python for Django
- Conclusion

Introduction to Python

Python is a strongly and dynamically typed language. Dynamically typed means that the type checking is being done at runtime and is strongly typed because it does not implicitly convert types under most circumstances.

	Statically Typed	**Dynamically Typed**
Strongly Typed	Java, C#, C++	Python, Ruby
Weakly Typed	C, C++	JavaScript, PHP

Table 1.1: *Categorization of programming languages based on two different typing characteristics*

Working with a dynamically typed language for the first time could be a shock for software developers used to statically typed, and it could feel incorrect. If you are coming from Java or C#, you must change your mindset and learn a new way of coding without private methods or interfaces in the traditional sense.

To contrast the difference between strong and weak typing, let's compare JavaScript and Python.

JavaScript:

```
console.log([] + []); // prints: ""

// things can get more interesting

console.log([] + {}); // prints: "[object Object]"

console.log({} + []); // prints: "[object Object]"
```

As you can see, JavaScript doesn't throw any errors, and the results of the operations are peculiar (and can seem unexpected).

However, with Python, things are quite different:

```
print([] + [])  # prints: []
```

```
print([] + {})  # Raises TypeError
```

Python's strongly typed nature leads to different behaviors than JavaScript's weakly-typed nature. The first operation returns expected, and refusing to convert values silently could prevent bugs.

Understanding variables as references

Python differs from other programming languages; it doesn't need to declare variable types beforehand. In Python, variables act as pointers to objects, not the objects themselves.

To understand how it works, check this simple Python code:

```
x=5

y=x  # At this point, x and y point to the same object 5.

print(id(x))  # outputs the integer 139691746963400

print(id(y))  # outputs the integer 139691746963400

x=10 # Now, x points to a different object, 10, but y still points to 5.

print(id(x))  # outputs 139691746963560
```

The id() function is used to print the unique identifier for objects that x and y are referencing. The first two call returns the same ID since x and y are referencing the same object. The third call of id prints a different id since x references a different object now.

Parameter passing

Python uses the **pass-by-object-reference** strategy when passing parameters. This approach means that references to the objects are passed and not the copies; this translates to cheaper function calls since object copy is expensive.

For immutable objects like strings or integers, Python doesn't modify the variable value beyond the function's scope:

```
def update_number(n: int) -> None:

   n = 10

x = 5

update_number(x)
```

```
print(x)  # prints: 5
```

However, extra caution is necessary when working with mutable objects. When a function or method changes a mutable object, it can produce unexpected side effects.

```
def update_list(numbers: list[int]) -> None:

   numbers.append(10)


x = [5]

update_list(x)

print(x) # prints: [5, 10]
```

Remember that the function directly interacts with the original object in memory, not a copy of it. Such behavior might not align with a programmer's intentions, and it's the reason for hard-to-detect bugs.

Mutability and immutability have been two approaches discussed for a long time. Immutability brings more safety and fewer side-effects to your code and therefore makes it easier to reason about. However, mutability can be interesting for performance and flexibility during development. Both approaches are valid and can co-exist. You will have to decide how to tackle your problems.

Interfaces or protocols

In Python, you can create an abstract base class as an interface for implementing subclasses. The ABC can specify some methods that any child classes must implement.

```
from abc import ABC, abstract method

class AbstractAnimal(ABC):

    @abstractmethod

    def make_sound(self) -> str:

        pass


class Dog(AbstractAnimal):

    def make_sound(self) -> str:
```

```
        return "Woof!"
```

Sometimes, you may not find any abstract base classes in Python codebases, and the contract could be implicit. This concept is often called duck typing - *If it walks like a duck and it quacks like a duck, then it must be a duck*. With duck typing, the type or class of an object is less important than its methods and properties. Duck typing enables a polymorphism where the developer doesn't require the object to be of a specific type but only to implement certain methods or properties. The implicit interface allows developers to replace objects with different implementations as long as the replacements fulfill the same contract, i.e., they have all the required methods and properties.

Duck typing is an inherent feature of Python and many other dynamically typed languages where type-checking is done at runtime. The principle allows for greater flexibility in code, but it also places more responsibility on the developer to ensure that objects are properly used.

Standard modules

Python's standard library is vast and includes numerous modules. Given its broad scope, covering all of it in an introductory segment is impossible. This section will show the most common modules used while working with a Django project.

Let's start with pathlib, an object-oriented module to handle filesystem paths. One of its common usages is in the settings of the project.

Let's see an example:

```
from pathlib import Path

# BASE_DIR is the project root (the directory containing manage.py)

BASE_DIR = Path(__file__).resolve().parent.parent

# This is how you would define the location of the static files directory

STATIC_ROOT = BASE_DIR / 'staticfiles'
```

As you can see, the `/` is the operator to join paths; the pathlib module was introduced in Python 3.4, and it offers a great way to handle the filesystem.

JavaScript Object Notation (JSON) is a universally recognized format for storing and transferring data. Converting objects to JSON is named serialization, while the reverse is called deserialization. The standard library has a module that works with JSON, the **`json`** module.

Here are some examples of how to use the JSON module:

```
import json

# let's create a dictionary to represent a person

person = {

    "name": "John",

    "age": 30

 }

# serialization of the object

person_json = json.dumps(person)

# deserialization of the json, loads returns a dictionary

person_dict = json.loads(person_json)

assert person == person_dict
```

When the object is not serializable, dumps will raise **TypeError.** To make the object serializable, you must provide a function that translates the object to a dictionary and pass it using the default parameter.

```
class Person:

    def __init__(self, name, age):

        self.name = name

        self.age = age


def person_serializer(obj: Any) -> dict:

    if isinstance(obj, Person):

        return {"name": obj.name, "age": obj.age}

    raise TypeError(f"Type {type(obj)} not serializable")

p = Person("John", 30)

import json

json.dumps(p, default=person_serializer)
```

The datetime module is another helpful module to learn. While Django provides several utilities for handling date-times, there might be occasions when it's necessary to resort to the functionalities of the standard datetime module. Let's see an example of the helpful timedelta class:

```
from datetime import datetime, timedelta

# with Django it's important to always use datetime timezone aware

current_datetime = datetime.utcnow()

# let's add 7 days to the current_datetime

future_datetime = current_datetime + timedelta(days=7)
```

Python offers a plethora of other modules to explore. We advise readers to consult the official **Python documentation** for a deeper understanding of these modules.

Error handling

When converting a string to an integer, one has to anticipate that the string is not a valid integer. Thus, it is important to understand Python's error-handling system.

Python is a strongly typed language that will raise an exception when an error occurs, like trying to convert a string to an integer that is not valid. In this case, it raises a **`ValueError`** exception. But fear not, for Python equips us with a way to catch and address these exceptions: the **`try/except/else/finally`** block.

Here is how to work with exceptions with Python:

```
def get_integer(raw_number):

    try:

        # Code that might raise an exception

        res = int(raw_number)

    except ValueError:

        # What to do if the exception occurs

        print("Not possible to convert to integer")

        res = None
```

```
    else:
        # Code to run if no exception was raised
        print("String to integer was successfully converted.")
    finally:
        # Code to run no matter what
        if res is not None:
            print(f"The integer is: {res}")
    return res
```

In our **get_integer** function, we enclose our code within this block. We optimistically try to convert the string to int. If all goes well, we log an informational message to say we've converted the string. If Python can't convert the string, it raises the ValueError exception, which we promptly catch. We log an error message, and instead of returning a default integer, we play it safe and assign None to our result.

No matter what happened in the try or except blocks, we move on to the final block. Here, if an integer is converted, we log its value. The function returns the result - the integer if it was converted or None if it wasn't.

And that's how you deftly handle errors in Python. So, when the unexpected happens, your program doesn't falter but takes a different path.

In *Chapter 9, Django Ninja and* APIs, we will see that we don't need to create this function to convert payloads to Python objects. We will use serializers that convert payloads to their respective objects.

It's important to note that catching the generic Exception is not always a good practice since it can silence bugs and it make troubleshooting bugs harder. Try to always be explicit when catching exceptions. The application should fail and detect the error rather than have a silent bug hidden deep in the application codebase.

List comprehensions

Suppose you have a list named 'numbers' with integers. Your mission is to generate a new list, **mod_results**, where each element is the modulus of the corresponding number from **numbers** when divided by a certain value, say 5. You could march down the traditional path, using a for-loop to calculate the modulus for each number and then appending it to **mod_results**. It's a decent method, but Python has syntactic sugar to write these types of loops in one line and keep the code more concise.

In a single code, you can generate the result:

```
numbers = range(0, 100)

mod_results = [n % 5 for n in numbers]
```

The last line will generate a list of integers with the computation of modulus with 5 for each number from 0 to 100.

Python also allows the inclusion of conditionals in list comprehensions. Want to compute the modulus for only the even numbers? Here is how to do it:

```
even_mods = [n % 5 for n in numbers if n % 2 == 0]
```

This feature can turn your multi-line tasks into one-liners, making your code compact, and readable.

Sometimes, list comprehensions can become cumbersome, especially when dealing with complex logic or multiple levels of loops and conditionals. If you find your list comprehension stretching over numerous lines or becoming so tricky that it's hard to understand at a glance, it might be time to reconsider using it.

F-Strings

Python f-strings, introduced in Python 3.6, provide a concise and convenient method to embed expressions inside string literals. The expressions are evaluated at runtime and formatted using the curly braces {}.

```
name = "Pepe"

age = 30

greeting = f"Hello {name}, you are {age} years old."

print(greeting)

# Output: Hello Pepe, you are 30 years old.
```

The f-string evaluates the variables' name and age within the string.

You can also have an expression inside the f-strings:

```
x = 5
```

```
y = 10

result = f"The sum of {x} and {y} is {x + y}."

print(result)

# Output: The sum of 5 and 10 is 15.
```

f-strings also support format specifiers, allowing more control over the formatting of the embedded expressions.

```
import math

pi_value = f"Pi value up to 10 decimal places: {math.pi:.10f}"

print(pi_value)

# Pi value up to 10 decimal places: 3.1415926536
```

Type hinting

As mentioned before, Python is dynamically typed, and taking over someone else's code can sometimes feel like solving a puzzle, especially if you are new to Python. Since no type is specified, the developer needs to read the code to infer the types of the argument or the return type.

Type hinting in Python serves as a specification. With type hinting, you can annotate your function definitions to specify what type of arguments the function expects and what type it will return.

Let's see an example to understand how it works:

```
def hello_world(person_name: str) -> str:

    return f'Hello, {person_name}!!'
```

The parameter **person_name** is expected to have type str in this function, but it could receive anything during runtime. Using the syntax with a colon is a way of telling that the **hello_world** function expects a string. The arrow after the function arguments -> **str** is another type hint that specifies a string as the return type.

Python 3.10 introduced the pipe operator (|) or **PEP 604 syntax** as a more readable way to denote Union types.

```
from typing import Union
```

```
print(int | str == Union[int, str])  # This will print: True
```

As you can see the pipe operator is the same as the Union.

Let's look at another example:

```
def get_task_details(task_id: int | str) -> dict[str, str | int]:

    # dummy data

    tasks = {

        '001': {'title': 'Write report', 'priority': 1},

        '002': {'title': 'Plan meeting', 'priority': 2},

        '003': {'title': 'Review code', 'priority': 3},

    }

    return tasks[str(task_id)]
```

In the **get_task_details** function, the type hint **task_id: int | str** means that the function accepts an integer or a string as the task ID. The function returns a dictionary indicated by -> **dict[str, str | int].** This dictionary maps to a string for the task title and an integer for the task priority. If the task isn't found, the function raises a KeyError exception.

Even when using type hints, Python is still a dynamically typed language. The interpreter doesn't enforce these types of hints during the code execution. Therefore, you can still pass arguments of any type to your function, and it will attempt to execute it. Python won't raise any errors because the argument type doesn't match the type hint.

Type hints serve as a form of documentation that can make the code more understandable and maintainable, and when used with a type checker like mypy (https://mypy-lang.org/), it can make it more robust.

Coding style

Writing Python code is not only understanding the syntax but also how the code is crafted and structured. Think of Python's style guidelines, glorified in PEP 8, as the dress code of the Python world–followed in writing clean, professional, and easy-to-read code.

Some of these guidelines include:

Indentation: Python sets the bar at four spaces per indentation level–not two, not eight, but four. Keeping to this rule results in a neat, organized code.

```
def example_function(arg1: Any, arg2: Any) -> None:
    if arg1 is not None and arg2 is not None:
        print("Both arguments are not None.")
```

Line Length: Keep lines within a limit of 129 at most. The line length limit facilitates reading.

Whitespace: Spaces around binary operators aren't just empty areas–they are bridges connecting parts of your code, making it easier to comprehend.

Variable names should be declarative, and the use of single characters should be avoided–they should be clear and self-explanatory.

```
# Better
box_cost = box_size**5 + 9
difference = (box_size + box_cost) * (box_size - box_cost)
# Avoid
box_cost=box_size**5+9
difference=(box_size+box_cost)*(box_size-box_cost)
```

By convention, function names should be lowercase letters, with underscores used as links between words to enhance legibility, known as **snake_case**.

```
# Preferred
def calculate_mean(numbers: list[int]) -> int:
    return sum(numbers) // len(numbers)
# Discouraged
def calc_m(n):
    return sum(n) // len(n)
```

Pairing well with these style guidelines are linters; the most common ones are flake8, pylint, and ruff. Linters ensures that your code stays clean, consistent, and up to the high-quality standards set by the Python community. A common practice in enterprise projects is to have a continuous integration pipeline with linters to check the code; this will prevent any developer from adding code, not PEP8 compatible.

As the wisdom of **PEP 8** puts it, A *Foolish Consistency is the Hobgoblin of Little Minds*. Remember to always find the right balance. Sometimes style guide recommendations just aren't applicable.

But it's important to remember that coding is as much an art as a science. While adherence to best practices is highly encouraged, there are moments when deviating slightly from a rule could lead to a more comprehensible piece of code.

It's all about finding the sweet spot–the perfect blend of consistency and adaptability.

Introduction to Django

Django is a high-level Python web framework loaded with features that allow you to immerse yourself in developing your application's functionality. Django comes with batteries included, which means it offers a full-featured and complete framework to build sophisticated web applications. Django makes building better web apps more quickly and with less code easier.

The framework comes with session management, Object-Relational Mapping (ORM), an automatic admin interface, a template engine and many more. This reduces the need for multiple third-party libraries and accelerates the delivery process.

The community around Django is a thriving ecosystem, making it an excellent choice for building an enterprise application. Since it is widely used, most errors and common gotchas are easy to find on the internet. The project has high-quality standards and a robust codebase demonstrating open-source success.

Even when the framework lacks certain features, the community has created thousands of libraries to expand the framework functionality and most of which have been actively maintained for years.

You can see the true power of a dedicated and creative community when you look at how they've taken this framework to this point.

Django's high-security standards are highly recognized in critical industries like finance. But also, for media companies, managing high-volume and dynamic content is easy through Django's user-friendly content administration features.

Fast-paced startups with high delivery velocity leverage this framework to turn those brainwaves into reality.

The Django Philosophy

Django documentation explains philosophies that encourage good practices and help to standardize projects. Adhering to these philosophies will keep the project healthy and easy to maintain but also facilitate the onboarding process for new developers into projects by reducing the learning curve.

Don't repeat yourself

The Don't repeat yourself (DRY) is a general principle to prevent duplication. The principle seeks to prevent the repetition of the same code in different parts of a project, or the re-implementation of a feature already provided by the framework or library.

However, sometimes it's hard to understand what constitutes duplication fully. Remember that duplication can appear anywhere - in code, architecture, requirement documents, or user documentation.

Using a feature-rich framework like Django may paradoxically increase the risk of violating the DRY principle. For instance, suppose that you need to capitalize a word in a template. Using the built-in feature the framework provides will uphold the DRY principle. A deep knowledge of the framework's capabilities and features is a must to prevent breaking the DRY.

Loose coupling and High cohesion

In software development, two essential principles exist for creating maintainable, modular, and efficient code. These principles are Loose Coupling and High cohesion.

Loose coupling refers to how much the modules or components of your application are independent of each other. Having Loose coupling allows developers to make changes to modules without affecting others.

High cohesion refers to how modules are functionally related. This means that a module performs a specific task. High cohesion goes hand in hand with The Single Responsibility Principle (SRP), which dictates that a class or module should have only one reason to change.

Loose coupling ensures that changes in one class or module don't cascade issues in others. Loose coupling promotes code that is easy to read, maintain, and test. Think of it as the butterfly effect. If adjusting one line of code causes problems in a separate module or class, you likely have a case of tight coupling. The same happens when you try to write a unit test, and it's tough to write it. Hard-to-write tests are a code smell sometimes related to coupling.

Design patterns exist in software development, functioning similarly to blueprints. Developers often rely on these patterns to simplify communication and systematically address common problems. A service layer is a design pattern encapsulating the application's business logic. It separates business logic from the user interface and data access layers. An interface within the service layer ensures that business logic is readily accessible to various applications in your project.

Many Django projects lack a service layer bringing maintenance problems since those projects tend to have coupling problems. Having a service layer helps to reduce coupling and increases cohesion, as we will see in later chapters.

Building a fully decoupled and cohesive system is complex, and could be expensive. Engineers often have to cut corners or work with an existing codebase. But don't worry - in this book, we'll work with good practices to keep coupling low and cohesion high.

Software engineering is the art of finding the right balance in decisions to deliver the project on time; sometimes, engineers often have to cut corners. A wholly decoupled and cohesive system could be expensive, especially if the project needed to follow good practices.

Less code and quick development

Every Django application should embrace the idea that **less is more**. Applications should be lean and without a boilerplate. The less the code, the less chance of having a bug. This idea applies to every aspect of the Django framework, and where there is too much code, most likely, you are missing a framework feature.

With the **batteries-included** philosophy Django is a framework that allows developers to focus on the problem they need to solve and not on technicalities, eliminating the need to build everything from scratch, like authentication and admin interfaces.

Explicit is better than implicit

Code should not hide its behavior or reply to implicit operations. When reading the code, there should not be any hidden operations and the programmer's intent should be transparent. This principle is part of the Zen of Python (**PEP-20**).

For example, Django models should declare all their attributes and properties; behaviors should be explicit in the code. When a model contains a title attribute, and since all titles are required, it should be explicitly set so that no blank titles are allowed in the attribute properties.

Models: Include all relevant domain logic

Models should be responsible for storing and retrieving themselves; this idea uses the Active Record architectural pattern, from the Ruby on Rails framework. This principle also applies to the operation that can be performed on the object, and the business logic should live in the model.

However, it's important to note that this principle works well for small projects. Moving the business logic to a service layer is essential when the project grows.

It's common to see many Django projects without a service layer since the principles are too open for interpretation. Both solutions are valid, but using a service layer goes hand in hand with the loose coupling.

Having a service layer helps provide an interface from other modules and will make future refactors easier since other modules will rely on the service layer's interface.

As we go deep into the following chapters, we will see how to think about interfaces first and the service layer's importance.

Separate logic from the presentation on templates

Templates control presentation and the logic it implements should relate to presentation and nothing else. Having business logic in the templates is a mistake and must be avoided. However, having some basic logic to control how to present the data is expected.

The template engine provides features to prevent code duplication, so if your website contains a common header or footer, ensure you are using the template engine to extend or include templates.

Views

A Django view is a function or a class that receives input from users via the web browser, makes a process of the input and returns a response to the user's browsers.

Views must be as simple as possible; its responsibility should be to translate the request and call the service layer. Views should not contain any business logic. The view implementation should not depend on the template engine.

Caching

The cache framework of Django provides a common interface across different cache backends and an easy way to extend it. Currently, the Django caching framework supports Memcached, database caching, filesystem, and local memory.

The framework does not provide a built-in solution for caching with Redis, but it offers an easy way to extend it and use Redis for caching. A well-known and battle-proven 3rd party library exists for that (https://github.com/jazzband/django-redis).

Django 4.2 highlights

Django 4.2, a long-term support release (LTS), that guarantees security and data loss fixes for an expected timeframe of about three years.

This Django version is compatible with Python versions from 3.8 to 3.11. Support for Python 3.11 was introduced, starting with Django version 4.1.3. You could opt for the more conservative route with Python 3.10. However, with the release of several patches for 3.11, choosing the most recent Python version could be valuable given its speed improvement of 1.22x as per standard benchmark tests.

Support for psycopg3

Psycopg is a popular PostgreSQL adapter for the Python programming language. The release of the major version of Psycopg brings significant changes. Its asyncio support enables Django's integration of asyncio into its framework. Django allows you to create async views using the **async def**, and for WebSockets, you can use the channel's library. Django 4.1 has introduced asynchronous database interaction methods, indicated by an **a** prefix, and extended in 4.2 to include more methods. Here is an example of async ORM:

```
async for task in Task.objects.filter(title__startswith="Story"):

    creator = await task.creator.afirst()
```

Comments on columns and tables

You can now annotate columns and tables with comments using the new Field attributes db_comment and models Meta.db_table_comment options. The comments are directly within the database. The annotated columns or tables improve the documentation of the database schema for future developers in the project.

In-memory file storage

Sometimes, when unit tests on Django apps need to access the hard drive, it slows testing down. This version added new in-memory file storage to accelerate test runs and reduce development times.

Custom file storages

Now, you can configure all storage settings in a dictionary, enabling the setup of multiple custom file storage backends in one place. *Chapter 3, Getting Started with Django Projects and Apps* will show how to configure this setting for managing static files.

Updates in password validation

Password reuse is a significant security risk, contributing to the potential for unauthorized access. In the past, leaks occurred in several databases, exposing that people tend to use common words as passwords. The framework provides a CommonPasswordValidator to prevent the use of common passwords, and this version introduces new common passwords.

Minor updates and additions

Like any other release, the developers have made numerous minor improvements concentrating on updating the request-response lifecycle for improved performance. There are refinements in the generation of sitemaps and handling of static files, along with enhancing error reporting and internalization. This minor release of the Django framework comes with many new features and improvements.

Python for Django

Python has an elegant and easy-to-read syntax, and Django philosophies fit perfectly, making it a natural fit.

Python's cross-platform compatibility makes Django able to run on any system making it easy to develop and deploy. The simplicity of Python enhances Django's framework, reducing the cognitive load, which allows one to focus on business logic. Its "batteries-included" philosophy aligns with the "don't reinvent the wheel" mantra, allowing the use of all the features that the language and framework provide.

Django has a healthy and extensive community that extends and improves the framework and libraries and makes the project more robust and secure.

The language enforces good coding practices, such as proper indentation, resulting in clean, understandable code. This coding practice aligns perfectly with Django's aspiration to be the **framework for perfectionists with deadlines**, emphasizing the importance of maintainable and readable code.

In a nutshell, Python complements Django like a well-crafted puzzle piece.

The language's core strengths–readability, an extensive support ecosystem, and simplicity–harmonize with Django's mission of simplifying web development.

Conclusion

Django is a framework with **batteries included**, which promotes good practices. Knowing those good practices will keep the project healthy and easy to maintain. Understanding the framework and language features will help you keep your application simple and striking to the DRY principle. Python is a dynamic and strongly typed language, and if you come from a statically typed language, it could be hard to read code without type annotations. The language has coding practices that it's essential to follow to maintain high levels of quality in your project, and several open-source tools can help you to follow them, like pylint, flake8, or ruff. Python and Django are a natural fit, and the framework follows **Python Zen** and both were built in harmony.

In the next chapter, our focus will be on configuring our development environment with tools that reproduce the production environment. We will explore the foundational aspects of team-based development processes, Git Flow, GitHub Flow and trunk-based development.

Questions

1. What are the purposes of Python's **`try/except/else/finally`** blocks in error handling?
2. When would it be considered good practice to catch the generic Exception in Python? When might it be harmful?
3. Explain in your own words what a list comprehension is and provide an example.
4. How does type hinting in Python help with code maintenance and robustness?
5. What are some of the key guidelines from PEP 8 for writing clean and professional Python code?
6. How can linters be used to enforce Python coding standards in enterprise projects?
7. How does the syntax and design of Python contribute to the effectiveness of the Django framework?
8. Describe what is meant by Python being a **dynamic and strongly typed language**. How can this be a challenge for developers coming from statically typed languages?
9. Why is Django referred to as a **framework for perfectionists with deadlines**?
10. How do Python and Django together contribute to the DRY (Don't Repeat Yourself) principle in software development?

CHAPTER 2
Setting Up Your Development Environment

Introduction

Reproducibility refers to consistently replicating the same output using the same source code and data. This is a foundational principle crucial for verifying and validating results in software.

This chapter will explain the importance of reproducibility and guide you in creating a development environment, mirroring your production setup as closely as possible.

We will walk you through steps to build your development environment to work on more than one project at the same time.

Using the dependency management tool Poetry, we will make our project dependencies easier to maintain.

Once we've covered the necessary tools for setting up a development environment, we'll set up the environment for working on our ongoing project within this book.

An overview of git, a control version system, will teach you primary use cases to start working on a Django project.

Finally, we will review different branching models, Git Flow, GitHub Flow, and trunk-based, essential for any team-oriented project. As a bonus, we show the git worktree feature to improve your git skills even further.

Structure

In this chapter, we will cover the following topics:

- Introduction to Development Environments
- Managing Python Versions with Pyenv
- Understanding Virtual Environments
- Introduction to Poetry for Dependency Management
- Setting Up a Django Project with Poetry
- Basic Configuration for a Django Project
- Introduction to Git for Version Control
- Creating a GitHub Repository
- Branching Models
- Advanced git usage: using worktree

Introduction to Development Environments

Dealing with development environments can sometimes feel like navigating a maze. There are vast options for hardware and software, a combination that can create all sorts of challenges. Have you noticed that certain things work fine on your computer but fail to operate on another one? A well-known phrase for it is *It works on my computer.* Usually, this phrase appears when everything works well, except in the production environment.

When we say **development environment**, we're talking about the specific setup we used to develop and test new software features. This setup is usually run on the developer's computer.

Docker is a popular platform for developing, shipping and running container applications. A container is a standalone package of software that includes everything needed to run an application, including the runtime, system tools, libraries, and settings.

Docker has become a standard way of fixing reproducibility problems. But as with everything, it could be better. There are other options in the ecosystem, like Nix, which focuses on making reproducibility as perfect as possible. Nix is a powerful package manager for Linux and other Unix systems, making package management reliable and reproducible. Nix provides isolation between different versions and configurations, addressing the **dependency hell** issue often encountered in traditional package managers.

We aim to build a flexible development environment that allows switching between Python versions for various projects. One of the big players in your development environment is your Integrated Development Environment or IDE for short. A whole bunch of open-source and commercial solutions work nicely with virtual environments. We will cover the virtual environment in this chapter.

Managing Python Versions with Pyenv

Pyenv is a version management tool that allows you to switch between Python versions.

Imagine you are working on a project coded in Python 3.8 and want to upgrade it to 3.9. The standard procedure is to upgrade your system interpreter to 3.9, which could remove 3.8. Changing your OS Python interpreter could bring other issues since other software depends on it. Using the system interpreter has some drawbacks. Pyenv isolates your environment and allows you to easily switch Python versions without changing your system Python interpreter.

The installation of Pyenv is straightforward. Curl is a tool used to fetch data from a server, and it's necessary to download the Pyenv installer.

Pyenv can be installed using the pyenv-installer, with steps documented in the official GitHub repository: https://github.com/pyenv/pyenv-installer

Pyenv allows you to install almost any Python version. It will download the source code and compile it. Pyenv also supports virtualenvs, but we will use poetry virtualenv in the following sections.

Let's install version 3.11:

```
pyenv install 3.11
```

Note: Your operating system will require some compilation dependencies for Pyenv to install Python. You can install it with the following commands:

Debian/Ubuntu

```
sudo apt install -y make build-essential libssl-dev zlib1g-dev \

libbz2-dev libreadline-dev libsqlite3-dev wget curl llvm libncurses5-dev
\

libncursesw5-dev xz-utils tk-dev libffi-dev liblzma-dev python-openssl
```

macOS

```
brew install openssl readline sqlite3 xz zlib
```

Now you are ready to switch your Python version to 3.11. Here are some common and helpful commands:

```
# switches the version for a specific application

# if your global is 3.10, opening a new terminal will not use 3.11

pyenv local 3.11

# changes the version to use it everywhere

# opening a new terminal will use this version

pyenv global 3.11

# test that the version was changed correctly

pyenv version

# verify that your python command is using the one installed by pyenv

which python

# it should output: /home/username/.pyenv/shims/python
```

Tip: With Pyenv you can install several Python interpreters. A good exercise is to play with other interpreters.

For example, Jython, a Python interpreter on the Java platform, enables integration with Java components. PyPy, another interpreter, often exceeds the standard Python interpreter (CPython) in execution speed due to Just-In-Time (JIT) compilation.

Understanding Virtual Environments

Projects have their dependencies, which are locked to specific versions to ensure reproducibility. Installing the dependencies for multiple projects in your existing global environment could lead to conflicts or create an environment that differs from the production environment. Virtual environments isolate projects' dependencies. Typically, you'll have one virtual environment per project. However, there could be exceptions, like when a project needs to migrate to a newer Python version.

Virtual environment, or **`virtualenv`**, is an additional layer that isolates the dependencies of your Python project.

Creating virtualenvs is straightforward, and there are multiple ways to do so. Pyenv has a plugin to manage virtual environments or you could use a dependency management like Poetry, which provides support for virtualenvs.

Introduction to Poetry for Dependency Management

Using a dependency management tool could make the project dependencies easier to maintain; some dependencies depend on others, and conflicts could go undetected. Versioning pinning is when the dependencies versions are fixed to a specific version; having this with all application dependencies could make the reproducibility of the environment easier to ensure.

Imagine not using versioning pinning, and everything works in your local environment. When you deploy the project to production, a new incompatible library release was added, and now your project is failing with errors.

Poetry is a dependency management tool that promotes good dependency management practices, like versioning pinning. The tool uses a file pyproject.toml to specify project settings and a .lock file to save the dependency tree. Most of the time, you will make changes via the poetry cli and are discouraged to manually modify the .toml file and the .lock file is prohibited from being changed.

Setting up a Django Project with Poetry

Let's configure our environment to use Poetry. Here are the steps to follow:

```
pip install poetry
```

Now, with Poetry installed, we can start a new project:

```
poetry new task_manager
```

Let's add our most awaited dependency, django:

```
cd task_manager

# let's add Django dependency

# this will automatically update the pyproject.toml and poetry.lock

poetry add django

# optionally, you can specify the version you want to install

poetry add django==4.2.2

# you can also specify dependencies only for the development environment

poetry add --dev pytest

# now we can install the dependencies with

poetry install

# spawns a new shell within the virtual environment

# where dependencies are isolated

poetry shell

# Test that Django was installed properly

python -c "import django"

# if no error code was returned, it means that Django was successfully installed!

echo $?

# it should print "0"

# if you want to see the tree of dependencies, use show

poetry show

# Another important command is the lock

# Locks the project's dependencies in the poetry.lock file,

# creating a snapshot of all dependencies and sub-dependencies
```

```
poetry lock
```

Tip: Semantic versioning or 'semver' is a versioning schema for software that communicates changes in a release. It comprises 3 parts using the format X.Y.Z, where:

`X` is the major version. This number changes when incompatible changes and some changes in your application could be required.

'Y' is the minor version. This number changes when new features are introduced that are backward-compatible.

'Z' is the patch version. This number changes when there are backward-compatible bug fixes. Typically, these upgrades are the safest to apply to your application; ideally, you should update it since it contains the latest security fixes.

Congrats! You are one step closer to starting with a Django project.

Basic Configuration for a Django Project

In this book, we will build a task management system, and the database to use is PostgreSQL. The basic configuration of our development environment should also use a PostgreSQL database to mimic the production environment; for this, we will use docker-compose.

Docker enables developers to build, package, and distribute applications in containers. A container is a software unit that packages code and its dependencies, enabling quick and reliable application setup and configuration.

Docker-compose is a tool that helps to define and share multi-container applications. Following good Docker practices, each container should have one application; you might have one container with the web server, a database in another, and a caching server in another. Docker is another layer in your development environment, and docker-compose is a tool for defining and managing multi-container Docker applications. Docker-compose allows users to define a multi-container application in a single file, and then spin up the application with a single command.

Our first step will be to install docker and docker-compose.

```
curl -fsSL https://get.docker.com -o get-docker.sh

sudo sh get-docker.sh
```

```
For macOS arm64

curl https://desktop.docker.com/mac/main/arm64/Docker.dmg

For macOS intel chip

curl https://desktop.docker.com/mac/main/amd64/Docker.dmg

sudo hdiutil attach Docker.dmg

sudo /Volumes/Docker/Docker.app/Contents/MacOS/install

sudo hdiutil detach /Volumes/Docker
```

docker-compose configuration is being done by a YAML file; this file specifies the configuration of each container. Let's see an example that we will use in this book.

All the code used here is in the public GitHub repository https://github.com/llazzaro/web_applications_django; by the end of this chapter, you will learn more about Git and how to use it.

Here is a simple Docker Compose configuration that sets up a PostgreSQL database:

```
version: '3.8'

services:

  db:

    image: postgres:latest

    restart: always

    environment:

      POSTGRES_USER: postgres

      POSTGRES_PASSWORD: mysecretpassword

      POSTGRES_DB: task_manager

    volumes:

      - postgres_data:/var/lib/postgresql/data/

    ports:

      - "5432:5432"
```

```
volumes:

  postgres_data:
```

In this Docker Compose file:

- We are using the official PostgreSQL image latest version.
- The restart: always policy ensures that the database container automatically restarts if it stops.
- Environment variables are used to set the username, password, and database name for PostgreSQL.
- We map a named volume **`postgres_data`** to **`/var/lib/postgresql/data`** to ensure that the data remains persistent across container restarts.
- We map port 5432 inside the Docker container to port 5432 on the host machine, allowing us to connect to the PostgreSQL server using local tools.

Remember to replace your_username, your_password, and your_database with your actual username, password, and database name.

Now you can test the docker-compose configuration by running:

```
# -d stands for "detached" mode

docker-compose up -d

# let's open a database client inside the container

docker-compose exec -u postgres db psql

# you should see the postgres prompt, try to show the current time

select now();
```

Introduction to Git for Version Control

When working with a team, multiple people work on the same project and make changes to different parts of the code, potentially to the same piece of code. Git is a tool that helps to share changes in an ordered way. There are several processes to use Git within a team; one of the most common is Git Flow, but today Trunk-Based development is gaining popularity.

Before going deeper into the processes, let's explain what Git is. Git is a distributed version control system that tracks file changes, typically used for source code. A repository is where Git saves and tracks all the changes, and you will always have a local repository that uses the **.git** directory and may optionally be connected to a remote repository.

Git is decentralized, meaning multiple local or remote repositories could store the code. Most companies choose one central repository as a source of truth.

You can think of a git repository as a timeline or history of changes. Every time you make some changes to your local project, those changes will be in a status called unstaged. Once you are sure your changes must be included in the history, you must add them to the stage. You can think of the stage status as a draft status. Finally, you create a snapshot using the commit command, creating a milestone in the repository's history.

Another critical concept to learn is the branches. A git branch is a pointer to a snapshot or commits of your changes.

To better understand, let's practice with our GitHub repository for the book.

Our first step is to clone the repository or repo. Since the GitHub repo is public, you don't need to authenticate now.

```
git clone https://github.com/llazzaro/web_applications_django

cd web_applications_django

# now let's check the current branch

git branch

# It should output 'main'

# let's create a new branch with switch

git switch -c update_readme

# let's check our current branch

git branch

# Now, open the README.md file with your favorite editor

# note there is a typo, search for "directory" and fix it

nano README.md

# save the changes and check that the file is shown as unstaged

git status

# You are now ready to stage the changes
```

```
git add README.md

# now let's add more changes to the README.md

vim README.md

# save the file and check for changes

> $ git status

>On branch main

>Changes to be committed:

> (use "git restore --staged <file>..." to unstaged)

>   modified: README.md

>

>Changes not staged for commit:

> (use "git add <file>..." to update what will be committed)

> (use "git restore <file>..." to discard changes in working directory)

>   modified: README.md
```

Now you will see that the file is shown with unstaged and staged changes. If you commit now, only the staged changes will be added to the snapshot.

Info:

- `init`: initializes a local directory as a Git repository. This operation is usually executed when starting a new project.
- `status`: Shows the state of the working directory and staging area.
- `clone`: Makes a copy of the project from an existing repository.
- `branch`: You can create, list, rename and delete branches.
- `checkout`: Switches branches and restores files from a commit. You can also create a new branch using **`git checkout -b <new_branch_name>.`**
- `switch`: Switches between branches. You can create a new branch using git **`switch -c <new_branch_name>.`**
- `restore`: Discards staged local changes when using **`--staged`** and unstashed without it.
- `add`: Adds changes to the staging.
- `commit`: Creates a snapshot in the repository's history.

- **pull**: Fetches the changes from the remote repository.
- **push**: Submits the local changes to the remote repository.
- **fetch**: Retrieves updates from a remote repository to your local repository without merging changes into your working directory.
- **stash**: Saves changes in your working directory that you're not ready to commit.

Now we are ready to commit our changes, let do it with:

```
git commit -m "fix: Correct typo in README.md"

# try again with git status

# you should only see the unstaged changes

# to see the history use log

git log

> Mon Jul 3 13:54:01 2023 +0200 f5142c2 (HEAD -> main) feat: Initialize project with poetry dependencies and README.md  [Leonardo Lazzaro]
```

Here, you can see information about the commit, like the date, the hash, and the commit message. The hash is important information since it allows you to uniquely identify the changes in the repository.

Info: Conventional Commits is a specification for the structure of commit messages. Adhering to this specification improves the readability of the messages since they follow a structured format.

This practice is particularly beneficial in improving collaboration when everyone in the team uses the same format, especially in large or open-source projects.

By improving communication, it makes code review easier, giving more context about the changes.

In Conventional Commits, each commit message includes a type, which indicates the changes made. Common types include **feat** (new feature), **fix** (bug fix), **docs** (documentation changes), **style** (formatting, missing semi-colons, etc.), **refactor** (code change that neither fixes a bug nor adds a feature), **test** (adding missing tests or correcting existing tests), **chore** (changes to the build process or auxiliary tools and libraries).

Throughout this book, we will consistently adhere to the Conventional Commits specification.

Up until now, your changes are committed to your local copy. The next step is to push it to the remote repository by using the **`git push`**.

```
git push origin update_readme
```

However, this command will fail since your remote called **`origin`** is a public repository with read-only access.

For fixing this issue you will need to create a fork or a new repository and change the remote.

Creating a GitHub repository

GitHub is one of the most popular platforms where developers can host and share code using Git. GitHub provides a space for developers to collaborate, contribute to open-source projects, and manage repositories both publicly and privately. It offers various tools and features to facilitate software development and collaboration among developers.

You will need to create a GitHub account or login to your account. Once you log in, go to the settings page: https://github.com/settings/profile

In the Access section, go to **`SSH and GPG keys`** and click **`New SSH`** Key.

Now you will need to generate a new SSH key, to do so follow these steps:

```
ssh-keygen -t ed25519 -C "email@example.com"
```

Replace email@example.com with your GitHub email, the command will generate two files; one file is the private key (**`id_rsa`**) and the other one is the public key (**`id_rsa.pub`**).

Now, you are ready to add the public key to GitHub.

Info: Remember to never share your private key or store it online, a common mistake is to push it into a public repository.

You are now ready to create a new repository, browse to the URL https://github.com/new, specify the name `web_applications_django` and click **`Create repository.`**

Once the repository is created GitHub will generate a URL, which could be HTTP or SSH. Switch to the SSH URL type and copy it.

Info: Usually, SSH URLs are like this one git@github.com:llazzaro/test.git

---

Now open a terminal and go to the **web_applications_django** that you clone before:

```
cd web_applications_django

# The remote named origin is pointing to book repository

# and needs to be deleted

git remote rm origin

# The next command will create a new remote named origin

# pointing to your repository

git remote add origin git@github.com:your_username/web_applications_django.git

# Now you can push the changes

git push

You should now see the code in your repository, congrats!
```

Branching models

Having standards makes communication and work more accessible since the rules and processes are well known by everybody. When using git, there are unique working methods called branching models. Each branching model has a particular use case, and a defined working method. Choosing the suitable model that best aligns with the features of a specific project is crucial.

Git Flow

Git Flow is a branching model that is widely used and is an ideal solution for projects requiring a scheduled release cycle, or for those that require maintenance across multiple versions.

Info: Organizations which design systems...are constrained to produce designs which are copies of the communication structures of these organizations...

Conway's Law

With Git Flow, there are at least 5 different types of branches. Let's describe them first:

- `main`: This branch represents the production-ready state.
- **`develop:`** This branch contains the latest delivered changes for the upcoming release.
- **`feature:`** Feature branches are where new capabilities for future releases are being developed.
- **`release:`** Release branches serve the purpose of preparing a new production release.
- **`hotfix`**: Hotfix branches emerge when a critical bug in production requires an immediate fix.

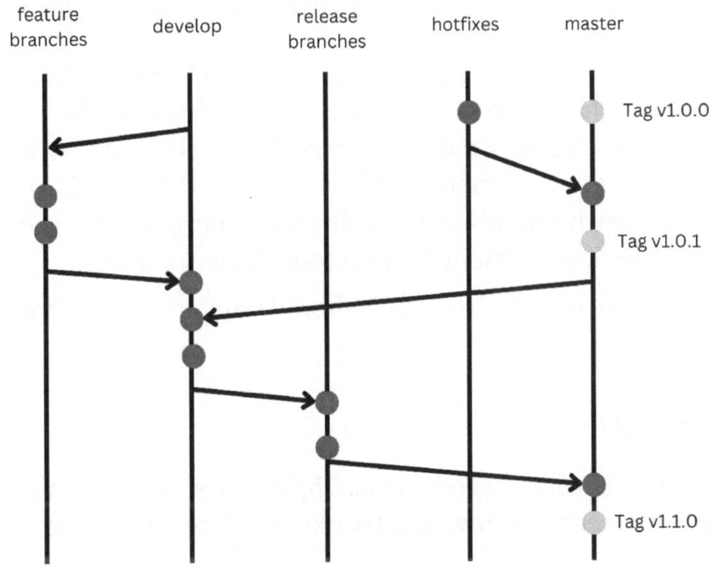

Figure 2.1: *The Git Flow Branching Model*

Suppose we need to develop a new feature called NewTask. We start by branching from the develop branch. As the feature undergoes development, commits occur in the local repository. Upon completion, we create a merge or pull request for the changes to be reviewed. After approval of the changes, it can be merged into the develop branch.

When the team determines the develop branch is ready for release, then a new branch will be created from the develop branch. Usually, these branches are named release/X.Y.Z. This branch undergoes thorough review and testing to confirm its readiness for production; once verified, it is then merged into the main branch.

Each time a release merges into the main branch, it requires a tag. The final step involves merging the main branch back into the develop branch.

Most projects should have a deployment pipeline that is triggered when any changes are merged into the main branch.

Info: CI/CD stands for Continuous Integration and Continuous Delivery. Continuous integration consists of checks on the code and the execution of tests. Typically, the checks on the code are static, like security checks, code formatting, type checking, running tests, and many more.

Continuous Delivery is a strategy in software development where changes to the software are automatically prepared for a release to production.

When a hotfix is required, the branch **`hotfix/name-of-the-hotfix`** is then created from the main branch. These changes usually go through the review process. Once approved, the changes can be merged into the main branch. Once all changes are in the main branch, a new tag will be created, and the patch's version number must be increased. Finally, the changes from the main branch are merged into the development branch to include the hotfix.

The changes applied to the main branch should trigger the pipeline to create the release as before.

GitHub Flow

Before diving into the trunk-based approach, let's first review GithubFlow, which sits somewhere between GitFlow and trunk-based development.

GithubFlow can be viewed as a trunk-based approach that simplifies the GitFlow process.

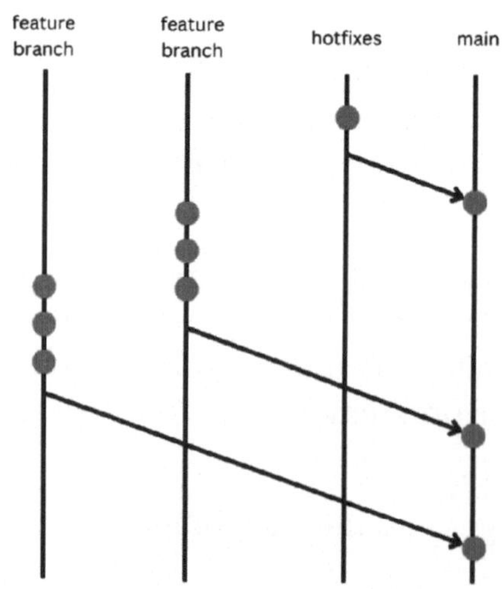

Figure 2.2: *The GitHub Flow Branching Model*

In GithubFlow, there is only one branch, the main branch. This branch contains production-ready code.

As you can see in the diagram, GithubFlow is a linear approach and utilizes far fewer branches than GitFlow, this makes this process a better fit for projects that require faster iterations.

Let's say that you need to develop the feature *NewTask* but using the GithubFlow, the first step is to create a branch from the main. As a developer, you will commit changes in your local repository, once the feature is ready, a new merge or pull request is usually created. This merge request will be reviewed by the team, and once it receives the necessary approvals, it will be merged into the main branch. Every time there is a commit in the main branch, the CI pipeline will run a set of tests and checks and finally deploy the changes into production.

When a hotfix is needed, the procedure mirrors the process used for feature development, which simplifies the process.

While this process is more straightforward, that doesn't necessarily make it better or worse–it depends on the specific needs of the project.

Trunk-based

With the trunk-based approach, things go faster than with GithubFlow. With the GithubFlow approach, a feature branch could be open for several days or weeks, which could bring problems like hard or longer reviews or even conflicts.

Trunk-based tries to solve these problems by splitting features into small steps and deploying them as soon as possible, ideally every day. To deploy an incomplete feature, the approach uses feature flags that are disabled in production.

Using these feature flags allows developers to deploy the feature in production even when it is not ready to use. This reduces the probability of breaking production since the changes are small and feature flags can be enabled incrementally.

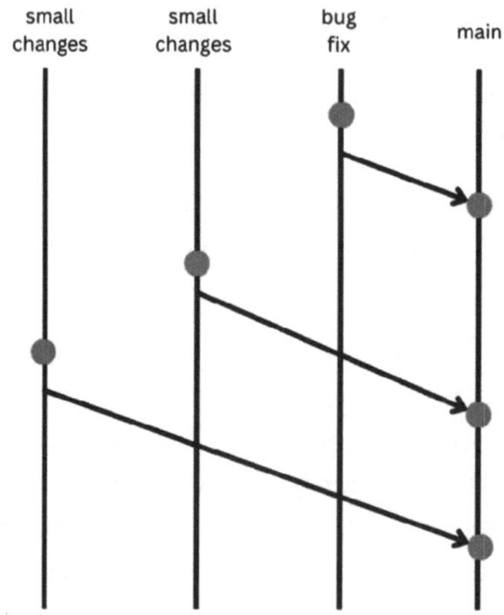

Figure 2.3: *The trunk-based branching model*

As you can see, each approach has its particular use cases and some of them are complex to maintain. If your project is a cloud-based web application, ideally you should go with a GithubFlow or Trunk-based. In the last few years, there has been a tendency to use trunk-based since it provides quicker feedback.

Some companies could have a different approach, but understanding some ways of working will allow you to quickly adapt.

Advanced Git Usage: Using Worktree

Sometimes, developers' lives are intense; you happily work on a new feature, but something goes wrong in production, and you need to create a hotfix branch. You have unstashed code changes for the new feature, and now you must commit incomplete work, stash or discard your changes.

A quick solution could be to clone the repository to a new directory, but this could take several minutes for a big project.

Info: If the clone of the project takes lots of time, you can shallow clone it by using the --depth flag

```
git clone --depth 5 git_repository_url
```

In this case, **`--depth 5`** means that Git will only clone the most recent 5 commits from each branch of the repository located at git_repository_url.

In most cases, Git has a solution for your daily problems; in this case, worktree is the solution. You need to use worktree from the beginning to switch between branches quickly. There are multiple ways to use worktree, but one particularly interesting is cloning the repository using bare.

```
git clone --bare https://github.com/llazzaro/web_applications_django
```

The git command will clone the repository; however, a bare repository can't be used to write code. This bare repository and worktree will allow us to write code.

Info: The `--bare` flag, when using the git clone command, creates a copy of the source repository without a working directory. The bare clone contains all the files, branches, and commit history. It contains only the .git contents. This clone type is used on server-side repositories or for backups, but it can be used with worktree.

Now let's add a worktree to create a new feature. Adding a worktree will create a new directory and branch. The branch will be created from the checked-out branch's tip or **HEAD**.

```
$ git worktree add new_task

$ ls

> FETCH_HEAD HEAD config description hooks info main new_task objects
packed-refs refs worktrees
```

Now you can go to the worktree to start working as usual.

```
$ cd worktrees/new_task

$ touch new_file

$ git add new_file

$ git commit -m 'feat: add new file'
```

Now let's see how to create a hotfix from the main branch using worktree

```
$ cd ..

# Let's create a worktree in the directory hotfix-user-not-able-to-login
from main # branch

$ git worktree add hotfix-user-not-able-to-login main
```

```
$ cd worktree/hotfix-user-not-able-to-login

# now you are ready to fix the code

# you can always go back to your feature branch

# by changing your directory

$ cd ..

$ cd new_task
```

As you can see, switching between branches is non-disruptive since it only requires you to change the directory and nothing else.

Once your hotfix is merged, it is recommended to delete the worktree by executing the command:

```
git worktree remove hotfix-user-not-able-to-login
```

Using Git worktree is optional, but it could improve your day-to-day development workflow and is a great feature.

Conclusion

Development environments can vary significantly, and ensuring reproducibility across different environments can be challenging.

Pyenv enables the management of multiple Python versions without disturbing the system interpreter. Virtual environments add a layer of isolation by keeping project-specific dependencies separate within the same Python interpreter. Poetry, a dependency management tool, helps to manage and resolve dependencies efficiently.

Starting a Django project with Poetry and Pyenv ensures an organized and isolated environment, setting a firm base for a smooth development journey.

Branching models are standards widely adopted. There is no best model, and the choice depends on the project's needs.

Git Flow is ideal for projects with scheduled releases. GitHub Flow is a simplification of Git Flow, and it's closer to a trunk-based approach, allowing faster iterations. The trunk-based process is for faster-paced changes, where each change is usually merged on the same day, even when the feature is not finished.

The next chapter will tackle an overview of the project we will work on in subsequent chapters. Exploring the distinctions between Django projects and applications, followed by an introduction to the Model-View-Template (MVT) design pattern.

Questions

1. What are the risks associated with not using version pinning in project dependencies?
2. How does using a virtual environment contribute to efficient Python project management?
3. How can a tool like Poetry help manage dependencies for a Django project?
4. Can you explain a tag in Git Flow, and why it's essential when merging a release into the main branch?
5. Why is adding an SSH key to your GitHub account important? How does it improve security?
6. How does Conway's Law relate to the Git Flow branching model?``
7. What kind of problems does Trunk-based development try to solve that might be encountered with GitHubFlow?
8. How can feature flags be beneficial for deploying incomplete features in Trunk-based development?
9. What is the role of feature flags in trunk-based development?
10. Describe a scenario where you would benefit from using Git's worktree feature. How does it improve the development workflow?

CHAPTER 3
Getting Started with Django Projects and Apps

Introduction

We will start by introducing the project we'll work on in the upcoming chapters, a task manager. After presenting the core idea of the task manager, we will explain two essential Django concepts: projects and applications.

We will go through a tour of the project's structure and create our first project. We will then start our first Django application following the best practices to keep our application independent and reusable.

You will learn about the Model-View-Template (MVT) design pattern, an important concept to understand when working with Django projects. We extend the idea of MVT by using a service layer to promote scalability and maintenance.

Using the development environment configured in the previous chapter, we start the initial configuration of the Django project to use the database provided by docker-compose.

With our environment configured, we launch our development server, preparing the path for creating our initial project pages—a home page and a help page.

Structure

In this chapter, we will cover the following topics:

- Introduction to the task manager
- Django project vs. Django application
- Creating a new Django project
- Understanding the Django project structure
- Starting your first Django app
- Understanding the Django app structure
- MVT design pattern in Django
- Extending the MVT pattern with a service layer
- Configuring your Django project
- Brief introduction to Django's development server
- Running your first Django app

Introduction to the task manager

We are ready to unveil our book project: a task manager, which serves as the forthcoming chapters' central theme. Task management software helps users to organize, track and complete tasks more efficiently.

Task managers are popular among software developers to keep track of tasks during the sprint cycles performed by team members.

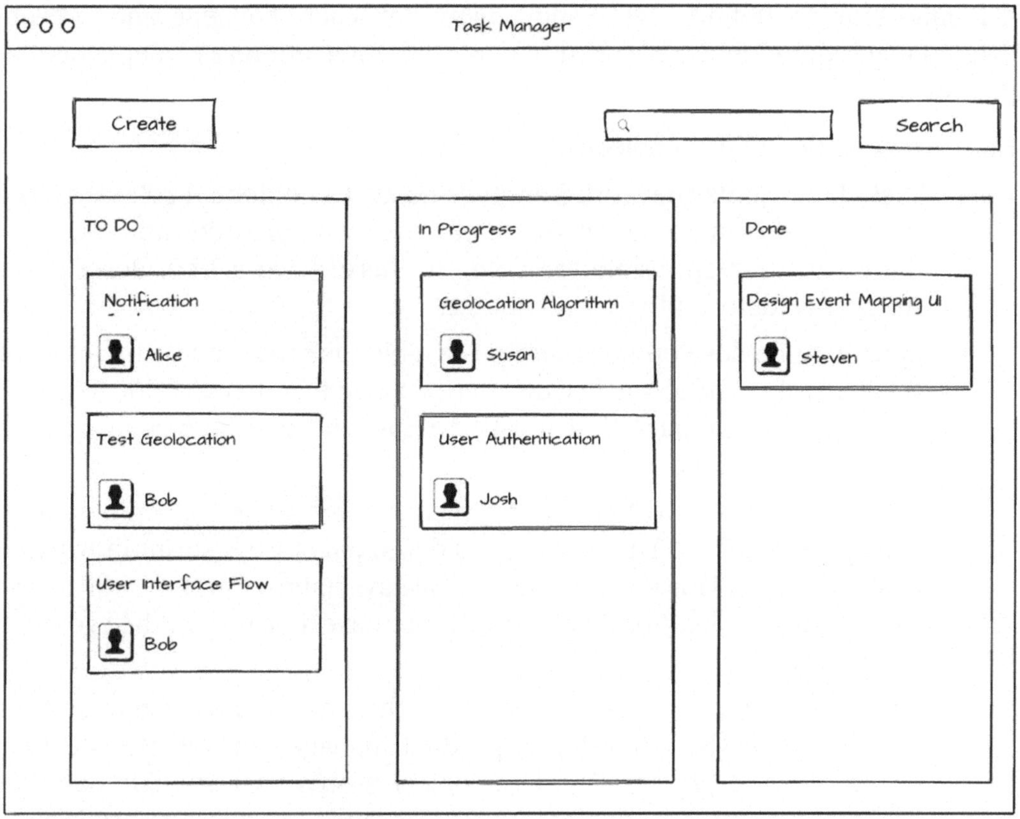

***Figure 3.1**: Task Manager Mockup*

The central concept of the task manager is the task itself and the objects around it, like users and comments. As we progress into the following chapters, we'll iteratively add and refine new features to the project.

An indispensable step before we move is to have a high-level overview of the project. Such a high-level overview empowers us to structure the Django project correctly.

Let's first list all the objects relevant to the problem:

- Task
- Epic
- Sprint
- User
- Comment

It's important to define one responsibility for each concept and prevent overlapping requirements. We need to make our applications as independent as possible.

Here is a definition of each object.

- **Task**: Represents the work item that needs to be done. Each task has a creator and owner. The creator is the user who created the task, while the owner is responsible for doing it. Tasks have a title, description, status, due date, and other attributes.
- **Epic**: In Agile development, an Epic is a big task that can be broken into smaller tasks. Those smaller tasks are usually taken in a sprint. The task can optionally be part of at most one Epic and one Epic could contain more than one task.
- **Sprint**: A sprint is a set period in which specific tasks are completed for deployment review. The task is considered part of the sprint in which it was completed. However, this doesn't always happen, and we will allow a Task to be part of more than one sprint to have a history of the evolution of the Task.
- **User**: Represent a person who uses the task management system. The user could be a developer, product manager, or any other person involved in the project. The User object stores user-specific data like username, password, contact information, and user roles or permissions. The Django framework provides this object.
- **Comments**: Each task could optionally have a note to it. The object provides a way for users to communicate. Each comment is associated with a specific task and the author (user). The Comment object stores the comment text, the user who created it, and the creation time. Having these attributes allows for a chronological ordering of the comments.

Django project versus Django application

A Django project comprises one more Django application, each serving a unique function. A project also has database settings, application-specific settings, templates, static files, and more. Conceptually, a Django project represents the entire application that you are building.

A Django application is a module made to perform a specific function. Due to its pluggable nature can be easily integrated into any Django project–enhancing its reusability across different projects.

Creating a new Django project

Creating a new project is relatively simple. As a first step, we need to enter the virtual environment and then use the command **`django-admin`** to start a new project:

```
poetry shell

django-admin startproject taskmanager
```

The command will create a new directory, **`taskmanager`** that includes some files for project configuration.

Throughout the project, we'll frequently interact with the **`settings.py`** and **`urls.py`** and regularly use Django's management commands.

Understanding the Django project structure

Upon executing the **`startproject`** command, you will create some files. Explore each resultant file and its purpose:

- **manage.py**: The Django command-line utility. With this command, you can start new applications, run a development server, create migrations, execute migrations, and more.
- **taskmanager/asgi.py**: This file stands for Asynchronous Server Gateway Interface, a standard interface for asynchronous Python web servers. It was introduced in Django 3.0 to support asynchronous features.
- **taskmanager/settings.py**: This file contains the configurations for your Django project. It includes settings for database connections, installed apps, middleware classes, template configs, and internationalization.
- **taskmanager/urls.py**: The URL declarations for this Django project; In this file, you'll define patterns for your URLs and associate them with your views.
- **taskmanager/wsgi.py**: This file stands for Web Server Gateway Interface. It's a specification that describes how a web server communicates with web applications. Django uses the WSGI standard as one of the interfaces to communicate with the web server.

Starting your first Django app

To start a new Django application, you need to be inside the virtual environment and use the manage.py **startapp** command:

```
poetry shell

cd taskmanager

python manage.py startapp tasks
```

We still need to configure the project to use the newly created **tasks** application. Later, we'll explore enabling this application in the project by modifying settings.py.

Understanding the Django app structure

A new application will create a new directory containing a new module, which includes:

- **admin.py**: The admin file is where you can define the admin interface for the application. In this file, you can specify how to display data in the admin related to the application and which actions can be made.
- **migrations**: Django creates files to change the database schema in this directory.
- **models.py**: This file defines the data models, which are then translated into database tables. Django detects any changes to these models and creates migrations to apply.
- **tests.py**: This holds the application's tests. Sometimes, you might change this to a directory for better organization of the tests.
- **views.py**: You can define Python functions or classes that take a request and return a response. Using the projects urls.py, you map a view to one or more URLs.

MVT design patterns in Django

Design patterns are repeatable solutions to common problems within software design. A pattern is like a blueprint, a schema, or a template for solving a problem applicable in many different situations. These patterns can improve communication and speed up the development process by providing a proven solution to problems already solved.

The Model-View-Controller (MVC) finds its roots in the 1970s, and the industry has widely adopted it. Many frameworks like Ruby on Rails, Laravel, Spring, and others adopt MVC. The design partitions application concerns improving maintainability, testability, and scalability.

The Model-View-Template (MVT) is a design pattern similar to the Model-View-Controller (MVC). The pattern defines clear separation on where the code should be written.

Django strongly focuses on why the framework adheres to MVT instead of MVC. In essence, the underpinning concept is strikingly similar.

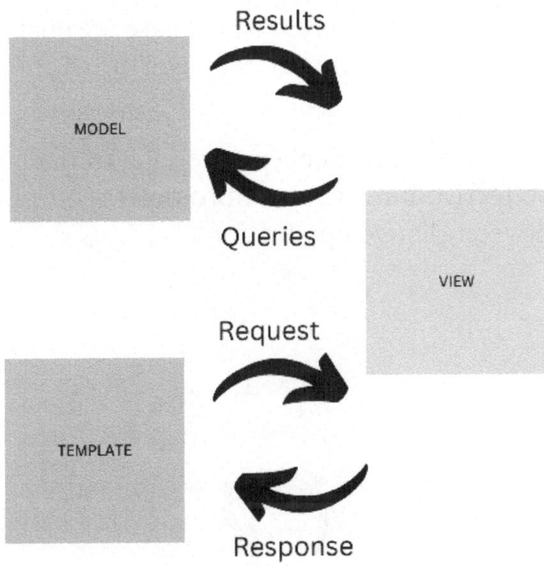

Figure 3.2: *Django MVT Design Pattern*

- **Model**: Defines the database structure. Models are the data access layer. This concept aligns with the **M** of MVC.
- **View**: The view is responsible for processing the request and creating a response. For modest-sized projects, it's common to place logic within the views, mirroring the **C** or Controller in the MVC paradigm. However, we will see that adding a layer called service is a better approach. This additional layer will structure the responsibilities better and allow us to have an interface for our application.
- **Template**: Determines the presentation of the data. By default, templates are text files to define placeholders with basic control structures. These templates use a context with data ready to render, which could produce an HTML, JSON or similar output.

Extending the MVT pattern with a service layer

The Service Layer pattern comes from the Domain-Driven Design (DDD) methodology, which Eric Evans explains in his book, *Domain-Driven Design: Tackling Complexity in the Heart of Software*, published in 2003.

However, the concept of the service layer does not belong exclusively to DDD. It's a typical pattern in many software designs and architectures, like hexagonal architecture.

The responsibility of a service layer is to encapsulate the business logic, providing a clear separation of concerns. The service layer provides an interface to the domain model.

When starting a project, it is an excellent exercise to first think of the service layer interface. An effective interface will promote good practices when using the service layer between Django applications.

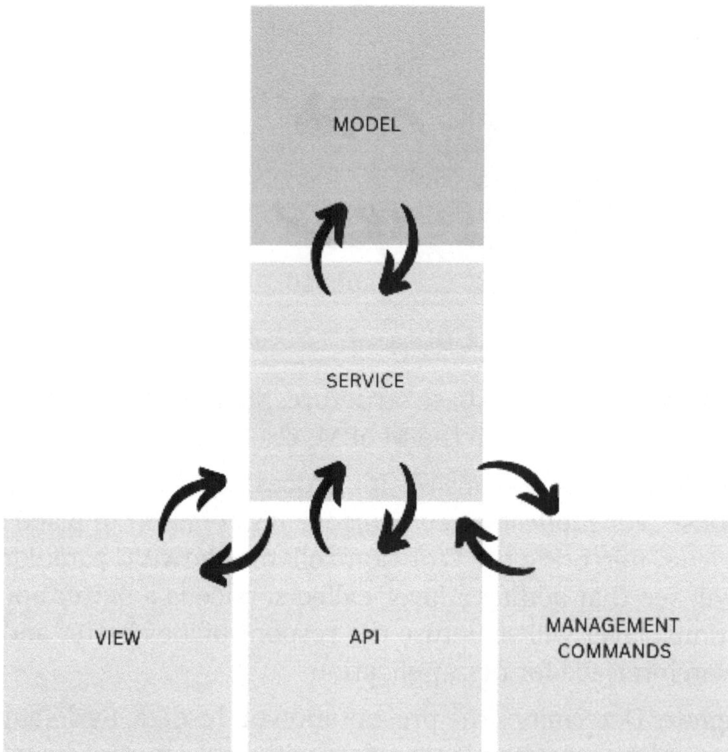

***Figure 3.3**: The MVT Pattern extended with a service layer*

One could perceive the service layer as an API, and it ideally should be the sole module imported from an external application. In large projects, importing from the model, rather than the service, could bring tight coupling, given that the model should ideally be considered private between applications. The service layer provides the interface; behind this interface, there could be anything, a model, a cache, another service, or even a queue. Importing the model from a Django application limits future changes in your project.

If you write all the business logic at the view and then you need to extend your project with a restful API or a management command, it will be hard to reuse the view code, or it could potentially cause duplicate business logic in your code base. A service layer will solve this problem since the view, API, or commands will use the service layer.

In the future, you may need to migrate specific segments of your projects to a different framework or language. A robust service layer will aid this transition because you must recreate the same interface in the new service.

Configuring your Django app

If you follow the previous steps, you should have an initial Django project with the `tasks` application created but not enabled.

The first step involves enabling the application by adding it to the **INSTALLED_APPS** list. Open the **taskmanager/taskmanager/settings.py** file with your favorite editor and search for the **INSTALLED_APPS**. Add to the end of the list the `tasks` string:

```
INSTALLED_APPS = [

    'django.contrib.admin',

    'django.contrib.auth',

    'django.contrib.contenttypes',

    'django.contrib.sessions',

    'django.contrib.messages',

    'django.contrib.staticfiles',

    'tasks',

]
```

The default settings come with some applications that the framework has, like the well-known Django admin.

A good way to verify if the settings were set up correctly is by attempting to create migrations for the **tasks** application:

```
$ python manage.py makemigrations tasks

> No changes detected in app 'tasks'
```

As evident, the application was located. Still, no changes were detected as we haven't altered the models.py file of the **tasks** application.

Now, it's time to configure the database. By default, Django uses SQLite, but in the previous chapter, we explained that it's better to use the same database engine than we use in production. We will use PostgreSQL for our project and have configured a Postgresql using docker-compose. Let's change the settings to use environment variables so we can use the PostgreSQL server of our local development environment.

Note: Employing environment variables is a best practice, and you should never commit secrets to the repository.

There exist several methods to store secrets. The most common ones are Hashicorp Vault and Cloud Secret Managers.

Using environment variables and a secret manager could be beneficial since some support automatic secret rotation.

Some might argue that environmental variables aren't optimal for storing secrets, given their potential accidental exposure. Another approach could be to use a secrets manager to retrieve and store the secrets.

Open the **docker-compose.yml** file and check for the PostgreSQL environment values. You should have these values set:

```
POSTGRES_USER: postgres

POSTGRES_PASSWORD: mysecretpassword

POSTGRES_DB: mydatabase
```

Reopen the **settings.py** file and locate the **DATABASES** dictionary; replace its existing content with the following:

```
DATABASES = {
```

```
    'default': {
        'ENGINE': 'django.db.backends.postgresql',
        'NAME': os.getenv('DB_NAME', 'mydatabase'),
        'USER': os.getenv('DB_USER', 'postgres'),
        'PASSWORD': os.getenv('DB_PASSWORD', 'mysecretpassword'),
        'HOST': os.getenv('DB_HOST', 'db'),
        'PORT': os.getenv('DB_PORT', '5432'),
    }
}
```

Note: The function getenv from the standard module `'os'` uses the second parameter as the default value when the environment variable was not set.

We are using localhost since we will run our development server in the host machine, and the **`docker-compose`** configuration for PostgreSQL exposes the database port to the localhost 5432.

```
# we need to install the PostgreSQL driver, psycopg3
poetry add psycopg
# let's spin up the database
docker-compose up -d
# initialize the database
python manage.py migrate
```

Provided everything is functioning as expected at this stage, you should observe a list of migrations that have been applied to the database:

```
>Operations to perform:
>  Apply all migrations: admin, auth, contenttypes, sessions
>Running migrations:
>  Applying contenttypes.0001_initial... OK
>  Applying auth.0001_initial... OK
>  Applying admin.0001_initial... OK
```

```
> Applying admin.0002_logentry_remove_auto_add... OK
> Applying admin.0003_logentry_add_action_flag_choices... OK
> Applying contenttypes.0002_remove_content_type_name... OK
> Applying auth.0002_alter_permission_name_max_length... OK
> Applying auth.0003_alter_user_email_max_length... OK
> Applying auth.0004_alter_user_username_opts... OK
> Applying auth.0005_alter_user_last_login_null... OK
> Applying auth.0006_require_contenttypes_0002... OK
> Applying auth.0007_alter_validators_add_error_messages... OK
> Applying auth.0008_alter_user_username_max_length... OK
> Applying auth.0009_alter_user_last_name_max_length... OK
> Applying auth.0010_alter_group_name_max_length... OK
> Applying auth.0011_update_proxy_permissions... OK
> Applying auth.0012_alter_user_first_name_max_length... OK
> Applying sessions.0001_initial... OK
```

Your Django project is now ready to start working with it.

Brief introduction to Django's development server

The Django framework has an integrated and ready-to-use development server. To initiate the server, execute the following commands:

```
# enter the poetry virtualenv

poetry shell

# start the development server

python manage.py runserver 0.0.0.0:3000
```

The **runserver** command includes optional arguments for specifying the listening address and port. The server will default to listening on localhost port 8000 if these are not provided.

Note: Not for production use: While the **`runserver`** command is a powerful development tool, it's not meant for production use. It has yet to be designed to be particularly secure, scalable, or robust and doesn't offer some advanced features provided by production-level servers.

If you navigate to http://localhost:3000 using your preferred browser, you should encounter the following welcome message:

***Figure 3.4**: Django default home page*

The development server has a reload feature. Each time the code undergoes modification, the server automatically refreshes itself. This auto-refresh feature proves extremely convenient during development, allowing you to review your changes without manually reloading the server and saving development time.

When DEBUG mode is on and an error occurs, Django displays a detailed traceback in the browser, helping to speed up the debugging process.

Tip: You can enhance your Django development environment by installing packages like django-debug-toolbar (https://github.com/jazzband/django-debug-toolbar) and django-extensions (https://github.com/django-extensions/django-extensions).

The Django Debug Toolbar is a third-party package that provides a configurable set of panels displaying various debug information about the current request/response. Once installed and configured, it appears as a toolbar at the top of the page. This package has a handy summary of the performance characteristics of the current page, such as the total time taken to serve the page, the number of SQL queries executed, and the number of static files used.

Django Extensions is another third-party package that adds a collection of custom extensions for the Django Framework. These include additional management commands, database fields, admin functionalities, and other useful utilities. The package includes some commands like `runserver_plus`, `show_urls`, and many more.

Remember that when using Poetry, you can install development dependencies by appending the `--dev` flag while adding them.

Running your first Django app

In the previous section, we manage to run our development server, but our application `tasks` is empty. At the beginning of this chapter, we introduced the project idea and a mock, now is the time to bring the mock to life. We will create a static template based on the mock that we will iterate throughout the book.

Remember, it's vital to keep our templates neat and straightforward. Having templates with thousands of lines can be tough. So, we'll create a base template and break it down into manageable, small-sized sections.

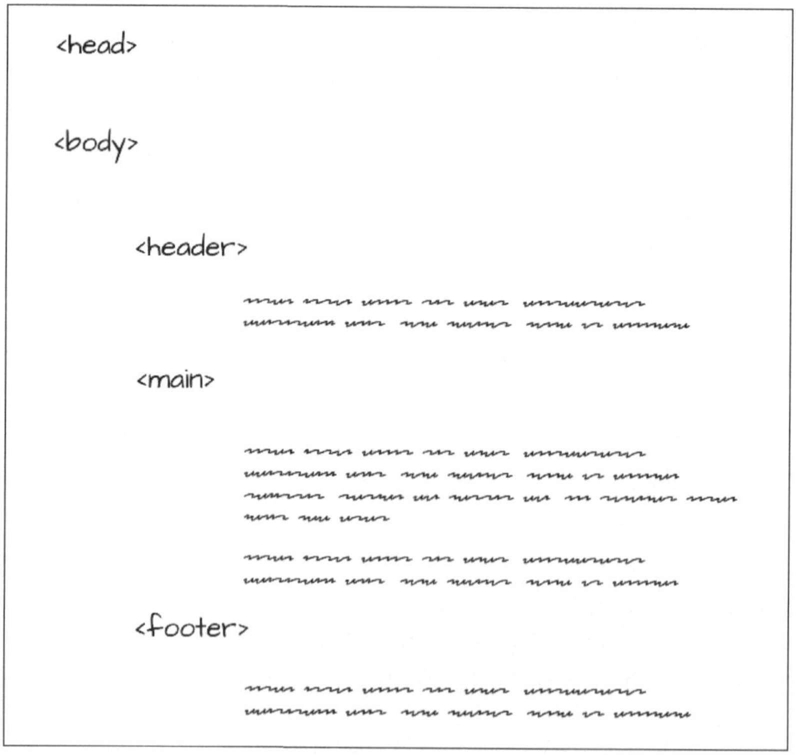

Figure 3.5: *Base HTML structure*

There's more than one way to structure a template, but we'll adhere to the layout presented in *Figure* 3.5. We'll establish three subsection templates, each with a distinct role.

- **header**: This section contains the navigation menu, typically shared across all project pages. It will contain the create button and the search bar.
- **main**: Displays the page's content, which is the list of issues in our case.
- **footer**: The footer will store helpful links for easy access.

The HTML code we will use is the following:

```
<!DOCTYPE html>

<html lang="en">

<head>

    <meta charset="UTF-8">

    <meta name="viewport" content="width=device-width, initial-
    scale=1.0">

    <title>Task Manager</title>

    <!-- CSS files -->

    <!-- Bootstrap CSS -->

    <link href="https://cdn.jsdelivr.net/npm/bootstrap@5.2.3/dist/
    css/bootstrap.min.css" rel="stylesheet" integrity="sha384-rbsA
    2VBKQhggwzxH7pPCaAqO46MgnOM80zW1RWuH61DGLwZJEdK2Kadq2F9CUG65"
    crossorigin="anonymous">

    <!-- <link rel="stylesheet" href="styles.css"> -->

</head>

<body>

    <% include "_header.html" %>

    <main>

        {% block content %}

        {% endblock %}

    </main>
```

```
    <% include "_footer.html" %>

    <!-- JS files -->

    <!-- jQuery and Bootstrap Bundle (includes Popper) -->

    <script src="https://code.jquery.com/jquery-3.5.1.slim.
    min.js" integrity="sha384-DfXdz2htPH0lsSSs5nCTpuj/
    zy4C+OGpamoFVy38MVBnE+IbbVYUew+OrCXaRkfj" crossorigin="anonymous"></
    script>

   <script src="https://cdn.jsdelivr.net/npm/bootstrap@5.2.3/dist/js/
   bootstrap.bundle.min.js" integrity="sha384-kenU1KFdBIe4zVF0s0G1M5b4h
   cpxyD9F7jL+jjXkk+Q2h455rYXK/7HAuoJl+0I4" crossorigin="anonymous"></
   script>

    <!-- <script src="script.js"></script> -->

</body>

</html>
```

The Django framework offers an **include** statement, letting you incorporate other HTML files. For our purpose, we'll include two files, **_header.html** and **_footer.html**.

Our base template leans on Bootstrap—a highly popular, open-source CSS framework instrumental in building responsive, mobile-first websites.

The main section contains a block, which a way to define an area for child templates can override. In this example, the block is called content. We will see how to override this content in the child templates main and help.

Now we are going to show the contents of the two files. Contents of the **file _header.html**:

```
<header class="d-flex justify-content-between align-items-center p-3">

    <!-- Left side -->

    <div>

        <button type="button" class="btn btn-primary">Create</button>

    </div>


    <!-- Right side -->
```

```
    <div class="d-flex">
        <input type="text" class="form-control" id="search"
        placeholder="Search">
        <button type="button" class="btn btn-success ml-2">Search</
        button>
    </div>
</header>
```

The header has a create button on the left and on the right side a search box. This header will be shared across all the project pages.

Contents of the **file _footer.html**

```
<footer class="footer mt-auto py-3 bg-light text-center">
    <div class="container">
        <a href="/help" class="text-dark">Help</a>
    </div>
</footer>
```

Our footer features a centered `Help` link, set to be the project's first page.

In *Chapter 6: Using the Django Template Engine*, we'll explore using the template engine to render dynamic content.

If you browse to http://localhost:3000/, the templates we've crafted won't be visible—we need to change our **settings.py**.

Head to **taskmanager/settings.py** and look for the `TEMPLATES` list. We must include the application path in the `DIRS` list to enable the framework to locate the templates.

```
TEMPLATES = [
    {
        'BACKEND': 'django.template.backends.django.DjangoTemplates',
        'DIRS': [BASE_DIR / 'templates', ],
        'APP_DIRS': True,
        'OPTIONS': {
```

```
            'context_processors': [
                'django.template.context_processors.debug',
                'django.template.context_processors.request',
                'django.contrib.auth.context_processors.auth',
                'django.contrib.messages.context_processors.messages',
            ],
        },
    },
]
```

Before our changes, the DIRS was set to the empty list [], now we added the path to the project templates. Without this configuration, the framework will raise an error that the file was not found since it was not in the template search path. Our project will have all the templates in the templates directory. Each app will have a sub-directory inside the templates directory. The directory hierarchy organizes the Task manager project's templates for easy access.

However, our Django project still cannot render the home page for the tasks application. We must configure the URL routes to guide the framework on the HTML to render.

Create a **urls.py** file in the tasks application containing:

```
# tasks/urls.py
from django.urls import path
from django.views.generic import TemplateView

app_name = 'tasks'  # This is for namespacing the URLs
urlpatterns = [
    path('', TemplateView.as_view(template_name='tasks/home.html'),
    name='home'),
    path('help/', TemplateView.as_view(template_name='tasks/help.html'),
    name='help'),
]
```

Our tasks application has two URL patterns, one for the home and the other for the help. Each time a request is processed, the framework checks the URL patterns in the order listed in **`urlpatterns`**. The first pattern–an empty string–matches only when the path is empty.

Note: The second pattern is '**`help/`**'–note the trailing slash. If a user accesses a URL without a trailing slash, and it matches a pattern with a trailing slash, Django will issue a redirect to the version with the trailing slash.

And we also need to change project **urls.py** to include the new URLs:

```
# taskmanager/urls.py

from django.contrib import admin

from django.urls import include, path


urlpatterns = [

    path('admin/', admin.site.urls),

    path('tasks/', include('tasks.urls', namespace='tasks')), # Including
    tasks URLs with a namespace

]
```

Our next step is to create the **home.html** and the **help.html**, for both of them, we are going to extend the **base.html** and use the block content.

Here is the **templates/home.html**:

```
{% extends "tasks/base.html" %}

{% block content %}

    <p>Lorem ipsum dolor sit amet, consectetur adipiscing elit, sed do
    eiusmod tempor ...</p>

{% endblock %}
```

Notice that our home HTML is quite straightforward to maintain. Since it extends the base, it includes all styles, JavaScript, menus, and footers. All content should be added to the **`content`** block. For now, we're sticking with just one content block, but remember, you can structure your page with multiple blocks.

Now let's look at the **help.html**:

```
{% extends "tasks/base.html" %}


{% block content %}

    <div class="container mt-4">

        <div class="card">

            <div class="card-header">

                Help Page

            </div>

            <div class="card-body">

                <h5 class="card-title">What is a task manager?</h5>

                <p class="card-text">A task management system is
                software that helps users organize and track the
                progress of tasks.</p>

                <a href="/" class="btn btn-primary">Go Home</a>

            </div>

        </div>

    </div>

{% endblock %}
```

Again, the help page extends the base template, inheriting the same look and feel as the other pages. Any changes made to base.html will reflect on the help page as well.

At this point, we have only dealt with static content, and some features, like the `Create` button, are not functional yet. Don't worry; by the end of this book, you will have a full-function task manager.

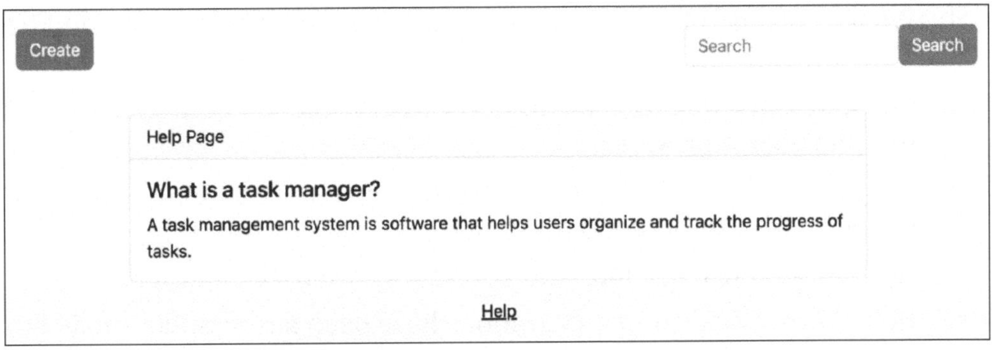

Figure 3.6: *Task manager project help page*

Conclusion

At the beginning of the chapter, we provided an overview of the task manager project and defined the critical objects of the project - Task, Epic, Sprint, User and Comment.

In the discussion on Django projects versus applications, we emphasized the modular nature of Django and how it promotes reusability across projects.

Understanding the MVT pattern is a must when working with Django projects, and extending it with a service layer promotes good practices to keep your application easy to maintain and scale.

We show best practices like environment variable usage for secret data, and the text underlines the importance of secure coding practices.

Finally, we learned the basics of templates and URL routing by creating basic static pages for the project.

In the next chapter, we will reiterate our project by creating the models to provide the data access layer for our future service layer. We will understand an object-relational-mapper (ORM) and how to use it effectively.

Questions

1. Why is it essential to have a high-level overview of the project before you start?
2. Why do the responsibilities of each object have to be defined to prevent overlapping requirements?

3. What are design patterns in software design?
4. What is Django's Model-View-Template (MVT) design pattern, and how does it work?
5. How does introducing a service layer extend the MVT pattern, and what benefits does it provide?
6. Why should the service layer be considered an API and the only module imported from another application?
7. How does Django use migrations, and why are they important?
8. How do you confirm that migrations have been successfully applied to a Django database?
9. Is enabling the DEBUG flag in environments not intended for development a good security practice?
10. Why is it not a good security practice to commit secrets to the git repository?

Exercises

1. Install the Django extensions application to your development environment and experiment using the command it provides. For example, try to use the `show_urls` command to list all the project URLs.
2. Install and configure the Django toolbar on your local environment, navigate to your task admin, and try to understand the information this excellent Django application shows.
3. Change the **home.html** to have a mockup as shown in *Figure 3.1*.
4. Incorporate an `About` page into the project.

CHAPTER 4
Django Models and PostgreSQL

Introduction

Understanding Django models is essential to create great web applications. We start this chapter with the foundational concepts of Django models. We then create our first model for the task manager project, the Task. Once our new model is ready, we deep dive into the framework database APIs. We shall then use the migration system of the framework by showing real-world use cases when making changes to the models.

The Django framework includes a built-in administrative interface. We'll explore this interface to manage our Task model and understand the framework's authorization tools.

The Object-Relational Mapper (ORM) stands as a pivotal component of the Django framework. After covering ORM, we'll analyze queries using aggregators and functions.

Database systems have rules to ensure data integrity. This chapter will discuss strategies to uphold database standards and prevent data corruption.

Finally, we review different relationships between models by introducing two new models, The Epic and the Sprint. With those new models, we will learn about one-to-one, one-to-many, and many-to-many relationships.

Structure

In this chapter, we will cover the following topics:

- Understanding Django models
- Creating your first model
- Django's database API: Create, retrieve, update, and delete operations
- Understanding Django migrations
- Running migrations to reflect model changes in the database
- Django's admin interface: Registering models and manipulating data
- Introduction to Django's ORM: Queries and aggregations
- Ensuring data integrity with model constraints
- Extending the models

Understanding Django models

The relational model organizes data using relations represented as tables. A table is a collection of tuples (or rows). Each table in the database represents a specific entity. For example, in our task manager, we will have a table for Tasks. Entities have attributes that are mapped to columns of the table. In a relational model, each entity has a unique identifier known as the primary key. Entities relate to one another using these keys, with foreign keys referencing other entities.

Operations on a relational database are carried out using a language such as SQL (Structured Query Language). This language allows for the manipulation and retrieval of data and can express a wide range of queries and commands.

Python is an object-oriented language that employs classes, objects, properties, methods, and inheritance. The Django framework provides a Model class that Python classes can inherit from. Consider a Python class named `Task` that inherits from the Django Model class. Then your class is a Django Model. Creating a new instance of a model class in Django and saving it will create a new row in the database. The data gets saved to the database when you invoke the `.save()` method on the object. Until saved, the object's data remains in the application's memory. If the application stops or restarts without saving, this data disappears.

Django's Object-Relational Mapping (ORM) bridges the relational model with the object-oriented paradigm. With ORM, your application can persist data and retrieve it across sessions or restarts. When you call `.save()` on a Django model object, the ORM translates this operation into a SQL command that the database can understand and sends this command to the database to store your data.

ORM allows intuitive data interactions through objects, enhancing code readability and maintenance. ORM offers a high-level API that minimizes the need for raw SQL, simplifying database operations. The database API through ORM ensures the project isn't tightly bound to a specific database, as ORM manages translations to the suitable database engine.

ORMs enhance security by promoting best practices and leveraging their maturity in the field.

In our project, each entity will correspond to a new class: Task, Epic, Sprint, and Comment.

- Task
- Epic
- Sprint
- Comment

For user management, we'll use the built-in User class provided by the framework, eliminating the need to create a custom one.

Creating your first model

The first model involves defining the class and creating and executing a migration.

Let's start with a minimal model that we will extend later. Open the models.py from the tasks directory and add the Task class:

```
from django.db import models

from django.contrib.auth.models import User


class Task(models.Model):

   STATUS_CHOICES = [

       ("UNASSIGNED", "Unassigned"),

       ("IN_PROGRESS", "In Progress"),
```

```
        ("DONE", "Completed"),
        ("ARCHIVED", "Archived"),
    ]

    title = models.CharField(max_length=200)
    description = models.TextField(blank=True, null=False, default="")
    status = models.CharField(
        max_length=20,
        choices=STATUS_CHOICES,
        default="UNASSIGNED",
        db_comment="Can be UNASSIGNED, IN_PROGRESS, DONE, or ARCHIVED.",
    )
    created_at = models.DateTimeField(auto_now_add=True)
    updated_at = models.DateTimeField(auto_now=True)
    creator = models.ForeignKey(
        User, related_name="created_tasks", on_delete=models.CASCADE
    )
    owner = models.ForeignKey(
        User,
        related_name="owned_tasks",
        on_delete=models.SET_NULL,
        null=True,
        db_comment="Foreign Key to the User who currently owns the task.",
    )
    class Meta:
        db_table_comment = "Holds information about tasks"
```

The Task class is a subclass of Django's Model, and its attributes are defined using Django Fields. Each field type specifies the data type for a corresponding database column. The framework provides a variety of types that can be used.

Let's review each attribute of the model:

- **Title**: Uses `CharField`, a type used for short strings of characters. The max title length is 200 chars, as specified in the attribute.
- **Description**: The description is a text that can be arbitrarily large. `TextField` is typically used when it is required to store a large amount of text.
- **Status**: The `Status` field has four predefined string options. Django's `CharField` type, when used with the `choices` option, restricts the values that can be stored, as demonstrated here. The choices parameter has to be a list of tuples containing the display string and the value to store.
- `Created_at`: We use the `DateTime` field with the `auto_now_add` set to True. This sets the current time to the attribute when the object gets created.
- `Updated_at`: Similar to the `created_at` but uses `auto_now` to True, the value is set to the current date time every time the object is modified.
- **Creator**: A foreign key linked to the User model. Setting this field is obligatory, as it cannot be null. The '`on_delete`' parameter dictates the action taken when the referenced user is deleted. In this case, we set the value to cascade, which will delete the Task. We chose to use `'cascade'`, but the appropriate action largely depends on specific project requirements.
- **Owner**: The User model via a foreign key. It can be set to null, especially if the task's owner is not determined at the time of its creation. When the owner object gets deleted, the owner is set to null to prevent deleting the Task object.

By default, Django provides an auto-increment primary key named `'id'` for every model. This can be overridden by specifying a custom primary key.

When designing models in Django, it's crucial to correctly set the null and blank attributes for each field. As a general guideline, minimizing the use of null values is advisable. Limiting null values can lead to more robust software because you won't have to deal with `IS NULL` or `IS NOT NULL` conditions in your queries. This also ensures that attributes will always have a value.

In our Task model, the relationship with the Owner is set to `null=True` because a task can exist without an owner.

The blank option serves a different purpose than null: it specifies whether a field is allowed to be empty when filled out in a form. For instance, our description field allows for empty values (**`blank=True`**) but disallows **`NULL`** values in the database (**`null=False`**). This field serves as a good example of when not to permit null values.

Allowing a field to be both blank and null is generally not recommended. This can create ambiguity, as both NULL and an empty string would be considered representations of an **`empty`** or **`no data`** state, complicating both data integrity and query logic.

Note: It's crucial to define the appropriate value for the **`on_delete`** property. Determining the appropriate values depends on the type of relationships defined in your relational model.

- **Aggregation**: In aggregation, one class (termed the **`whole`**) can contain instances of another (the **`part`**), but the **`part`** can also exist without the **`whole`**. In Django, this is similar to **`models.SET_NULL`**, **`models.SET_DEFAULT`**, or **`models.SET()`** (a function that returns a value). If the **`whole`** is deleted, the **`part`** still exists, but the foreign key is set to **`NULL`**, its default value, or the result of a provided function, respectively.
- **Composition**: In composition, one class (the **`whole`**) owns or comprises objects of another class (the **`parts`**), where the **`parts`** cannot exist without the **`whole`**. In Django, this is similar to **`models.CASCADE`**. If the **`whole`** is deleted, the **`parts`** are also deleted.

Neither of these concepts neatly maps onto the **`models.PROTECT`** behavior. It would prevent deletion of the **`whole`** if there are any existing **`parts`**, which is not typically a behavior in either aggregation or composition.

Finally **`models.DO_NOTHING`** also doesn't directly map onto these concepts. It would leave the **`part`** inconsistent if the **`whole`** is deleted. This behavior is not typically associated with either aggregation or composition in object-oriented programming.

Remember, these are not exact mappings and the behaviors of aggregation and composition can vary.

Next, let's guide the framework to generate the necessary migrations:

```
poetry shell

python manage.py makemigrations
```

```
> Migrations for 'tasks':
>   tasks/migrations/0001_initial.py
>     - Create model Task
```

Info: You can also revert migrations if you need to with:

```
python manage.py migrate tasks zero
```

Since it was the initial migration, we need to use the `zero`. Otherwise, you need to specify the prefix of the migration file name corresponding to the migration number.

Django automatically detects model changes and crafts the migration code suitable for the database.

To apply these changes to the database, run the migrate command:

```
python manage.py migrate

# let's verify that the tables were created

python manage.py dbshell

# this will give us a SQL shell

localhost postgres@mydatabase=# \d+ tasks_task
```

The last command should output the created database showing the columns, primary key, indexes, and foreign keys.

Info: The `'dbshell'` command provides direct access to the database configured in `settings.py`, making it handy for troubleshooting and verifying modifications during development.

Django's database API: Create, retrieve, update, and delete operations

Django offers two primary ways to interact with the database: using the `.save()` method of an object and the object manager.

This manager is your primary interface to the database, accessed via `Model.objects`. The manager allows you to make queries to the database. Each Django model has a manager that you can access via the **Model.objects** which can be used to retrieve instances of the model.

Creating Objects. Django comes with a shell that allows you to manipulate objects, let's create a new Task using this shell:

```
python manage.py shell

>>> from django.contrib.auth.models import User

>>> creator = User.objects.create_user("developer", "email@example.com", "password")

>>> from tasks.models import Task

>>> Task.objects.create(title="Implement User Profile Picture Uploading", description="Design and implement a feature that allows users to upload, change, and delete their profile picture on their user account.", creator=creator)

<Task: Task object (1)>

>>> task = Task.objects.get(title="Implement User Profile Picture Uploading")

>>> task.status

'UNASSIGNED'
```

Here, we create a user and a task, setting the newly created user as the task's creator. Since the creator is mandatory, we set the creator as the just-created user. Then we get the Task by its title and print the status attribute set to **UNASSIGNED**, the default value.

Using the **.save()** Method:

```
>>> task = Task(title="Implement User Profile Picture Uploading", description="Design and implement a feature that allows users to upload, change, and delete their profile picture on their user account.", creator=creator)

>>> task.id is None

True

>>> task.save()
```

```
>>> task.id
3
```

After instantiating a Task object and verifying its id is None (meaning it's not yet in the database), the **.save()** method saves it to the database. Subsequent interactions will update the existing database entry.

You can retrieve objects directly from the model using the objects manager. Using the object manager has two common ways to retrieve the objects: the get or filter.

The filter method will return a **QuerySet** and it could zero or multiple results. It should be used to fetch multiple objects from the database.

The get method retrieves one object from the database; if no object is found, the method will raise the exception **DoesNotExist**.

Let's use the object manager filter:

```
>>> Task.objects.filter(id=3)
<QuerySet [<Task: Task object (3)>]>
>>> Task.objects.get(id=3)
<Task: Task object (3)>
>>> Task.objects.get(id=100)
Traceback (most recent call last):
  File "<console>", line 1, in <module>
  File "/Users/mandarina/Library/Caches/pypoetry/virtualenvs/task-
  manager-ox-Othme-py3.10/lib/python3.10/site-packages/django/db/models/
  manager.py", line 87, in manager_method
    return getattr(self.get_queryset(), name)(*args, **kwargs)
  File "/Users/mandarina/Library/Caches/pypoetry/virtualenvs/task-
  manager-ox-Othme-py3.10/lib/python3.10/site-packages/django/db/models/
  query.py", line 637, in get
    raise self.model.DoesNotExist(
tasks.models.Task.DoesNotExist: Task matching query does not exist.
```

The filter method, as shown, returns a **QuerySet** containing a Task with an object id of 3. The get method returned the Task object with an id equal to 3. However, the get method raised an exception when we tried to get the object with an id that does not exist in the database.

With the object manager, you can fetch or count all the Tasks:

```
>>> Task.objects.all()

<QuerySet [<Task: Task object (8)>, <Task: Task object (9)>, <Task: Task object (10)>]>

>>> Task.objects.count()

3
```

In the first line, we used the **all** method to get a **QuerySet** with all the stored Tasks in the database. The second operation returns an integer with the number of Tasks stored in the database.

Our object was linked to the database row with a primary key value of 3. Let's update the title by using the model **.save()**:

```
>>> task.title = "New title"

>>> print(task.title)  # prints "New title"

>>> task.refresh_from_db()

>>> print(task.title)  # prints "Implement Picture Uploading"
```

The Django framework only persists in attribute changes when the **.save()** method is explicitly called. After calling the **.save()** an update query is performed to the database and the new title will be persisted. Optionally you can call **refresh_from_db**, which will read the object from the database and refresh all its attributes.

Alternatively, the update operation can also be performed using the object manager:

```
>>> Task.objects.filter(id=3).update(title="Implement Picture Uploading")

1
```

When updating using the object manager, exercise caution; the update method can affect multiple objects. In our example, the integer one **(1)** was returning, informing that only one object was affected by the update operation. We used the primary key to filter objects to guarantee that the operation would affect only one object.

Now let's try to delete the task with an id equal to 3:

```
>>> task = Task.objects.get(pk=3)

>>> task.delete()

(1, {'tasks.Task': 1})
```

The method returns a tuple of two elements:

- The number of objects deleted.
- A dictionary describing the number of deletions made per object type.

Instead of using `'id'`, you can filter by `'pk'`, a shorthand for 'primary key'.

Using the object manager to delete one Task can also be used and it is similar to the update example:

```
>>> Task.objects.filter(pk=2).delete()

(1, {'tasks.Task': 1})
```

Since we used the primary key to filter the object, only one object was deleted. You can also call the delete without filtering, which will delete all the tasks:

```
>>> Task.objects.all().delete()

(5, {'tasks.Task': 5})
```

In the previous example, we swapped `'filter'` with `'all'`, which fetches a `QuerySet`. Subsequently, we instructed the manager to delete all objects returned by this `QuerySet`.

Understanding Django migrations

Relational databases use a specific schema, wherein each table has columns with defined data types. SQL provides queries to manipulate the database schema, such as creating or altering tables.

The way to change the schema with Django is through database migrations. Django has an amazing migration system that detects the changes in the models of your application. If you create or modify a model, Django's migration system detects these changes, creating versioned files to capture schema alterations.

Migrations are atomic, meaning that each migration is treated as a single transaction to the database.

Each Django application has a **'migrations'** directory containing files that track incremental schema changes.

We have already created and applied the initial migration to our local database for our **tasks** application.

Info: The **makemigrations** command creates new migrations based on the changes detected in your models. Django maintains a record of your schema in the **django_migrations** table, and **makemigrations** essentially differ your models against the schema stored in this table to decide what changes need to be made.

To generate the new migration files, execute:

```
python manage.py makemigrations
```

To apply the migration to the database:

```
python manage.py migrate
```

Migrations can also be reversed, undoing the applied changes.

```
python manage.py migrate yourappname 0017   # migrate to the state after applying 0017 migration

python manage.py migrate yourappname zero   # unapply all migrations and revert to the initial database schema
```

Django's migration system also supports inter-migration dependencies. This means you can make and apply changes to your schema in any order and Django will ensure everything gets applied properly.

Data migration modifies the data itself while keeping the schema unchanged, typically to correct or adjust it. For instance, if you want to change the status of all **'Archived'** tasks to **'Completed'** in your Task model, you would use data migration. You would do this using a data migration.

You can create a data migration with the following command:

```
python manage.py makemigrations tasks --empty
```

The preceding command will create an empty migration. We can then instruct the migration system to execute certain Python operations. In this case, we'll be using the migration to change the status of **'Task'** from **'Archived'** to **'Done'**.

```
from django.db import migrations


def change_archived_tasks(apps, schema_editor):
    # Get the Task model from the apps registry
    #  the app registry is used to ensure that you're
    # working with the correct version of your model
    Task = apps.get_model('tasks', 'Task')
    # Update all 'Archived' tasks to 'Done'
    Task.objects.filter(status='ARCHIVED').update(status='DONE')


class Migration(migrations.Migration):

    dependencies = [
        ('tasks', '0001_initial'),
    ]

    operations = [
        migrations.RunPython(change_archived_tasks),
    ]
```

Execute the 'migrate' command to update the Task status to 'Done'.

Tip: A common mistake is to create a loop that calls the save method. Looping and querying are considered bad practices and will lead to the problem known as nplus one queries.

When you need to batch update an object it is better to use the objects manager, which was meant to affect more than one instance.

Over time, a Django application accumulates many migrations, potentially slowing down tests and impacting local environment performance. `'Squashing'` combines multiple migrations, capturing the same changes, to optimize test runs and local setup.

For squashing migration, Django has a command **squashmigrations**:

```
./manage.py squashmigrations app_label start_migration_name end_
migration_name
```

If **start_migration_name** and **end_migration_name** are omitted, all the migrations for the app are squashed.

The squash command creates a new migration file that is equivalent to the squashed migrations and a replaces attribute is added to the Migration class of the latest migration. The command will keep the original migration files since other systems could require those files when squashing. The recommended process is to squash, maintain the old files, commit and release. Once all the systems have been upgraded, you can remove the old files, commit the changes, and perform a second release.

Django's admin interface: Registering models and manipulating data

The Django admin interface is an intuitive alternative to the shell for managing objects. To set it up, open the file **tasks/admin.py** and add the following class:

```
from django.contrib import admin

from tasks.models import Task


class TaskAdmin(admin.ModelAdmin):

    list_display = ("title", "description", "status", "owner", "created_
    at", "updated_at")

    list_filter = ("status",)


admin.site.register(Task, TaskAdmin)
```

After saving the changes in admin.py; your development server should automatically reload. Before you can access the admin interface, you'll need to create a superuser account:

```
$ poetry shell

$ python manage.py createsuperuser

Username (leave blank to use 'mandarina'): admin
```

```
Email address: admin@example.com
Password:
Password (again):
Superuser created successfully.
```

Once you have input your chosen password twice, you'll have a new superuser account. Browse to http://localhost:8000/admin and log in with the user you have made before.

Once you open the admin URL, you should see the login page:

Once you login with the superuser account just created, the home page of the admin will be shown.

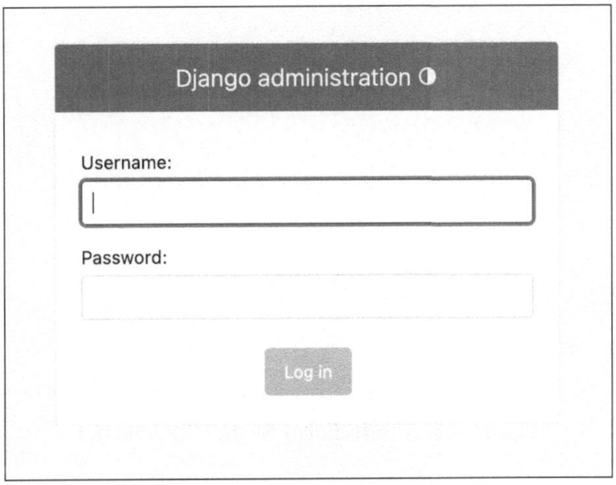

Figure 4.1: *Admin login form*

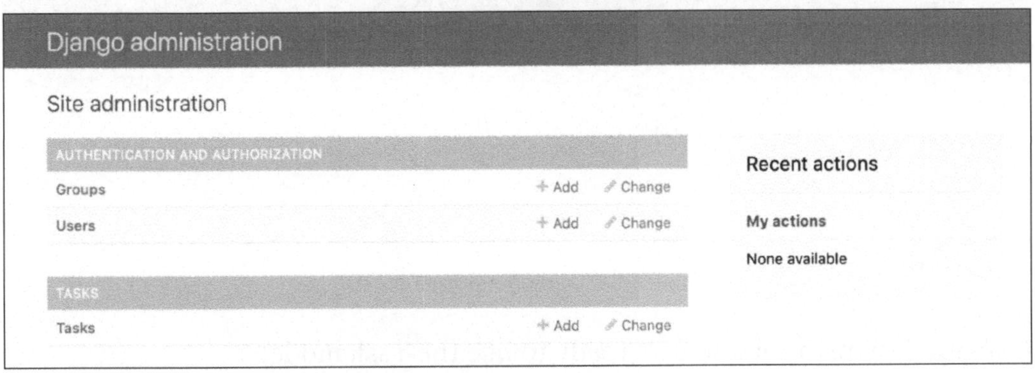

Figure 4.2: *Admin home page*

To create a new task via the admin, click on the **Tasks** link in the model list of the admin (http://localhost:8000/admin/tasks/task/add/); you'll be presented with a form.

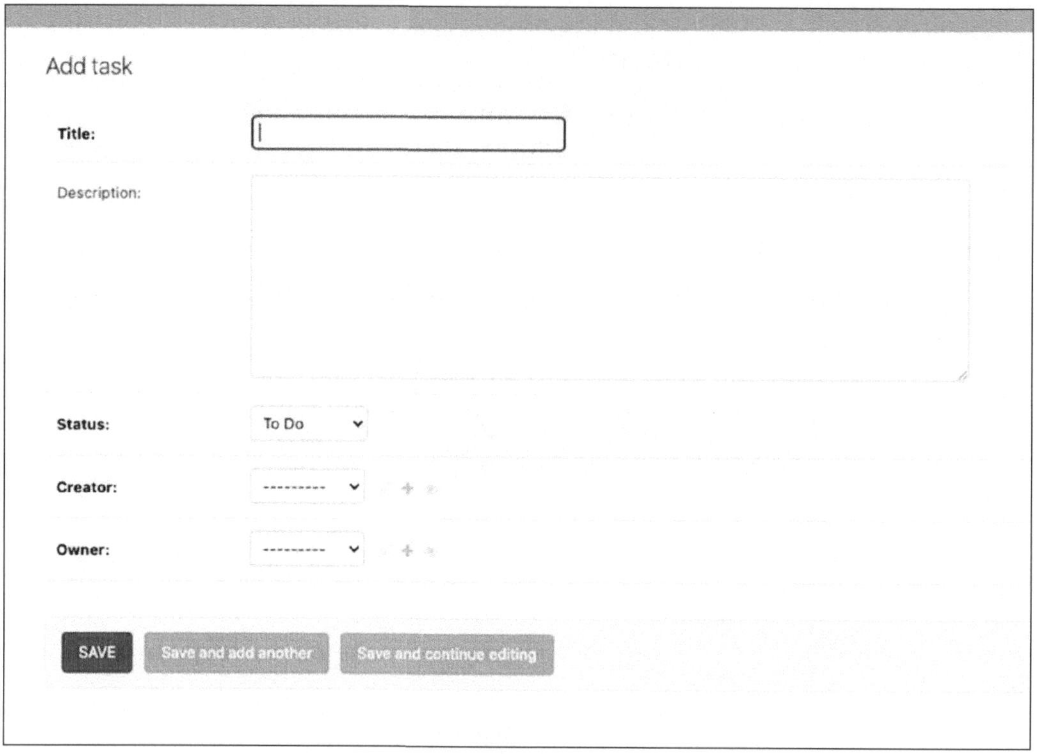

Figure 4.3: *Admin Form for the Task model*

Browse back to the list and confirm that you created your new **Task**.

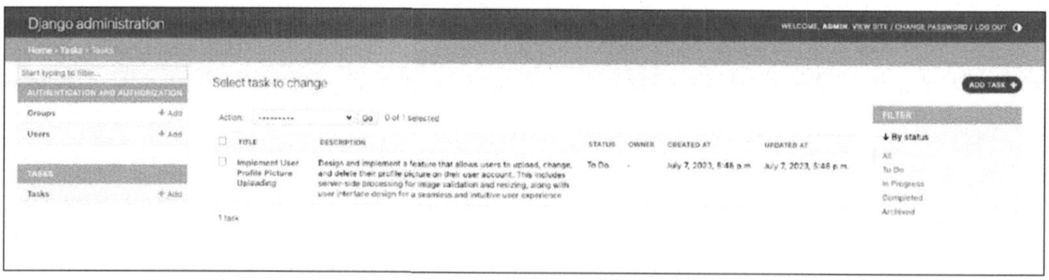

Figure 4.4: *Django Admin Task list*

Congratulations! Your admin is ready to use the Task model.

The admin lets you define your actions for objects. An action method can modify the selected object in the admin list. Suppose that we want our admin to mark the selected Tasks as archived. You have to extend the **TaskAdmin** with a new method and configure the following actions:

```
from tasks.models import Task


class TaskAdmin(admin.ModelAdmin):

    list_display = ("title", "description", "status", "owner", "created_
    at", "updated_at")

    list_filter = ("status",)

    actions = ['mark_archived']

    def mark_archived(self, request, queryset):

        queryset.update(status='ARCHIVED')

    mark_archived.short_description = 'Mark selected tasks as archived'


admin.site.register(Task, TaskAdmin)
```

By setting `actions = ['mark_archived']`; we add a new action to the admin interface. The string **make_archived** refers to the method of the **TaskAdmin** class. The method receives two parameters: **'request'** and **'queryset'**. The **queryset** contains all the tasks the admin user chose from the list. Optionally, write a short description of the action using the **.short_description** on the method.

Django's framework includes a built-in authentication system that allows you to set and verify specific permissions for each user.

The authentication system provides a Group model where users can be added to those groups. In your project, you can create different groups to manage the permissions.

In Django, each model automatically comes with a set of predefined permission created for it. These are the permissions:

- **Add**: Permission to add new instances for the model
- **Change**: Permission to edit the existing instances
- **Delete**: Permission to delete

These permissions for each model are created as part of Django's built-in authentication system. You can use this permission not only in the admin, but also in the views and templates.

You could have **Admins** and **Editors**, each with the corresponding permissions. If a user is part of the Admin group, they have extensive permissions, allowing them to change and delete anything within the admin area.

We'll set up two groups: Admins and Editors. The first allows adding, modifying and deleting Tasks, while the Editors can only change Tasks.

You can use a superuser account to create Groups within the admin interface. However, we also show how to programmatically create a data migration to create all the required groups programmatically.

The **ModelAdmin** has three methods that can be overridden to check for permissions, the **has_change_permission**, **has_add_permission**, and **has_delete_permission**. We will check for the corresponding permissions for each of those methods. Then we are going to have three groups: **Creator**, **Editor**, and **Admin**.

First we need to define our groups and their permissions. We have different ways to achieve this creation of groups, one is via the admin page or via code. We will first review how to do it via the admin and then we will see an alternative way using a data migration.

Browse to the admin page http://localhost:8000/admin and on the home page click on **Groups**, this will open the Groups views. Next to the **Groups** in the left side click on **+Add** or navigate to http://localhost:8000/admin/auth/group/add/, this will open to following group creation page:

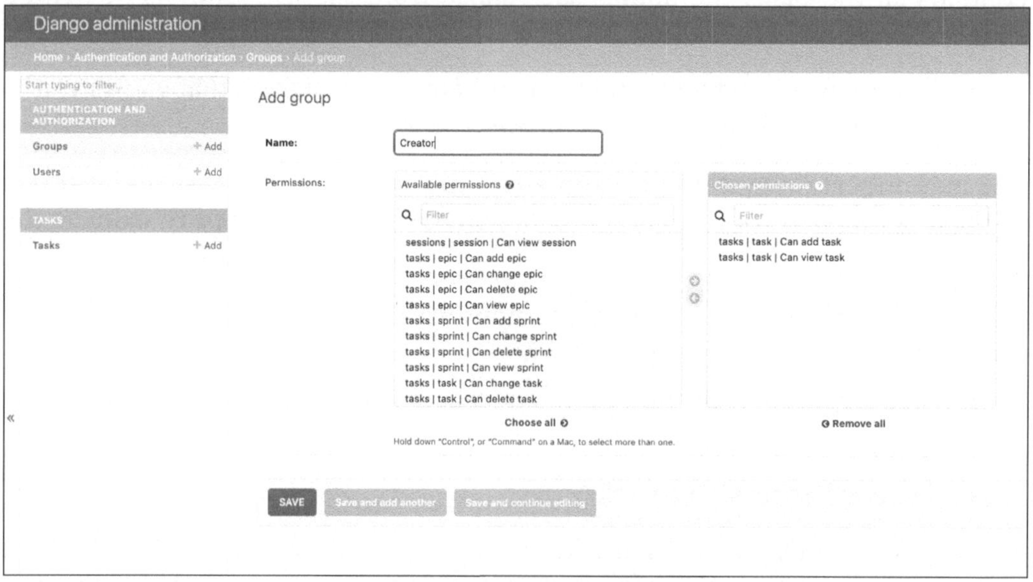

Figure 4.5: *New group creation page*

In *Figure* 4.5, we are about to create a new **`Creator`** permission with the **`tasks.add`** and **`tasks.view`** permissions. All available permissions were provided by the framework, but you can also add your custom ones.

Sometimes it's useful to configure the groups and permission via a data migration. First, let's play with the Group and Permission model to understand how they work. Once we understand how they work, we can easily create a data migration.

Users inherit all permissions from any group they join. Let's play with the shell to understand how it works:

```
>>> from django.contrib.auth.models import Group, Permission

>>> from django.contrib.contenttypes.models import ContentType

>>> from tasks.models import Task  # assuming your app name is tasks

>>>

>>> # create a new group

>>> task_admin_group, created = Group.objects.get_or_
create(name='TaskAdmins')

>>>

>>> # get the content type for the Task model

>>> content_type = ContentType.objects.get_for_model(Task)

>>>

>>> # get the permissions for the Task model

>>> permissions = Permission.objects.filter(content_type=content_type)

>>>

>>> # assign the permissions to the group

>>> task_admin_group.permissions.set(permissions)

>>>

>>> # save the group

>>> task_admin_group.save()

>>> # let's check that the user is not in any group

>>> user = User.objects.get(pk=2)
```

```
>>> user.groups.all()
<QuerySet []>
>>> user.has_perm("tasks.add_task")
False
>>> # Adding the user to the admin group will give permissions
>>> user.groups.add(task_admin_group)
>>> user.has_perm("tasks.add_task")
True
```

Once the user is added to the group, it inherits permission from that group. You can configure your application using the admin interface and configure the groups from it or create a data migration.

Firstly, you need to create an empty migration:

```
python manage.py makemigrations tasks --empty
```

Open the newly created migration file with your favorite editor and add the following:

```
from django.db import migrations
from django.contrib.auth.models import Group, Permission


def create_groups(apps, schema_editor):
    # create "Creator" group with "add_task" permission
    creator_group = Group.objects.create(name='Creator')
    add_task_permission = Permission.objects.get(codename='add_task')
    creator_group.permissions.add(add_task_permission)

    # create "Editor" group with "change_task" permission
    editor_group = Group.objects.create(name='Editor')
    change_task_permission = Permission.objects.get(codename='change_
    task')
    editor_group.permissions.add(change_task_permission)
```

```
    # create "Admin" group with all permissions
    admin_group = Group.objects.create(name='Admin')
    all_permissions = Permission.objects.filter(content_type__app_
    label='tasks')
    admin_group.permissions.set(all_permissions)


class Migration(migrations.Migration):

    dependencies = [
        ('tasks', '0005_task_status_check'),
    ]

    operations = [
        migrations.RunPython(create_groups),
    ]
```

Once you have your groups created, we need to add the methods that check for the **permissions**:

```
class TaskAdmin(admin.ModelAdmin):
    list_display = ("title", "description", "status", "owner", "created_
    at", "updated_at")
    list_filter = ("status",)
    actions = ['mark_archived']
    def mark_archived(self, request, queryset):
        queryset.update(status='ARCHIVED')
    mark_archived.short_description = 'Mark selected tasks as archived'
    def has_change_permission(self, request, obj=None):
        if request.user.has_perm('tasks.change_task'):
```

```
            return True
        return False

    def has_add_permission(self, request):
        if request.user.has_perm('tasks.add_task'):
            return True
        return False

    def has_delete_permission(self, request, obj=None):
        if request.user.has_perm('tasks.delete_task'):
            return True
        return False

admin.site.register(Task, TaskAdmin)
```

Now, you can add users to a particular group to limit the admin actions. For example, a user on the **`Creator`** Group will only be allowed to create Tasks.

Tip: Django users need the **`is_staff`** flag enabled to access the admin. You can enable it on the admin interface for the User model.

Introduction to Django's ORM: Queries and aggregations

Django's ORM offers a powerful API for model querying. As we have previously explored its capabilities for retrieval, updates, and deletions, mastering this API ensures clearer and more efficient code.

The most common way to query the models is via the objects manager, which is accessed via the **`objects`** attribute of the model. We already reviewed how the get and the filter works and how useful they are. Django uses the double underscore is a notation to indicate a separation in the query and it could be used to perform comparisons:

```
from datetime import datetime, timedelta

from django.utils import timezone


# Get today's date and time in the timezone-aware format

today = timezone.now().replace(hour=0, minute=0, second=0, microsecond=0)

# Query to get tasks created before today

tasks_created_after_today = Task.objects.filter(created_at__lt=today)
```

The previous query will return all the tasks created before today. The **lt** means less than and Django has many operators to use like:

- **gt**: Greater than
- **gte**: Greater than or equal to.
- **lte**: Less than or equal to
- **contains**: Field contains the value. Case-sensitive
- **in**: Within a range
- **isnull**: is NULL (or not)

The previous list is the most common ones, but the framework ORM supports more options.

You could have noticed by now that if you use multiple filters Django ORM will use the AND operator in the query:

```
# Query to get tasks with status "IN_PROGRESS" and created before today

tasks_in_progress_before_today = Task.objects.filter(

    status="IN_PROGRESS",

    created_at__lt=today

)
```

The query the ORM will generate is and it will use the **AND** operator:

```
SELECT"tasks_task"."id","tasks_task"."title","tasks_task"."description",
"tasks_task"."status", "tasks_task"."created_at", "tasks_task"."updated_
at", "tasks_task"."creator_id", "tasks_task"."owner_id" FROM "tasks_task"
WHERE ("tasks_task"."created_at" < 2023-08-29 00:00:00+00:00 AND "tasks_
task"."status" = IN_PROGRESS)
```

If you need to use the OR operator, you will need to use Django's Q, which is usually used to create complex queries. As an example, let's get all the Tasks with status **IN_PROGRESS** and with title **Implement Dijkstra Algorithm**:

```
from django.db.models import Q

from .models import Task  # adjust the import based on your project structure


# Query to get tasks with status "IN_PROGRESS" or title "Implement Dijkstra Algorithm"

tasks_filtered = Task.objects.filter(

   Q(status="IN_PROGRESS") | Q(title="Implement Dijkstra Algorithm")

)
```

The previous query will use the SQL OR operator:

```
>>> print(tasks_filtered.query)

SELECT "tasks_task"."id", "tasks_task"."title", "tasks_task"."description", "tasks_task"."status", "tasks_task"."created_at", "tasks_task"."updated_at", "tasks_task"."creator_id", "tasks_task"."owner_id" FROM "tasks_task" WHERE ("tasks_task"."status" = IN_PROGRESS OR "tasks_task"."title" = Implement Dijkstra Algorithm)
```

Let's say we want to fetch tasks that are not archived. We could use the filter method, but the framework also provides the exclude method:

```
# let's filter Tasks that are not archived

tasks = Task.objects.exclude(status='ARCHIVED')

# an alternative with filter, but less intuitive

from django.db.models import Q

tasks = Task.objects.filter(~Q(status='ARCHIVED'))
```

For those new to Django's ORM, filtering with Q might seem less intuitive. The use of 'exclude' is more straightforward and doesn't require extensive knowledge of the framework.

Tip: If you need to print the SQL raw query, it is possible by using the query method on a QuerySet object:

```
>>> print(Task.objects.exclude(status='ARCHIVED').query)
```

```
SELECT"tasks_task"."id","tasks_task"."title","tasks_task"."description",
"tasks_task"."status", "tasks_task"."created_at", "tasks_task"."updated_
at", "tasks_task"."creator_id", "tasks_task"."owner_id" FROM "tasks_task"
WHERE NOT ("tasks_task"."status" = 'ARCHIVED')
```

Often, for the tasks model, we might want to retrieve unarchived tasks, ordered by their creation date, in descending order:

```
tasks = Task.objects.exclude(status='ARCHIVED').order_by('-created_at')
```

Using **order_by** allows the result to be ordered by the specified column. The '-' sign indicates the order we want the results (from newest to oldest).

Django's ORM also offers aggregation functions, letting you operate on grouped objects within your database. You can compute sums, averages, counts, minimums, maximums, etc., across multiple records. These functions can be used with a group by clauses, allowing you to group records by specific values before performing the aggregation.

Let's say we are curious about the average tasks each user has:

```
from django.db.models import Count, Avg

avg_tasks_per_user = Task.objects.values('owner').annotate(task_
count=Count('id')).aggregate(avg=Avg('task_count'))
```

The **values('owner')** is equivalent to a **'group by'** clause, **annotate(task_count=Count('id'))** counts the tasks per user, and **aggregate(avg=Avg('task_count'))** computes the average.

With Django's ORM, you can craft complex queries. Suppose we were requested to calculate the average time it takes for a task to move to the **DONE** status. Let's assume that when the status changes to **DONE** the **updated_at** is also updated. Having this in mind, we can calculate the requirement with the following query:

```
from django.db.models import Avg, F, ExpressionWrapper, fields

# Annotate each task with its duration from creation to completion

tasks_with_duration = Task.objects.filter(status='DONE').annotate(

    duration=ExpressionWrapper(F('updated_at') - F('created_at'),
```

```
    output_field=fields.DurationField())
)

# Calculate the average duration

average_duration = tasks_with_duration.aggregate(average_
duration=Avg('duration'))

# Caution: If any attribute alters, 'updated_at' updates too, potentially
skewing our query results and necessitating model adjustments.
```

The F object allows you to refer to the value of a model field within a query.

`ExpressionWrapper` is used to wrap the subtraction operation in a new field called duration.

`fields.DurationField()` is the output type of the **`ExpressionWrapper`**.

`filter(status='DONE')` ensures that we only consider tasks that have reached the 'DONE' status.

`aggregate(average_duration=Avg('duration'))` calculates the average duration across all tasks.

Note that if any attribute alters, **`updated_at`** updates too, potentially skewing our query results and necessitating model adjustments.

Extending the models

To cater to epics and sprints, we need to enhance our application. We will add two new models, Epic and Sprint. Separate models are in place since epics and sprints have unique behaviors and attributes. Having two models allows us to set up different relationships between models. For instance, multiple tasks could belong to an epic, each to a specific sprint.

Before diving deeper, let's touch upon some essential concepts about models and their relationship types.

Django's ORM offers three relationship types: one-to-one, one-to-many, and many-to-many.

The One-to-One Relationship (`OneToOneField`): A one-to-one relationship implies that one object is related to exactly one other object. This can be seen as a constrained version of the **`ForeignKey`**, where the reverse relation is unique.

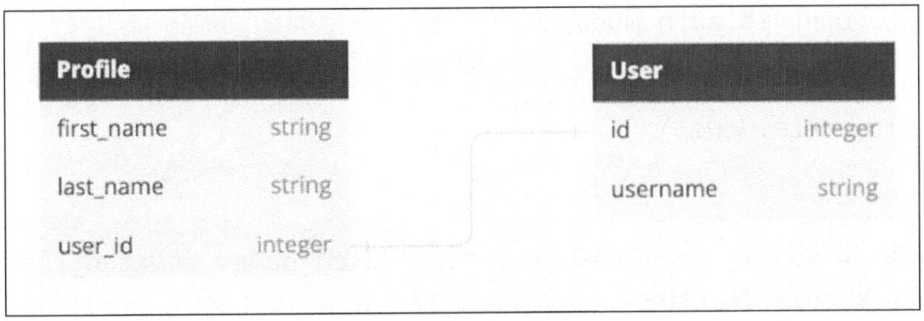

Figure 4.6: *One to one*

A typical example of Django is the User Profile:

```
from django.db import models

from django.contrib.auth.models import User


class Profile(models.Model):

    user = models.OneToOneField(User, on_delete=models.CASCADE)

    # Other fields...
```

A One-To-Many relationship implies one object can be related to several others.

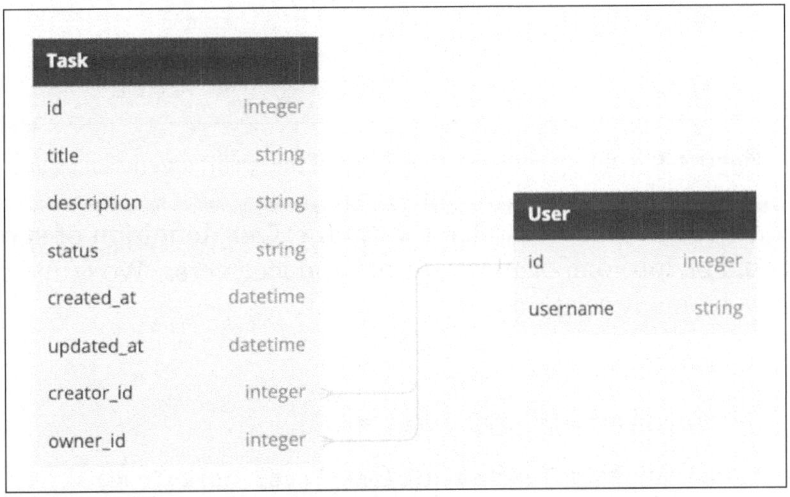

Figure 4.7: *One to many relationships of the Task and User model*

We already use this relation type with the Task model when we specify the creator and the owner:

```
from django.db import models
```

```
from django.contrib.auth.models import User


class Task(models.Model):

    ...

    creator = models.ForeignKey(User, related_name='created_tasks', on_
    delete=models.CASCADE)
```

Many-to-Many (**ManyToManyField**): In this relationship, objects can relate to several others, which, in turn, can associate with multiple entities.

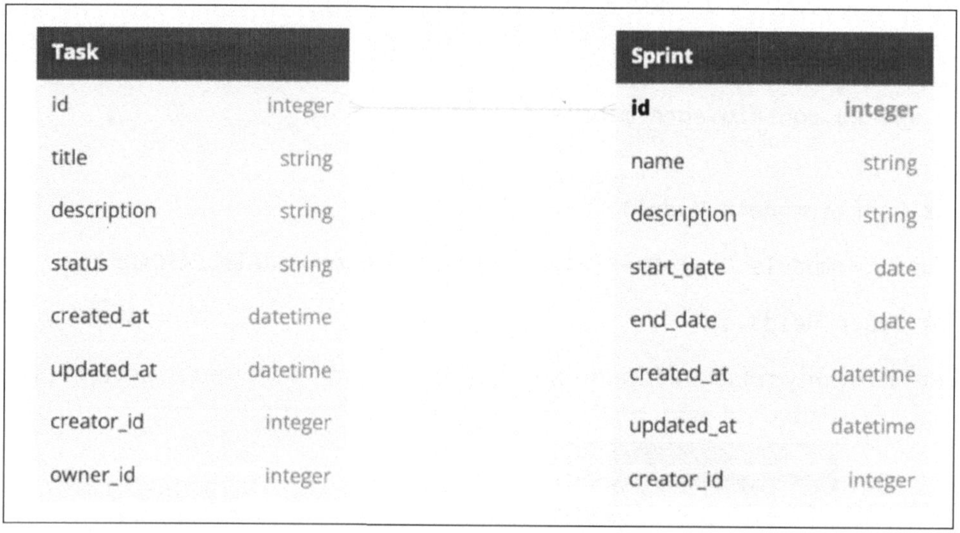

Figure 4.8: *Many-to-many relationships of the sprint and task models*

Here, we introduce our first model, the **Sprint**. Our definition of sprint is that one task could be into one or more sprints and vice versa. We found a use case for the many-to-many relationship:

```
class Sprint(models.Model):

    name = models.CharField(max_length=200)

    description = models.TextField(blank=True, null=True)

    start_date = models.DateField()

    end_date = models.DateField()

    created_at = models.DateTimeField(auto_now_add=True)

    updated_at = models.DateTimeField(auto_now=True)
```

```
    creator = models.ForeignKey(User, related_name='created_sprints',
    on_delete=models.CASCADE)

    tasks = models.ManyToManyField('Task', related_name='sprints',
    blank=True)
```

Info: Many-to-Many relationship in a relational database is implemented using a join table.

The junction table consists of at least two columns, each being a foreign key to the primary key of the tables being related. Each row in the junction table represents a relationship between one row in the first table and one in the second.

The next model to introduce is the **`Epic`**. By our definition, a Task can belong to only one Epic:

```
class Epic(models.Model):

    name = models.CharField(max_length=200)

    description = models.TextField(blank=True, null=True)

    created_at = models.DateTimeField(auto_now_add=True)

    updated_at = models.DateTimeField(auto_now=True)

     creator = models.ForeignKey(User, related_name='created_epics', on_
delete=models.CASCADE)
```

We need to modify the Task model to add a foreign key that references the Epic model:

```
class Task(models.Model):

    ...

    epic = models.ForeignKey(Epic, on_delete=models.SET_NULL)
```

As we've explored the relationship types, it's vital to note potential querying issues that can impact your web application's performance.

Imagine wanting to display all tasks alongside the associated epics for users. Typically the query will be something like this:

```
Task.objects.all()
```

When querying a database, if you retrieve a list of objects and then, for each object, query its related objects separately, you end up with N+1 queries. 'N' represents the number of objects, and '**+1**' is the initial query. This common performance snag is dubbed the "N+1 selects" issue.

Various methods detect the N+1 issue. You can log queries by tweaking project settings or use the **django-tool-bar** to view the framework's total query count.

Tip: Logging slow queries in PostgreSQL can be invaluable for diagnosing performance issues. By keeping track of queries that take an unusually long time to run, you can focus your optimization efforts where they're most needed.

Django provides optimization tools to solve the N+1 problem, the **select_related** and the **prefetch_related**.

- **select_related**: Uses a join query to return all the data from the objects and their relationships. This operation gets all the objects in one query, which could make the initial query more time-consuming and memory-intensive if the relationship has lots of objects. This type of operation can be done when the model has one-to-one or many-to-one.
- **prefetch_related**: Performs separate lookup and Python does the join. Using **prefetch_related** could be faster for one-to-many or many-to-many.

In summary, for foreign keys or one-to-one relationships, **select_related** is ideal. For reverse foreign key lookups or many-to-many relationships, opt for **prefetch_related**.

Here is an example of using it:

```
Task.objects.prefetch_related('epic').all()
```

Info: The open-source community has created amazing packages to detect the N+1 problem, like the **nplusone** or **django-perf-rec**. **nplusone** is a Python library that automatically detects the N+1 queries problem, while **django-perf-rec** is more like a regression testing tool for performance

---

You can also filter using relationship models by using double underscore "__".

Let's suppose that we need to filter all the Tasks of the Sprint with name **"Amsterdam"**:

```
Task.objects.filter(sprint__name="Amsterdam")
```

The previous query will select the tasks that are in the sprint with the name **"Amsterdam"**. This query will perform a join:

```
python manage.py shell

>>> from tasks.models import Task

>>> print(Task.objects.filter(sprints__name="Amsterdam").query)

SELECT "tasks_task"."id", "tasks_task"."title", "tasks_task"."description", "tasks_task"."status", "tasks_task"."created_at", "tasks_task"."updated_at", "tasks_task"."creator_id", "tasks_task"."owner_id" FROM "tasks_task" INNER JOIN "tasks_sprint_tasks" ON ("tasks_task"."id" = "tasks_sprint_tasks"."task_id") INNER JOIN "tasks_sprint" ON ("tasks_sprint_tasks"."sprint_id" = "tasks_sprint"."id") WHERE "tasks_sprint"."name" = Amsterdam
```

Ensuring data integrity with model constraints

A database constraint is a rule used to ensure data integrity. Using constraints restricts the type of data stored in the database, which prevents accidental storing of invalid data.

Without constraints, our models could have invalid values. Think of a sprint ending before its start or tasks with unacceptable statuses.

Several types of constraints exist in databases:

- **Primary Key**: One of the most important constraints defining the model's identity that uniquely identifies a record in the table.
- **Foreign Key**: Identifies a record in another table.
- **Unique**: Ensures that all the values in a column are unique.
- **Not null**: Ensures that a column cannot have null values.
- **Check**: A rule that verifies whether the values in a column meet a specific condition.
- **Default**: This constraint sets a value when none was previously defined.

Let's now implement constraints for the Sprint model, ensuring logical start and end dates:

```
class Sprint(models.Model):
```

```
    ...
    start_date = models.DateField()
    end_date = models.DateField()

    class Meta:
        constraints = [
            models.CheckConstraint(check=models.Q(end_date__
            gt=models.F('start_date')), name='end_date_after_start_
            date'),
        ]
```

Place all configurations that are unrelated to fields within the model's optional Meta options. The meta options are not only for constraints but also for setting a different table name, ordering, verbose name or many more.

Constraints get listed as **CheckConstraint** objects, and they all must be valid. The **CheckConstraint** accepts a **Q** instance, which is a way to encapsulate a SQL condition into a Python object. In Django, the function **F** lets you directly reference model field values and perform related database operations. **F('start_date')** refers to the value of the **start_date** field.

After adding constraints to the class meta, regenerate the migrations:

```
python manage.py makemigrations
# add the constraints to the database
python manage.py migrate
```

If a sprint is saved with a start date that is not less than the end date, Django will raise an **IntegrityError**.

```
>>> from tasks.models import Sprint
>>> from django.utils import timezone
>>>
>>> from datetime import timedelta
>>> current_time = timezone.now()
>>> one_day_ago = current_time - timedelta(days=1)
```

```
>>>

>>> from django.contrib.auth.models import User

>>> creator = User.objects.get(pk=1)

>>> Sprint.objects.create(name="Eternals epic", start_date=current_time,
end_date=one_day_ago, creator=creator)

Traceback (most recent call last):

  File "/Users/mandarina/Library/Caches/pypoetry/virtualenvs/task-
  manager-ox-Othme-py3.10/lib/python3.10/site-packages/django/db/
  backends/utils.py", line 89, in _execute

    return self.cursor.execute(sql, params)

  File "/Users/mandarina/Library/Caches/pypoetry/virtualenvs/task-
  manager-ox-Othme-py3.10/lib/python3.10/site-packages/psycopg/cursor.
  py", line 723, in execute

    raise ex.with_traceback(None)

psycopg.errors.CheckViolation: new row for relation "tasks_sprint"
violates check constraint "end_date_after_start_date"
```

This demonstrates the effectiveness of the constraint we added.

Let's now consider the status field of the Task object:

```
>>> from tasks.models import Task

# let's try to filter with a status that is not defined in the choice field

>>> Task.objects.create(title="test", creator=creator, status="INVALID")

<Task: Task object (14)>
```

Like the Sprint model, we'll integrate a Meta class into the model, constraining the status attribute values:

```
class Meta:

    constraints = [

        models.CheckConstraint(

                check=models.Q(status='UNASSIGNED') |
                models.Q(status='IN_PROGRESS') | models.Q(status='DONE')
                | models.Q(status='ARCHIVED'),
```

```
                name='status_check',
            ),
        ]
```

Next, generate the migrations once more:

```
python manage.py makemigrations

# add the constraints to the database

python manage.py migrate
```

If your database has any Task instance with an invalid status, the migrate command will fail with an **IntegrityError**, and you will need to proceed with data migration to fix the invalid status.

Conclusion

Models are foundational to your web application. Models bring life to your project. The framework provides many tools to work with these models, like the migration system and the database API.

The admin interface is user-friendly. With just a few lines of code, you can create a versatile admin panel with various roles.

The ORM lets you craft high-level object operations, which can be easily understood and converted to SQL. It adds a layer that enables the use of any database engine behind it.

Using model constraints to enforce rules and maintain data consistency is essential.

In many projects, you'll often need to know how to set up relationships between Django models. Knowing how these relationships work will enable you to build more efficient web applications.

Databases have three relationship forms: one-to-one, one-to-many, and many-to-many. For data integrity and effective operations, these relationships control the specific and shared associations between data records in various tables.

In the next chapter, we'll explore how to link URLs with views. We will tour different ways to implement views, with function views and class-based views. With this knowledge, we will implement our first views.

Questions

1. What is the role of a primary key in a relational database and how does it relate to Django models?
2. Explain how Django's ORM translates Python code into SQL commands. Use the `.save()` method as an example.
3. What are the differences between `models.CASCADE`, `models.SET_NULL`, and `models.PROTECT` with regards to `on_delete` property in a `ForeignKey` field?
4. What is the difference between the get and filter methods in Django, and what do they return?
5. What is the result of calling the `.delete()` method on a Django model instance or a QuerySet? What does the returned tuple represent?
6. What are Django migrations and what purpose do they serve in Django projects?
7. What does **squashing** migrations mean in Django, and how can it be done? What are the benefits of squashing migrations?
8. What is the purpose of the `has_change_permission`, `has_add_permission`, and `has_delete_permission` methods in Django's `ModelAdmin` class?
9. Why is the `is_staff` flag important for Django users, and how can it be enabled?
10. What is Django's built-in authentication system, and how can it be utilized with Group models to manage permissions?
11. Can you explain the difference between the `exclude` method and the `filter` method in Django's ORM? Why might one be more intuitive than the other?
12. How is a Many-to-Many relationship implemented in a relational database?
13. How does the `related_name` attribute function in Django's ForeignKey and `ManyToManyField` relations?
14. What is the purpose of a database constraint and why is it important?
15. What is the role of the Meta class in a Django model?

Exercises

1. Extend the Task model by adding a new field `due_date` to represent when the task is due. You must generate and apply migrations, verify that the changes were applied as expected, and add the field to the admin. Think about the default values for this new attribute.
2. Play more with the Django shell and try to create a Task without an owner. Does Django raise any errors? Was it possible to create the Task?
3. Configure the Django Admin to filter Task by `created_at` date.
4. Create a constraint that the `due_date` has to be greater than the `created_at`.

Squash all the migration created in this chapter.

CHAPTER 5

Django Views and URL Handling

Introduction

We begin the chapter with a precise definition of a view and its responsibilities. We'll then explore the framework's various generic views for common scenarios.

We will write our first views using Django's generic views and configure the URL paths to allow users to interact with tasks in our project management project.

With a path converter, we will understand how to pass arguments to the views and, with namespaces, how to prevent name clashing between URLs from multiple applications.

Through function-based views with a service layer, we will implement our first business logic to add a Task to a Sprint atomically

Tackling concurrent data access is a challenging problem to solve. Utilizing pessimistic and optimistic locking techniques, we'll engineer a robust solution for concurrent data access, employing Django views and a service layer.

Lastly, we will customize HTTP error codes to better align with the aesthetics of our project.

Structure

In this chapter, we will cover the following topics:

- Understanding Django Views
- Introduction to Django's Generic Views
- Writing Your First Django View
- Class-based Views Mixins
- URL Configuration in Django
- Creating URL Patterns for Your Views
- Using Django's `HttpRequest` and `HttpResponse` Objects
- Handling Dynamic URLs with Path Converters
- Understanding Django's URL Namespace and Naming URL Patterns
- Introduction to Function-based Views
- Using Function-based Views with a Service Layer
- Pessimistic and Optimistic Locking Using Views and a Service Layer
- Error Handling with Custom Error Views

Understanding Django Views

Before understanding views, it's crucial to understand the Hypertext Transfer Protocol (HTTP). HTTP is an application-level protocol in the OSI model and forms the backbone of the World Wide Web (WWW). The protocol is the foundation of any data exchange and transmits different hypermedia documents, like HTML and JSON.

HTTP follows a client-server model, where the client submits a request to the server and the server returns a response. The protocol is stateless, meaning each command is executed independently without referencing previous ones.

HTTP uses methods for its requests. The most common methods are `GET`, `POST`, `DELETE`, and `PUT`. Once the server processes the request, it will return a response with a status code that helps us understand what happened on the server. Well-known response codes are 200, 404, and 500, for example.

To adhere to best practices for views, we need to define their responsibility. They handle the request, delegate it to the suitable service layer, and return a response. Views will take everything related to the HTTP world, directing authentication, producing the correct HTTP code, and making redirects. Our recommendation is to avoid adding business logic to the view. There are multiple reasons not to add business logic to the views. Some of them are:

- Reusability: Embedding business logic directly into the view severely hampers its reusability elsewhere, given that views are tightly coupled with HTTP requests and responses.
- Testability: If you have the business logic in the view, it is more difficult to test, since it requires mocking the response object. When your logic is in a service layer or domain model, you can test it in isolation.
- Coupling: If you have the business logic in the views, changing the business logic will require changes in the view and vice-versa.

Note: In the MVC architecture, the onus of managing HTTP requests falls squarely on the controller. Given that MVC also employs a component called 'view,' it's easy to get confused when you toss the MVT pattern into the mix–especially since the terminology overlaps. In the MVT pattern, the view is the controller.

Now that we know business logic has no place in our views, we're prepared to construct lean, laser-focused components that coordinate requests and responses. We are ready to learn about the framework's different views.

Introducing Django's Generic Views

The framework provides class-based views for common scenarios, allowing you to create fewer code views.

Generic views can handle much boilerplate code, like pagination, processing forms, and more. Generic views will make your code easier to maintain but sometimes more challenging to understand if you are unfamiliar with the framework.

Note: Class-based views tempt you to write the business logic in the class implementation. Remember that class-based views are still views, so avoid writing business logic in class-based views.

Applying them judiciously fast-tracks the implementation of robust solutions. As a rule of thumb, use generic views when you don't need to customize them often.

Let's review the generic views the framework provides.

List and detail views:

- `ListView`: A view that displays a list of objects from a model.
- `DetailView`: A view that shows a single object and its details.

Date-based views:

- `ArchiveIndexView`: A date-based view that lists objects from a date-based queryset in the "latest first" order.
- `YearArchiveView`: A date-based view that lists objects from a year-based queryset.
- `MonthArchiveView`: A date-based view that lists objects from a month-based queryset.
- `WeekArchiveView`: A date-based view that lists objects from a week-based queryset.
- `DayArchiveView`: A date-based view that lists objects from a day-based queryset.
- `TodayArchiveView`: A date-based view that lists objects from a queryset related to the current day.
- `DateDetailView`: A date-based view that provides an object from a date-based queryset, matching the given year, month, and day.

Editing views:

- `FormView`: A view that displays a form on GET and processes it on POST.
- `CreateView`: A view that shows a form for creating a new object, which is saved to a model.
- `UpdateView`: A view that shows a form for updating an existing object, which is saved to a model.
- `DeleteView`: A view that shows a confirmation page and deletes an existing object.

The base view:

- `TemplateView`: A view that renders a specified template. This one does not involve any kind of model operations.

As we'll uncover later, class-based views and the service layer concept are far from a match. We advise you to learn how to use the framework's tools correctly.

Writing Your First Django View

Generic class-based views usually fit the most common scenarios. We'll develop Task views to handle typical scenarios: creating, modifying, updating, and deleting Task instances. For now, we won't delve into authentication; however, *Chapter 8: User Authentication and Authorization in Django* will revisit these views and add security.

```
# Code for tasks/views.py

from django.urls import reverse_lazy

from django.views.generic import DetailView, ListView

from django.views.generic.edit import CreateView, DeleteView, UpdateView


from .models import Task


class TaskListView(ListView):

    model = Task

    template_name = "task_list.html"

    context_object_name = "tasks"


class TaskDetailView(DetailView):

    model = Task

    template_name = "task_detail.html"

    context_object_name = "task"


class TaskCreateView(CreateView):

    model = Task

    template_name = "task_form.html"

    fields = ("name", "description", "start_date", "end_date")


    def get_success_url(self):
```

```
        return reverse_lazy("task-detail", kwargs={"pk": self.object.
        id})


class TaskUpdateView(UpdateView):

    model = Task

    template_name = "task_form.html"

    fields = ("name", "description", "start_date", "end_date")


    def get_success_url(self):

        return reverse_lazy("task-detail", kwargs={"pk": self.object.
        id})


class TaskDeleteView(DeleteView):

    model = Task

    template_name = "task_confirm_delete.html"

    success_url = reverse_lazy("task-list")
```

Adhering to the Single Responsibility Principle (SRP), each class has a distinct function. The class name and its parent class signify the view's specific operation.

For each view in Django, there is usually a corresponding HTML template that the view uses to generate the webpage. Here's an example of how you might structure the HTML templates for each view:

templates/tasks/task_list.html: This template displays a list of tasks.

```
{% extends "base.html" %}


{% block content %}

  <h1>Task List</h1>

  <ul>

  {% for task in tasks %}

    <li>

      <a href="{% url 'task-detail' task.id %}">{{ task.name }}</a>
```

```
    </li>
  {% empty %}
    <li>No tasks available.</li>
  {% endfor %}
  </ul>
{% endblock %}
```

The template will iterate all the tasks and show a link for each task to see more details using the template tag **`URL`**. If there are no tasks, it will show **`No Tasks available`**.

templates/tasks/task_detail.html: This template displays the details of a single task.

```
{% extends "base.html" %}

{% block content %}
  <h1>{{ task.name }}</h1>
  <p>{{ task.description }}</p>
  <a href="{% url 'task-update' task.id %}">Edit</a>
  <a href="{% url 'task-delete' task.id %}">Delete</a>
{% endblock %}
```

The task detail template will show the name and description of the task with two links, one to update the task and the other to delete the task. Both links use the template tag **`url`** and the URL name to refer to the appropriate view.

templates/tasks/task_form.html: This template is used for creating and updating tasks.

```
{% extends "base.html" %}

{% block content %}
  <h1>New Task</h1>
  <form method="post">
```

```
  {% csrf_token %}
  {{ form.as_p }}
  <button type="submit">Save</button>
  </form>
{% endblock %}
```

The update task renders the task form and shows a **Save** button to perform the update operation.

templates/tasks/task_confirm_delete.html: This template asks the user to confirm before deleting a task.

```
{% extends "base.html" %}

{% block content %}
  <h1>Delete Task</h1>
  <p>Are you sure you want to delete the task "{{ task.name }}"?</p>
  <form method="post">
  {% csrf_token %}
  <button type="submit">Yes, delete</button>
  </form>
  <a href="{% url 'task-detail' task.id %}">No, take me back</a>
{% endblock %}
```

Using generic views is simple and it will keep your project code lean. Use them when there is no need for custom logic. Later in this chapter, we will see how to use a service layer with function-based views.

Class-based Views Mixins

A way to provide code reusability using inheritance is through the `mixin` concept. A mixin is a class with defined properties and methods that provides a particular generic behavior and is not meant to be instantiated. Mixin does not require a hierarchical relationship between those classes; you can add as many as you want to extend your class behavior.

In object-oriented design, inheritance should be used to model an **is-a** relationship based on the behavior. The idea is that a class should inherit from another class based on the behavior.

As an example, we will create a **SprintTaskWithinRangeMixin**. This mixin ensures a task being created or updated is within the date range of its associated sprint.

```
# tasks/mixins.py

from django.http import HttpResponseBadRequest

from django.shortcuts import get_object_or_404

from .services import can_add_task_to_sprint


class SprintTaskWithinRangeMixin:

    """

        Mixin to ensure a task being created or updated is within the
        date range of its associated sprint.

    """

    def dispatch(self, request, *args, **kwargs):

        task = self.get_object() if hasattr(self, "get_object") else None

        sprint_id = request.POST.get("sprint")

        if sprint_id:

            # If a task exists (for UpdateView) or is about to be
            created (for CreateView)

            if task or request.method == "POST":

                if not can_add_task_to_sprint(task, sprint_id):

                    return HttpResponseBadRequest(

                        "Task's creation date is outside the date range
                        of the associated sprint."

                )
```

```
        return super().dispatch(request, *args, **kwargs)
```

In Django's class-based views, the dispatch method is the entry point for the incoming HTTP requests. When the framework processes a request, the dispatch method will delegate the request to the appropriate method (**get**, **post**, **put**, **delete**) based on the HTTP method.

Our Mixin overrides the dispatch method, checking sprint start and end date using the service layer before invoking the relevant method via the super call.

We will return a wrong HTTP response if the interval is invalid.

Using the mixing is simple. You need to inherit from it:

```
# tasks/views.py

from django.views.generic import CreateView, UpdateView

from .models import Task

from .mixins import SprintTaskMixin


class TaskCreateView(SprintTaskMixin, CreateView):

    model = Task

    template_name = "task_form.html"

    fields = ("name", "description", "start_date", "end_date")


    def get_success_url(self):

        return reverse_lazy("task-detail", kwargs={"pk": self.object.
        id})


class TaskUpdateView(SprintTaskMixin, UpdateView):

    model = Task

    template_name = "task_form.html"

    fields = ("name", "description", "start_date", "end_date")


    def get_success_url(self):
```

```
        return reverse_lazy("task-detail", kwargs={"pk": self.object.
        id})
```

The code for the service layer is the following:

```
from django.shortcuts import get_object_or_404

from .models import Sprint


def can_add_task_to_sprint(task, sprint_id):
    """

    Checks if a task can be added to a sprint based on the sprint's date
    range.

    """

    sprint = get_object_or_404(Sprint, id=sprint_id)

    return sprint.start_date <= task.created_at.date() <= sprint.end_date
```

It's a simple check using the **`start_date`** and **`end_date`** using the task creation date.

Info: Inheritance is a powerful object-oriented tool that can help reduce code duplication. However, overuse of inheritance for code reuse can lead to several problems.

Whenever you want to inherit from a class, don't think about code reusability; think more about behavior.

Invalid inheritance could lead to:

- Tight coupling: Inheritance creates a strong relationship between the parent and child classes. Any changes in the parent class may unintentionally affect the behavior of the child classes.
- Exposing too many public methods: When a class inherits from another, it gets access to all its public methods, even those it doesn't need.

For code reusability, composition often beats inheritance. Composition creates complex objects by using other, more simple objects.

For example, in terms of object-oriented design, one might be tempted to make Sprint a subclass of **`Epic`** to reuse fields like **`name`**, **`description`**, **`created_at`**, **`updated_at`**, and **`creator`**.

However, it is incorrect to model this relationship with inheritance because a Sprint is not a type of Epic. In terms of Agile methodology, they are different. Understanding the business domain you are trying to model is crucial to creating the right abstractions in your application.

If the application evolves to a point where **`Epic`** and **`Sprint`** share a lot of expected behaviors, consider using a mixing to share a common code.

When crafting a mixin, aim for a singular responsibility and strive for generality. A mixin class that solves multiple problems could be a sign of bad design or a code smell. Another essential convention to follow when creating a mixin is to use the postfix "Mixin". This will denote the usage of the class. Not adding this postfix is a mistake, leading developers to create a hierarchy from this class instead of adding it for behavior.

Note: There is an anti-pattern called the god object when the object knows or does too much. This anti-pattern is an example of poor design, as it contradicts modular design principles.

Not using mixins with a single responsibility could lead to an object that contains all the standard methods and attributes just for the sake of code reuse and it might become a god object.

The key is to ensure that each class adheres to the Single Responsibility Principle (SRP). Django's framework furnishes an abundant array of mixins for augmenting view behaviors.

Here is a list of the most common and valuable mixins the framework provides:

Attribute Mixins:

- **`ContextMixin`**: Adds extra context data to the view.
- **`TemplateResponseMixin`**: Renders templates and returns an HTTP response.
- **`SingleObjectMixin`**: Provides handling to get a single object from the database.

Data Modification Mixins:

- **`FormMixin`**: Used to handle form submission and validation.
- **`ModelFormMixin`**: Extends FormMixin to deal with model forms.
- **`CreateModelMixin`**: Used to save a new object to the database.
- **`UpdateModelMixin`**: Used to update an existing object in the database.
- **`DeleteModelMixin`**: Used to delete an object.

Fetching Data:

- **`SingleObjectMixin`**: Used to fetch a single object based on the primary key or slug
- **`MultipleObjectMixin`**: Used to fetch multiple objects (often used for listing views)
- **`Pagination`**
- **`MultipleObjectMixin`**: Provides pagination functionality if the **`paginate_by`** attribute is set

Redirect and Success URL Handling

- **`RedirectView`**: Used to handle simple HTTP redirects.

- `SuccessMessageMixin`: Used to display a success message after acting successfully.

The `ListView` that we use to list the Task objects inherits the `MultipleObjectMixin` and the `TemplateResponseMixin`. Doing this will give you the pagination behavior and template rendering capabilities.

URL Configuration in Django

We have already touched upon URL configurations in previous chapters. However, to delve deeper into the subject, it's crucial to understand regular expressions.

A regular expression, often abbreviated as regex, is a sequence of characters forming a search pattern. The sequence of characters is used to match a pattern in a text. Regex can be straightforward, like matching `help` as we did in *Chapter 2, Setting Up Your Development Environment*, or a complex one, like the ones used to identify an email address within a document.

Understanding regex may initially be challenging, but vital for effective URL manipulation.

Let's review some fundamental components of regular expressions:

- **Literal characters:** These are the most straightforward, matching in any text string. For instance, the regex 'a' would match 'a' in any text containing 'a'.
- **Special characters**: These are reserved characters that carry special meanings. For instance, '.' represents any character except a newline.
- **Quantifiers**: Dictate the number of instances for a character or group of characters you want to match. Examples include '*', '+', '?', '{n}', '{n,}', and '{n,m}'.
- **Character classes**: Set of characters enclosed between square brackets []. It will match any one character in the brackets. For example, '[abc]' will match any of 'a', 'b', or 'c'.
- **Escape sequences**: Sometimes, you will need to match special characters that are reserved. You will need to use the backslash (\) to do this. For example, if you want to search for a period, you'd need to use '\.' in your pattern.
- **Anchors**: Anchors are used to specify the position of the pattern concerning a line of text. '^' is used to check if a string starts with a

specific character, and '$' is used to check if a string ends with a particular character.

- **Groups and capturing**: Parentheses define groups and capture specific character sets. These captured groups can be reused through numbered back-references.
- **Alternation**: The pipe character (|) defines alternatives matching the pattern.
- **Flags**: These are options to modify the behavior of the pattern match. For example, 'i' is used for case-insensitive matches, 'g' for global search, and so on.

Django URL configuration uses regex to match the URL's path to a specific view.

The following is a Django example that retrieves tasks archived in a specific year:

```
from django.urls import re_path

from . import views


urlpatterns = [

    re_path(r'^tasks/(?P<year>[0-9]{4})/$', views.year_archive),

]
```

The regex begins with '^', indicating that the path should start with `'tasks/'`. The next part `(?P<year>[0-9]{4})` will match a four-digit number and it will pass this value as a `year` parameter to the view. The `$` specifies that the end of the URL has to have "/" at the ending to match this pattern.

Note: That the '`r`' preceding the string is a flag, informing Python that this is a raw string. In raw strings, backslashes are treated as literal characters. Raw strings are useful because regular expressions often contain a lot of backslashes; without this flag, Python would try to interpret these backslashes as escape sequences.

It's important to note that for most basic URL patterns, complex regex is not required. However, as your application grows or when dealing with more intricate routing requirements, the versatility of regex becomes invaluable. Regular expressions offer a powerful tool for matching various string patterns, allowing greater flexibility and control over your URL configurations.

Creating URL Patterns for your Views

Having set up our class-based views, we can now proceed to create their corresponding URL patterns:

```
from django.urls import path

from django.views.generic import TemplateView


from .views import (

    TaskCreateView,

    TaskDeleteView,

    TaskDetailView,

    TaskListView,

    TaskUpdateView,

)


urlpatterns = [

    path("", TemplateView.as_view(template_name="tasks/home.html"),
    name="home"),

    path("help/", TemplateView.as_view(template_name="tasks/help.html"),
    name="help"),

    path("tasks/", TaskListView.as_view(), name="task-list"),  # GET

    path("tasks/new/", TaskCreateView.as_view(), name="task-create"),  #
    POST

    path("tasks/<int:pk>/", TaskDetailView.as_view(), name="task-
    detail"),  # GET

    path(

        "tasks/<int:pk>/edit/", TaskUpdateView.as_view(), name="task-
        update"
```

```
    ),  # PUT/PATCH
    path(
        "tasks/<int:pk>/delete/", TaskDeleteView.as_view(), name="task-delete"
    ),  # DELETE
]
```

Each view is associated with a unique URL pattern.

Notably, generic class-based views are only engineered to handle one HTTP method within a single class. Therefore, we adhere to the Single Responsibility Principle (SRP) by utilizing different classes for each operation. The angle brackets in the URL patterns signify dynamic segments, capturing portions of the URL to be passed as arguments to the view functions.

These generic views in Django are each designed for a specific type of request:

- **`DetailView`** and **`ListView`** are designed to handle **`GET`** requests.
- **`CreateView`**, **`UpdateView`**, and **`DeleteView`** are designed to handle **`GET`** and **`POST`** requests. We need the **`GET`** to ask the user for the data to submit in the **`POST`**.

Notice that our **urls.py** file does not import any models, adhering to Django's best practices by avoiding tight coupling between the URL patterns and the models.

Although the URLs we've defined are not strictly RESTful, we'll delve into designing a RESTful API in *Chapter 9, Django Ninja and APIs*.

Handling Dynamic URLs with Path Converters

When using the path function in the URL patterns, it is possible to use the angle brackets to define parts of the URL that can be captured and passed as a parameter to the view:

```
path('tasks/<int:pk>/', TaskDetailView.as_view(), name='task-detail'),
```

In this case, **`<int:pk>`** is a path converter. The first part, **`int`** is the converter type telling the framework what type to match. The second part, **`pk`**, serves as the variable name to which the matched value is assigned; this variable is then passed as a parameter to the view.

Django has several built-in converters:

- **str**: Matches any non-empty string, excluding the path separator, '/'.
- **int**: Matches zero or any positive integer.
- **slug**: Matches any ASCII alphanumeric string, hyphens and underscores.
- **uuid**: Matches a formatted UUID.
- **path**: Matches any non-empty string, including the path separator, '/'.

If the built-in converters fall short of your needs, you can also roll out your custom path converter.

Let's see how to create a custom path converter for the date type. The converter we are going to define handles dates in the format "YYYY-MM-DD", where "**YYYY**" is the 4-digit year, "**MM**" is the 2-digit month, and "**DD**" is the 2-digit day.

To craft your custom path converter, either inherit from one of Django's built-in converter classes or independently implement two requisite methods.

Let's see the implementation of the **DateConverter** class by implementing the class protocol:

```
# tasks/converters.py

from datetime import datetime


class DateConverter:

    regex = "[0-9]{4}-[0-9]{2}-[0-9]{2}"


    def to_python(self, value):

        return datetime.strptime(value, "%Y-%m-%d")


    def to_url(self, object):

        return object.strftime("%Y-%m-%d")
```

You'll need to implement two core methods: **to_python** and **to_url**. The former takes a string and morphs it into an object, while the latter transforms a datetime object into a string. The regex is designed to match strings formatted as dates in the "YYYY-MM-DD" pattern.

To use the converter, you will need to register it:

```
# tasks/urls.py

from django.urls import path, register_converter


from . import views, converters


register_converter(converters.DateConverter, "yyyymmdd")


urlpatterns = [

    # ...

    path("tasks/<yyyymmdd:date>/", views.task_by_date),

    # ...

]
```

The **task_by_date** view will be spotlighted in this chapter's *Introduction to Function-based Views* section.

Understanding Django's URL Namespace and Naming URL Patterns

URL patterns can be organized in a friendly way using namespaces and names. Each URL has an optional parameter **name**:

```
path("tasks/", TaskListView.as_view(), name="task-list"),
```

Once you have named a URL, you can use this alias across various parts of your application, a lifesaver for future changes to the URL path. Using the name is a good practice since if you decide to change the path in the future, you will not need to change it somewhere else:

Suppose we want to redirect the user to the task list view:

```
from django.shortcuts import redirect

from django.urls import reverse
```

```
def task_home(request):

    return redirect(reverse("task-list"))
```

Info: HTTP redirects instruct the client to stop loading the current page and start loading a different URL.

Redirects are used for many different purposes. For example, it could be used to ensure that users always use HTTPS or when they are not authenticated to show the login page.

The HTTP status codes for redirect are in the range of 3xx. The most common ones are:

- 301: Moved permanently, meaning the resource is permanently located at the new address.
- 302: Moved temporarily: This indicates that the resource has moved temporarily to a new URL, but future requests should still target the original URL.

In this case, **home_view** shuttles the user off to the Task List view; notably, the view references the URL by its name rather than its explicit path. This allows the user to change the path in the future without changing all its usage.

Within a multi-app environment, you could run into clashing URL names. The framework uses the namespace to differentiate URLs with the same name but from different applications.

To set the namespace for URLs, use the **app_name** variable in the urls.py file:

```
app_name = "tasks"  # namespace


urlpatterns = [

    path("tasks/home/", task_home, name="task-home"),

   path("tasks/<int:pk>/", TaskDetailView.as_view(), name="task-detail"),

    #...

]
```

Utilizing a namespace alters how you reference the URL:

```
from django.shortcuts import redirect

from django.urls import reverse
```

```
def home_view(request):
    return redirect(reverse("tasks:detail"))
```

A colon is the delimiter between the **tasks** namespace and the URL name. In this way, if there is another view with the name **detail** it won't clash with the task's detail view.

Using Django's HttpRequest And HttpResponse Objects

The framework provides valuable object representations of the HTTP request and response. These objects are meant to exist within the scope of the view functions and shouldn't be passed beyond that boundary.

Whenever a request hits the Django server, the framework instantiates an HttpRequest object, passed as the first argument to the view function.

Let's review some crucial attributes of the **HttpRequest**:

- **method**: An upper case string with the method used in the request sent to the server, for example, **GET**, **POST**.
- **user**: An instance of the framework User class representing the logging-in user. When the user is not logged in, instead of the User instance, you will find an AnonymousUser instance. We will see more on how to handle authentication in *Chapter 8, User Authentication and Authorization in Django.*
- **path**: A string with the requested URL path.
- **GET**: A dictionary-like object containing all available GET parameters.
- **POST**: A dictionary-like object containing all available POST parameters.
- **FILES**: A dictionary-like object containing all available file upload input parameters.
- **headers**: A dictionary-like object containing all available HTTP headers.

Using the HttpRequest object, you gain straightforward access to incoming request data, simplifying your view logic.

The HttpResponse object is the view return type, encapsulating Django's HTTP response to the client.

Here is an example that returns an HTML-rendered template using the **`HttpResponse`**.

```
from django.http import HttpResponse

from django.template import loader


def example_view(request: HttpRequest) -> HttpResponse:

    template = loader.get_template("example.html")

    context = {"name": "Test"}  # data to inject into the template

    html = template.render(context, request)

    return HttpResponse(html)
```

The **`HttpResponse`** object accepts a parameter that contains the content destined for the client. The function **`example_view`** is a function-based view, we will see more about this type of function in the next section.

Info: Instead of using the template loader and rendering the template, you can use a Django frameworks shortcut **`render`**:

```
from django.shortcuts import render

def example_view(request):

    context = {"key": "value"}  # data to inject into the template

    return render(request, "example.html", context)
```

The HttpResponse has a `status_code` and `content_type` parameters that can be used to return different types of responses, like not found 404. For some exceptional common cases, the framework provides other objects that can be useful:

- **`HttpResponseRedirect`**: Redirect the user to a different URL. The status code is 302.
- **`HttpResponseNotFound`**: Used to inform that the resource was not found. The status code is 404.
- **`HttpResponseBadRequest`**: This response is used to inform that the server cannot or will not process the request due to something that is perceived

to be a client error. The status code is 400.

- **`HttpResponseForbidden`**: Indicates that the server understands the request but refuses to authorize it. The status code associated with the response is 403.
- **`HttpResponseServerError`**: When an unexpected error occurs on the server side, there is a status code (500) to inform about it.
- **`JsonResponse`**: This class converts a serializable Python object into a JSON-formatted HTTP response. This type of response will add the content-type header to the response with the value application/json.

Info: The **`Content-Type`** header plays a crucial role in ensuring the correct interpretation of data. Specifically, when this header is set to **`application/json,`** it means that the data being sent or received is formatted as **`JSON.`** By specifying **`application/json,`** developers ensure that the receiving end understands that the transmitted data should be treated as a **`JSON`** object.

Django offers additional subclasses of **`HttpResponse`** tailored for various common scenarios. You can always use the HttpResponse to return any response type, but using the built-in classes makes the code lean and easy to understand.

Introducing to Function-based Views

The framework has two different ways to implement views: function-based views (FBV) and class-based views (CBV).

Since the introduction of CBV in March 2011, Django's official documentation has promoted its usage, and many developers in the Django community prefer CBVs. There is a tendency to reject FBV, saying it's the old way and everything should be implemented using CBV. This statement is not entirely true; sometimes, it's better to use FBV than CBV.

Function-based views are the most straightforward way to define a view with Django. FBVs are simply Python functions that accept an **`HttpRequest`** object as an argument and return an **`HttpResponse`** object.

Let's see one example of FBV:

```
from datetime import date

from django.http import HttpRequest, HttpResponse

from django.shortcuts import render
```

```
def task_by_date(request: HttpRequest, by_date: date) -> HttpResponse:
    tasks = services.get_task_by_date(by_date)
    context = {"tasks": tasks}
    return render(request, "task_list.html", context)
```

The function takes a **HttpRequest** object and uses the `render` shortcut to return a **HttpResponse** object. The `render` function allows you to render a template with a context. In *Chapter 6, Using the Django Template Engine*, we will learn more about the template engine that the framework provides.

Path converters feature can be used with function and CBV. However, when using function views with type hints, you no longer have to check the URLConf to be sure about the type.

You can't define argument types in the method signature with class-based views, as CBVs don't include these parameters. This can make the code more challenging to read.

Now, let's suppose we need to process a **POST** request that receives the task's ID to check the task using the service layer:

```
from django.http import HttpRequest, HttpResponse, HttpResponseRedirect
from django.shortcuts import render
from django.urls import reverse


def check_task(request: HttpRequest) -> HttpResponse:
    if request.method == "POST":
            # Extract the 'task_id' parameter from the POST data.
            task_id = request.POST.get("task_id")
                 if services.check_task(task_id):
                     return HttpResponseRedirect(reverse("success"))
       if task_id:
                 return HttpResponseRedirect(reverse("success"))
       else:
```

```
            # If no ID was provided, re-render the form with an error
            message.
            return render(
                    request, "add_task_to_sprint.html", {"error":
                    "Task ID is required."}
            )
    else:
          # If the request method is not POST, just render the form.
          return render(request, "check_task.html")
```

First, our code checks for the method type to equal POST. When it's not, we render the template with the HTML form.

The request method can be **POST**, while no data is sent; therefore, we need to check if the **task_id** is present in the payload. If we find the expected payload in the request, we can do something with it and then redirect the user to the success page; otherwise, we show an error to inform the user that the first name is required.

The template code of the **check_task.html** with the form to request the user for the **task_id** is:

```
<form method="post">
  {% csrf_token %}
  <label for="name">Please insert Task ID:</label>
  <input id="id" type="text" name="id">
  <input type="submit" value="Submit">
  {% if error %}
    <p>{{ error }}</p>
  {% endif %}
</form>
```

Our template contains an HTML form that prompts the user for data. When the user clicks the submit button, the browser generates a POST request to the server. In *Chapter 7: Forms in Django*, we will see an alternative, more Django way to implement form and explain the security mechanism of the CSRF token in depth.

Using function-based views gives you more direct control over the request and response objects since it allows you to manipulate the objects with no abstraction layer. But more control also gives you more responsibility for handling different cases and, therefore, a foot gun. It requires rigor to avoid too much code duplication and long function-based views that contain too much logic.

Starting with FBVs is advisable for Django beginners because they are straightforward and don't require in-depth knowledge of the framework's API.

Deciding when to use FBV is a challenging task. When the view is simple or the framework class views don't match the behavior you need to implement, using functions as views could be a good idea. Keeping your code lean and easy to understand is part of the framework's philosophy.

Don't hesitate to use functions as views; simplicity is the key.

Using Function-based Views with a Service Layer

Using function-based views with a service layer is ideal, as there is no need to override or change the behavior of class-based views to integrate the service layer. Our views will only handle the request and generate a response based on the return values of the service layer. The models will be small and straightforward, and their purpose will be as data holders.

Let's consider the use case where we must create a new task and associate it with an active sprint. An `active` sprint is defined as a Sprint with a start date on or before today and an end date on or after today.

Let's first start with the **services.py** to implement the business logic of our use case:

```
# tasks/services.py

from datetime import datetime

from django.contrib.auth.models import User

from django.db import models, transaction

from django.core.exceptions import ValidationError
```

```
from .models import Task, Sprint, User


def create_task_and_add_to_sprint(
    task_data: dict[str, str],
    sprint_id: int,
    creator: User
) -> Task:
    """
    Create a new task and associate it with a sprint.
    """

    # Fetch the sprint by its ID
    sprint = Sprint.objects.get(id=sprint_id)

    # Get the current date and time
    now = datetime.now()

    # Check if the current date and time is within the sprint's start
    and end dates
    if not (sprint.start_date <= now <= sprint.end_date):
            raise ValidationError("Cannot add task to sprint: Current
            date is not within the sprint's start and end dates.")
    with transaction.atomic():
        # Create the task
        task = Task.objects.create(
                title=task_data["title"],
               description=task_data.get("description", ""),
```

```
            status=task_data.get("status", "UNASSIGNED"),
            creator=creator
        )

        # Add the task to the sprint
        sprint.tasks.add(task)

    return task
```

Our function **`create_task_and_add_to_sprint`** will create a new Task and add it to the sprint using a transaction. Using the **`transaction.atomic`** ensures that all operations are completed successfully or not at all; no intermediate states will exist. For example, a task not added to a sprint will not be created.

Info: Transactions ensure that a series of database operations either all occur successfully or none at all, preserving the **all-or-nothing** principle. This is particularly vital in scenarios involving multiple related changes, where the failure of one part could lead to data corruption or inconsistency.

However, it's important to exercise caution when employing transactions, especially in high-traffic systems. Transactions can become a bottleneck in database performance. When a transaction is in progress, it can lock certain parts of the database, preventing other operations from proceeding until the transaction completes.

Let's move on to our view implementation:

```
from django.http import HttpRequest, HttpResponseRedirect, Http404
from django.shortcuts import render, redirect
from .services import create_task_and_add_to_sprint


def create_task_on_sprint(request: HttpRequest, sprint_id: int) -> HttpResponseRedirect:
    if request.method == 'POST':
        task_data: dict[str, str] = {
```

```
            'title': request.POST['title'],
            'description': request.POST.get('description', ""),
            'status': request.POST.get('status', "UNASSIGNED"),
        }
        task = create_task_and_add_to_sprint(task_data, sprint_id,
        request.user)
        return redirect('task-detail', task_id=task.id)
    raise Http404("Not found")
```

All our views are public, allowing any unauthenticated user to create, update, view, or delete tasks. In *Chapter 8, User Authentication and Authorization in Django* we will make all our views secure by adding authentication and authorization using Django's security features.

The first thing you should notice is that there is no import of models for the function-based views. We only import things related to HTTP, authentication, and the service helpers.

The code then checks if the HTTP request method is POST. If it is POST, it converts the POST parameters to a dictionary, otherwise it returns 404. Using the **`task_data dictionary`** and **`sprint_id`**, we call the service layer function. Finally, we redirect the user to the task-detail view, passing the ID of the newly created task.

It's important to note that views.py has no implementation related to the business logic. The function **`create_task_and_add_to_sprint`** can be easily used from an API or a management command.

We will work extensively with services and function-based views in the following chapters. Class-based views are not inherently wrong; they may be the better choice sometimes. Your choice between function-based and class-based views should depend on your specific requirements, but remember always to keep your implementation simple.

Finally, our URL pattern for this new view:

```
# tasks/urls.py
urlpatterns = [
    # ...
```

```
    path("tasks/sprint/add_task/<int:pk>/", create_task_on_sprint,
    name="task-add-to-sprint")
]
```

Pessimistic and Optimistic Offline Locking using Views and a Service Layer

We should introduce the problem it solves to understand pessimistic and optimistic offline locking. Let's consider multiple team members trying to claim ownership of a task. If they do it simultaneously, they could claim the task simultaneously and the result is not guaranteed, a condition known as a race condition.

Pessimistic and optimistic locking ensures that only one team member can claim a task at any moment. Once the task has an owner set, nobody else can claim ownership.

Understanding race conditions and finding them are not simple tasks. When a race condition exists, it is hard to detect it due to some randomness of the bug. The easiest way to understand a race condition is to consider context switches and invalid variable states in your server.

Database managers provide generic concurrency control mechanisms that might not be tailored to specific application needs. For instance, your application might have complex business rules or workflows that need custom handling of concurrent accesses which goes beyond what the DBMS offers. Implementing optimistic or pessimistic locking at the application level allows for finer control and integration with these business rules.

Let's add a new view to our task manager project to claim ownership of a task:

```
from django.http import JsonResponse, HttpResponse

from rest_framework import status


from .services import claim_task


def claim_task_view(request, task_id):

    user_id = request.user.id  # Assuming you have access to the user ID
```

```
    from the request

    try:
        claim_task(user_id, task_id)
        return JsonResponse({'message': 'Task successfully claimed.'})

    except Task.DoesNotExist:
        return HttpResponse("Task does not exist.", status=status.
        HTTP_404_NOT_FOUND)

    except TaskAlreadyClaimedException:
        return HttpResponse("Task is already claimed or completed.",
        status=status.HTTP_400_BAD_REQUEST)
```

The view will use our service **claim_task** using the **user_id** and the **task_id**. If the service claims the task, it will return a JSON response. The function **claim_task** could raise two exceptions, one when the task was already claimed and the other if the task was not found.

Now let's see the service implementation:

```
# tasks/services.py
from django.db import models, transaction
from django.contrib.auth.models import User

class TaskAlreadyClaimedException(Exception):
    pass

@transaction.atomic
def claim_task(user_id:int, task_id:int) -> None:
    # Lock the task row to prevent other transactions from claiming it
    simultaneously
    task = Task.objects.select_for_update().get(id=task_id)
```

```
    # Check if the task is already claimed
    if task.owner_id:
        raise TaskAlreadyClaimedException("Task is already claimed or
        completed.")

    # Claim the task
    task.status = "IN_PROGRESS"
    task.owner_id = user_id
    task.save()
```

Our service uses the transaction.atomic decorator to encapsulate the service inside a database transaction without it, `select_for_update` will not work as expected. The first thing the service does is `select_for_update`. This uses a database query that will lock the selected rows at the database level. With the locked rows, we proceed with updating the task.

When the function execution ends, the transaction gets committed and the lock is released. Since the owner was set to the task, we also moved the task status to **IN_PROGRESS**.

Using pessimistic offline locking has advantages and disadvantages. Let's review them:

Advantages

- **Data Integrity**: Guarantees that once a process holds a lock, it can safely read and update the resource without interference from other processes.
- **Simplicity**: Easier to implement and to understand how it works.
- **No Dirty Reads**: Prevents scenarios where one transaction reads uncommitted data from another.

Disadvantages

- **Reduced Throughput**: Each resource can be accessed only one process at a time.
- **Deadlocks**: If not managed carefully, it can lead to situations where two or more processes are waiting indefinitely.
- **Resource Intensive**: Managing locks can consume system resources, and holding locks for extended periods can block system resources.

Optimistic offline locking uses a different approach. The code will not lock the database record. Optimistic offline locking will check that no other transaction has changed the record since you read it before you try to commit any changes.

Since we are using a service layer, we can implement an additional service that will use optimistic locking and you can reuse the same view.

However, optimistic locking requires a change in the model. We need to add a new column to the Task model to add a versioning.

```
class VersionMixing:
    version = models.IntegerField(default=0)


class Task(VersionMixing, models.Model):
   # ... (other fields remain the same)
```

Now let's create the migration and execute them:

```
poetry shell
python manage.py makemigrations
python manage.py migrate
```

Once we have our Task model migrated, we can add our new service **claim_task_optimistically**:

```
from django.db import transaction
from django.db.models import F
from django.core.exceptions import ValidationError


def claim_task_optimistically(user_id: int, task_id: int) -> None:
   try:
       # Step 1: Read the task and its version
       task = Task.objects.get(id=task_id)
       original_version = task.version

       # Step 2: Check if the task is already claimed
```

```
        if task.owner_id:
            raise ValidationError("Task is already claimed or completed.")

        # Step 3: Claim the task
        task.status = "IN_PROGRESS"
        task.owner_id = user_id

        # Step 4: Save the task and update the version, but only if the
        version hasn't changed
        updated_rows = Task.objects.filter(id=task_id, version=original_
        version).update(
            status=task.status,
            owner_id=task.owner_id,
            version=F('version') + 1  # Increment version field
        )

        # If no rows were updated, that means another transaction changed
        the task
        if updated_rows == 0:
            raise ValidationError("Task was updated by another transaction.")

    except Task.DoesNotExist:
            raise ValidationError("Task does not exist.")
```

The implementation is straightforward. First, we get the Task and its version. We then check if the owner was set before and raise an error if the task has an owner set.

We then set the new status and the owner, but instead of using the same method, we use an update query. The key is that the update query is filtered by the original version, and we also use the database function to increment the value which is made through an atomic operation.

The ORM will return the number of update rows, and we can check against this number to verify if the operation was performed.

If you are interested in learning more about Pessimistic and Optimistic Offline Locking, I highly recommend exploring Chapter 16 of '*Patterns of Enterprise Application Architecture*'. This chapter provides an in-depth analysis and comparison of both locking strategies. It covers the scenarios where each approach is most effective, illustrating how they can be implemented in various enterprise applications. The chapter also discusses the trade-offs and considerations associated with each pattern, helping you understand when to use one over the other.

Advantages:

- **High Concurrency**: Allows multiple transactions to read the data simultaneously.
- **Resource-Efficient**: This does not require the system to manage locks.
- **No Deadlocks**: Records are not locked.
- **Better Responsiveness**: Transactions are less likely to be blocked, which can lead to better system responsiveness.

Disadvantages:

- **Complexity**: More complex to implement correctly, particularly in systems with multiple operations that must be performed as a unit.
- **Potential for Conflicts**: If two transactions read the same record and then attempt to update it, the latter will fail and typically will have to retry, adding complexity and potentially reducing efficiency.
- **Stale or Dirty Reads**: Without additional controls, there's the potential to read stale or "dirty" data being updated by another transaction but hasn't been committed yet.
- **Eventual Consistency**: Unlike pessimistic locking, the system's consistency is eventual and may require additional effort.

Choosing between the two often depends on your specific requirements. If consistency and simplicity are more important and you can afford to queue or serialize transactions, pessimistic locking might be more appropriate. Optimistic locking may be better if you require high concurrency and are okay with handling the occasional update conflict.

Error Handling with Custom Error Views

By default, Django comes with predefined views for handling HTTP error codes such as **`Page Not Found (404)`** and **`Internal Server Error (500)`**.

You can customize these views to integrate seamlessly with the overall aesthetic of your web application.

Let's see how to create custom error views:

```
# tasks/views.py

from django.shortcuts import render


def custom_404(request, exception):

    return render(request, '404.html', {}, status=404)
```

This function-based view is configured to render the **`404.html`** template when invoked. However, don't forget to update your urls.py to set this function as the 404 handler:

```
# tasks/urls.py

handler404 = 'tasks.views.custom_404'
```

For handling internal errors, you can adopt a similar approach; just replace **`'handler404'`** with **`'handler500'`**.

Info: When the DEBUG setting is set to True, the framework displays detailed error messages with views. You must select the DEBUG settings to False to see the custom errors.

Be cautious with the data you reveal in custom error views; disclosing too much can pose security risks. As a rule of thumb, try to customize the error views for the look and feel and keep it as simple as possible.

Go ahead and create a **404.html** file, then place it in the **templates** directory of your Django project:

```
{% extends "base.html" %}
```

```
{% block content %}
  <h1>Page Not Found</h1>
  <p>We're sorry, but the page you were looking for doesn't exist.</p>
  <p><a href="{% url 'home' %}">Return to the homepage</a></p>
{% endblock %}
```

Conclusion

The key to architecting a robust Django project is crafting clean, lean views without any business logic. We delved into the realm of generic opinions on how to develop our initial Django views and tinkered with URL configurations to use them.

Next, we embarked on an exploratory tour of **HttpRequest** and **HttpResponse** objects, using path converters for dynamic URL management and leveraging URL namespaces to prevent clashes across multiple applications.

Both pessimistic and optimistic locking serve as potent solution to race conditions amidst a torrent of simultaneous server requests.

Finally, we discovered how to handle errors effectively through custom error views.

In the next chapter, we'll augment our task manager project by utilizing the features of the framework's template engine. Furthermore, we'll explore the art of serving static assets such as CSS, JavaScript, and images.

Questions

1. What is the stateless nature of requests and how does it affect the interaction between client and server?
2. What are the primary responsibilities of views in Django?
3. Why is it not recommended to add business logic in Django views?
4. In the context of class-based views in Django, why is inheritance not recommended purely for code reuse? What problems could arise from invalid inheritance?
5. What is the **god object** antipattern and how does it contradict the Single Responsibility Principle (SRP)? How does Django Mixins help avoid this problem?

6. How can dynamic URLs be handled with path converters in Django?
7. What are the roles of `to_python` and `to_url` methods in a custom Django path converter?
8. What are some advantages of using function-based views in Django?
9. How can function-based views be used with a service layer in Django?
10. When might it be better to use class-based views instead of function-based views in Django?
11. How is a race condition described when multiple team members try to claim the same task? Why is it hard to detect?
12. How does optimistic locking differ from pessimistic locking regarding database record locking?
13. In what scenarios might one prefer pessimistic locking over optimistic locking and vice versa?

Exercises

1. Refactor the services.py to a directory and create a new module with the services for the sprint, task and epic.
2. Implement a service layer to implement the business logic for Sprint.
    a. `create_sprint`: This service should take the sprint details like `name`, `description`, `start_date`, `end_date`, and the user creating the sprint. It should create a new Sprint object and return it. Make sure to validate the dates - the end date should be after the start date.
    b. `remove_task_from_sprint`: This service should take a sprint ID and a task ID. It should validate both IDs, check if the task exists in the sprint, and then remove the task from the sprint.
    c. `set_sprint_epic`: This service should take a sprint ID and an epic ID. It should validate both IDs and then assign the sprint to the epic.
3. Create the views to call the services created in point 2.

CHAPTER 6
Using the Django Template Engine

Introduction

Django templates define the application's front end, allowing us to present information to users. Understanding the interplay between contexts, tags, and filters in the template system accelerates web application development.

The Django framework offers myriad features, simplifying the process of serving static content. We'll delve into employing CDNs and compressing and optimizing static content, ensuring our web apps run fast. Template inheritance and inclusion make maintaining our web application easier, ensuring a consistent look and feel across all pages.

Additionally, we'll dive into the when and how of crafting custom template tags and filters, elevating the efficiency of our template designs.

As this chapter winds down, we'll cover the **debug** template tag, essential for troubleshooting template issues. By presenting our checklist, we'll cover various techniques to supercharge the rendering performance and slash your app's load times. By the end of the chapter, we'll dissect the nuances of templates, aligning them with the high standards of security practices.

Structure

In this chapter, we will cover the following topics:

- Introduction to Django Template Engine
- Creating Your First Django Template
- Django Template Language: Variables, Tags, and Filters
- Using Static Files in Django Templates: CSS, JavaScript, Images
- Inheritance in Django Templates
- Including Templates: Reusing Template Code
- The home page view: Showing Tasks by status
- Custom Template Tags and Filters
- Django Template Context Processors
- Debugging Django Templates
- Optimizing Template Rendering
- Securing Django Templates

Introduction to Django Template Engine

The Django framework boasts two primary template engines: Django Template Language (DTL) and Jinja2. The framework also allows creation of custom template backends, allowing third parties to support more template languages.

Since DTL is Django's inherent template system, it'll be our focus in this chapter. Jinja2 remains an option, hinging on your project's specifics; however, its usage isn't on our current book's agenda.

Tip: You can mix DTL and Jinja2, but it's not recommended. Using only one template engine is better since it will make maintainability easier and reduce the probability of making mistakes.

For consistency's sake, opt for a single template engine for your project.

Django templates are text files that contain a mix of HTML and template language. These files are used to define your web application's structure and layout. Context comes into play when these templates render into the final HTML. That's what browsers tap into, bringing our web application to the end-users.

Fast forward to *Chapter 3, Getting Started with Django Projects and Apps*. There, we birth our core HTML file: base.html. The base.html file contains all the boilerplate for our web application and all our templates will extend this base template, making the look and feel of our application the same over all the pages. This base template will make our maintenance easier since changing something in the base will be reflected in all other pages extending the base.

In Django's MVT paradigm, when a user requests, the view determines which template to use and what context data to provide. The template then renders this data, producing the HTML sent back to the user.

Django Template Language: Variables, Tags, and Filters

There are three essential constructs in the template language: variables, tags, and filters.

The best way to understand variables is to consider how they work with the template context. The context refers to a dictionary passed to the template engine during rendering. A dictionary is a key-value data structure; each key will be a variable name and the value will be the value of the template variable. Let's see an example:

```
# views.py

from django.shortcuts import render


def custom_view(request, exception):

    context = {'task_name': 'Develop GeoPathFinder'}

    return render(request, 'my_view.html', context, status=200)
```

Then, in our template, if we want to show our task_name:

```
{% block content %}

<p>Task Name: {{ task_name }}</p>

{% endblock %}
```

As you can see, the keys of the context dictionary will translate to variables in your template.

Dictionaries could contain other types of values, such as lists, instances of objects, or even a dictionary. The template language allows access to this data structure:

```
# views.py

from django.shortcuts import render


def custom_view(request, exception):

    user = request.user

     context = {'tags':['backend', 'frontend'], 'scores': {101: 5, 105:
13}, 'user': user}

    return render(request, 'my_view.html', context, status=200)
```

In our template, here's how we can access these data structures:

```
{% block content %}

<h1>Welcome, {{ user.username }}!</h1>

<p>The first tag is {{tags.0}} and the score for the task with pk 101 is:
{{score.101}} </p>

{% endblock %}
```

The template language lets you access attributes of objects, as well as indexes and keys of lists and dictionaries. Django templates fail silently. This means that if you access the index "0" of a list and the list is empty, it will not raise an error.

Info: Django templates have a peculiar characteristic that can be both a benefit and a pitfall - they fail silently. This means that if an error occurs in your template, instead of raising an explicit error, Django will often ignore the problem and continue rendering the rest of the template as if nothing happened. While this can keep your application running smoothly in the face of minor issues, it can also make debugging quite challenging, as errors in your templates might not be immediately apparent.

Filters are functions that take one or more arguments and are used to transform the values of variables.

Let's see some common examples of using template filters:

```
{% block content %}

<h1>{{ task.title|title }}</h1>

<p>Description: {{ task.description|truncatechars:25 }}</p>

<p>Created on: {{ task.created_at|date:"F j, Y"}}</p>

{% endblock %}
```

In the preceding example, we use two filters: the **`truncatechars`** and date. The first one, **`truncatechars`**, will trim a string after a certain number of characters and add an ellipsis (...). The date filter will change the string representation of the date object and has a lot of flexibility to change the format. The format we are using is "`F j, Y`", which means:

- `F`: Full textual representation of a month, such as 'January' or 'March'.
- `j`: Day of the month without leading zeros.
- `Y`: A full numeric representation of a year, consisting of 4 digits.

The filter will output:

```
<p>Published on: September 21, 2023</p>
```

Info: The available string formats for the template language are very extensive and you can always check the framework's documentation. The format was designed to be compatible with PHP.

Here are some common format characters:

- `j`: Day of the month without leading zeros, for example, 7
- `l`: Day of the week in textual long, for example, Monday
- `S`: Ordinal suffix for the day, for example, 'st'
- `F`: Month in textual long, for example, March
- `Y`: Year in 4-digit long, for example, 2023
- `H`: Hour in 24 hours with leading zeros
- `i`: Minutes
- `s`: Seconds in 2-digit format with leading zeros
- `e`: Timezone name

Here is a list of the most useful filters provided by the framework:

- **length**: Returns the length of the object.
- **slugify**: Converts the string to a format compatible with URLs.
- **upper/lower**: Returns a string or char's uppercase or lowercase.
- **title**: Converts a string into title case by making words start with an uppercase character and the remaining characters lowercase.
- **default**: Returns the value if available; otherwise, it returns the default value.
- **first/last**: Returns a collection's first/last element.
- **filesizeformat**: Allows to convert the size of files to human-readable format.

Django template tags are a way to provide functionality to the templates. You can loop objects, inherit from templates, use conditional operators, and more with tags. Tags are noted with braces and percent signs (**{% %}**).

Here are some of the commonly used Django template tags:

- **{% for %}** and **{% endfor %}**: These are used to create a loop in the template.
- **{% if %}**, **{% else %}** and **{% endif %}**: These tags are used for conditional rendering in the template.
- **{% url %}**: This tag generates URLs. You pass in the name of a view and, optionally, any arguments or named arguments.
- **{% block %}** and **{% endblock %}**: These tags define a block that can be overridden in child templates.
- **{% extends %}**: This tag is used for template inheritance. It allows you to use the structure of a parent template and override parts of it.
- **{% load %}**: This tag makes custom template tags and filters accessible within the template.
- **{% include %}**: This tag allows you to include the contents of another template file.

Best practices suggest keeping heavy logic out of templates. Instead, service layers should handle this logic, passing only the necessary processed data to templates for rendering. This ensures a separation of concerns and maintains both clarity and efficiency.

Inheritance in Django Templates

The template language allows you to reuse parts of your HTML using inheritance with the **{% extends %}** template tag. As previously mentioned, it's common practice to utilize a base template containing the boilerplate and then override specific sections using blocks. Using a base template allows you to perform easier maintenance.

Though we have touched **base.html** earlier, we can enhance it with additional template tags:

```
<!DOCTYPE html>
<html lang="en">
<head>
    <meta charset="UTF-8">
    <meta name="viewport" content="width=device-width, initial-scale=1.0">

    {# Using a block for the title allows child templates to provide
    their specific titles. We use the default filter to set a fallback
    title if not provided. #}
    <title>{% block title %}{{ page_title|default:"Default Title" }}{%
    endblock %}</title>

    {# This block is intended for page-specific CSS. Override in child
    templates as needed. #}
    {% block extra_css %}{% endblock %}

    <!-- Bootstrap CSS -->
    <link href="https://cdn.jsdelivr.net/npm/bootstrap@5.2.3/dist/
    css/bootstrap.min.css" rel="stylesheet" integrity="sha384-rbsA
    2VBKQhggwzxH7pPCaAqO46MgnOM80zW1RWuH61DGLwZJEdK2Kadq2F9CUG65"
    crossorigin="anonymous">
</head>
```

```
<body>

    {# Use of the 'include' tag helps in modularizing the HTML, making
    maintenance easier by breaking the layout into smaller parts. #}
    {% include "tasks/_header.html" %}

    <main>
        {# Main content block can be overridden in child templates to
        provide page-specific content. #}
        {% block content %}{% endblock %}
    </main>

    {% include "tasks/_footer.html" %}

    {# A block for adding custom JavaScript ensures flexibility for child
    templates to introduce or override scripts. #}
    {% block extra_javascript %}{% endblock %}

    <!-- Using external libraries can be beneficial for consistency and
    speed. Always ensure they're from trusted sources. -->
    <script src="https://code.jquery.com/jquery-3.5.1.slim.
    min.js" integrity="sha384-DfXdz2htPH0lsSSs5nCTpuj/
    zy4C+OGpamoFVy38MVBnE+IbbVYUew+OrCXaRkfj" crossorigin="anonymous"></
    script>
    <script src="https://cdn.jsdelivr.net/npm/bootstrap@5.2.3/dist/js/
    bootstrap.bundle.min.js" integrity="sha384-kenU1KFdBIe4zVF0s0G1M5b4h
    cpxyD9F7jL+jjXkk+Q2h455rYXK/7HAuoJl+0I4" crossorigin="anonymous"></
    script>
</body>
</html>
```

In this updated base template, we've incorporated additional blocks. Specifically, the title is now dynamically set by **`{{ page_title|default:"Default Title" }}`**, which either displays the **page_title** or defaults to **Default Title**. To customize the title block, simply override it in your child template.

We've also introduced two new blocks, **extra_css** and **extra_javascript**, for incorporating custom CSS and JavaScript.

Template blocks, especially those intended for overriding, should be adequately explained using comments to ensure clarity for developers who might work with the template in the future.

In a child template, this block can be overridden to include page-specific scripts:

```
{% extends "base.html" %}


{% block extra_javascript %}

{{ block.super }}

<script src="path/to/custom/script.js"></script>

{% endblock %}
```

Sometimes, you might want to include the content from the base template's block and add to it. The **{{ block.super }}** tag allows you to do it.

Including Templates: Reusing Template Code

Our base template uses the `include` for the header and footer. Using the include is very useful for reusing common template parts. It also makes the template simpler to understand and structure.

Using the include is very simple:

```
{% include "tasks/_footer.html" %}
```

Using an underscore as a filename prefix is not mandatory, but it is commonly used for templates meant to be included by other templates.

The included tag has some limitations and drawbacks. The tag uses the current context to render the included template. You will get an error if the included template refers to some variables not included in the context.

For every template inclusion, the system triggers a file read operation. Overusing template inclusions can lead to performance bottlenecks. As best practice, avoid including templates within loops.

Another limitation arises when the "**include**" usage makes you hardcode the filename of the intended template. Using the filename in the template will make future refactoring more difficult if you want to change the filename.

There are ways to circumvent the hardcoding issue on the template inclusion. One of them is to define the template parts in the settings.py and then pass the template filename as a context variable from the views.

Add template names to Django's settings:

```
# settings.py


TEMPLATE_PARTS = {

    "footer": "tasks/_footer.html",

    # other template parts can be added here

}
```

Then, in your views:

```
from django.conf import settings


def my_view(request):

    context = {

        "footer_template": settings.TEMPLATE_PARTS["footer"]

    }

    return render(request, "my_template.html", context)
```

This way, you centralize the template paths in the settings and avoid hardcoding them in the templates or views. When you need to refactor or change paths, it's done in one place in the settings.

However, remember that over-abstracting can make the code harder to follow for some developers. The key is to strike the right balance based on the project's needs

The **include** tag is a handy tool for reusing template code in Django and is widely used.

One of the potential issues with the included tag is that the included template relies on the current context to render. Any variable not available in that context can result in an error. To mitigate this issue, Django offers context processors. In the upcoming sections, we will dive deeper into context processors. This will provide a robust solution to avoid variable availability issues in included templates, ensuring smoother and more reliable template rendering.

The Home Page View: Showing Tasks by Status

We have all the tools to build a functional task manager home page to show our tasks, as we introduced in *Chapter 3, Getting Started with Django Projects and Apps*.

First, let's change our home view implementation to this:

```
def task_home(request):

    # Fetch all tasks at once

    tasks = Task.objects.filter(status__in=["UNASSIGNED", "IN_PROGRESS",
    "DONE", "ARCHIVED"])


    # Initialize dictionaries to hold tasks by status

    context = defaultdict(list)


    # Categorize tasks into their respective lists

    for task in tasks:

           if task.status == "UNASSIGNED":

                 context["unassigned_tasks"].append(task)

           elif task.status == "IN_PROGRESS":

                 context["in_progress_tasks"].append(task)

           elif task.status == "DONE":
```

```
                context["done_tasks"].append(task)
            elif task.status == "ARCHIVED":
                context["archived_tasks"].append(task)

    return render(request, "tasks/home.html", context)
```

We structured our implementation to use a context where the tasks are pre-filtered by their status. Using this context during template rendering avoids unnecessary duplicate iterations for each task status.

Now, our new **tasks/home.html** template is as follows:

```
{% extends "tasks/base.html" %}

{% block content %}
    <div class="container mt-5">
        <h2>Tasks by Status</h2>
        <div class="row mt-4">

            <!-- Unassigned Tasks -->
            <div class="col-md-3">
                <h4>Unassigned</h4>
                {% for task in unassigned_tasks %}
                    <div class="card mb-2">
                            <div class="card-body">
                                <h5 class="card-title"><a href="{% url
                                'tasks:task-detail' task.pk %}">{{ task.title
                                }}</a></h5>
                                <p class="card-text">Owner: {{ task.owner.
                                username|default:"None" }}</p>
                            </div>
                    </div>
```

```
    {% endfor %}
</div>

<!-- In Progress Tasks -->
<div class="col-md-3">
    <h4>In Progress</h4>
    {% for task in in_progress_tasks %}
        <div class="card mb-2">
                <div class="card-body">
                    <h5 class="card-title"><a href="{% url
                    'tasks:task-detail' task.pk %}">{{ task.title
                    }}</a></h5>
                    <p class="card-text">Owner: {{ task.owner.
                    username|default:"None" }}</p>
                </div>
        </div>
    {% endfor %}
</div>

<!-- Completed Tasks -->
<div class="col-md-3">
    <h4>Completed</h4>
    {% for task in done_tasks %}
        <div class="card mb-2">
                <div class="card-body">
                    <h5 class="card-title"><a href="{% url
                    'tasks:task-detail' task.pk %}">{{ task.title
                    }}</a></h5>
                    <p class="card-text">Owner: {{ task.owner.
```

```
                                username|default:"None" }}</p>
                            </div>
                        </div>
                    {% endfor %}
                </div>


            </div> <!-- End of row -->
        </div> <!-- End of container -->
{% endblock %}
```

Our updated home template showcases three distinct columns, with each column representing a specific task status. Each task title provides a link to its detailed page, displaying the task owner.

To populate your project with tasks, simply use the admin page to add either tasks or users. In *Chapter 8, User Authentication and Authorization in Django*, we will add authentication and the task create form will allow us to create new tasks as normal users.

Here is the result of our new home tasks page:

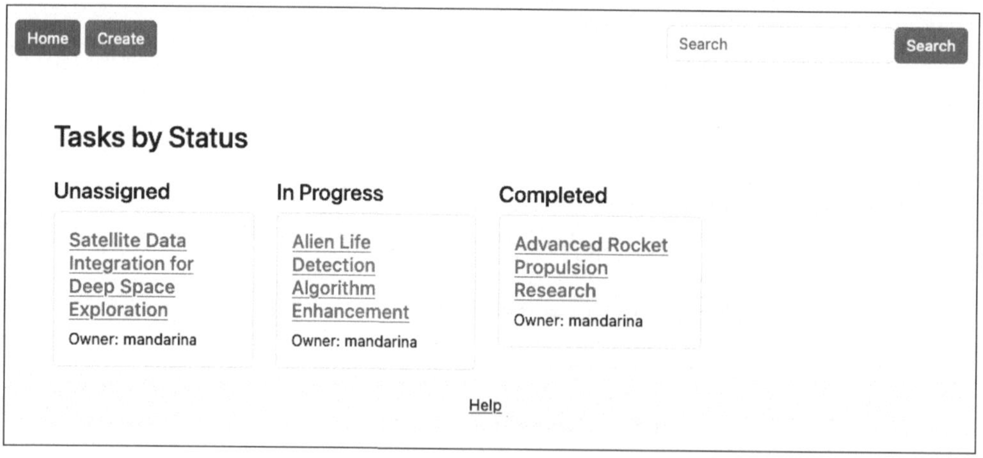

Figure 6.1: *The Task homepage*

You can always check the GitHub repository, **git@github.com:llazzaro/web_applications_django.git**, and check out the branch chapter_6 to see the project code.

Custom Template Tags and Filters

Creating custom template tags can significantly aid in structuring and organizing your project. For example, we will create a mini-report to summarize tasks of a particular sprint.

We must review our requirements carefully before designing custom template tags or filters.

Since we need to create a mini report of the sprint tasks, it is more complex than a simple transformation of one value to another, and using a tag is more suitable.

Tip: While crafting a filter for the mini-report is technically feasible, doing so is more complicated since the operation goes beyond a basic transformation. Creating a filter for the mini-report will be difficult and its implementation messy, which needs to be aligned with the framework's philosophy.

If you are in doubt and it feels hard to implement a filter, you could create a tag instead.

In your application's root directory, establish a `'templatetags'` directory and include an `__init__.py` file. Django will search for custom template filters for each installed application in this directory.

Inside the `templatetags` directory, create a new file called **sprint_tags.py**. This file will contain the custom tag implementation:

```
from django import template

from django.db.models import Count


from taskmanager.tasks.models import Sprint


register = template.Library()


@register.simple_tag

def task_summary(sprint: Sprint) -> dict:

    # Group tasks by status and count each group

    task_counts = (
```

```
        sprint.tasks.values("status").annotate(count=Count("status")).
        order_by()
    )

    # Convert the result into a dictionary: {status: count}
    summary = {item["status"]: item["count"] for item in task_counts}

    return summary
```

The new filter **task_summary** takes a sprint as a parameter and returns a dictionary to be merged into the context. It is required to register the template tags by using a decorator that the framework provides. The code just counts the tasks of the sprint by status using a query.

For using the template tag in your template, you need to load it first:

```
{% load sprint_tags %}

{% task_summary sprint as summary %}

<p>Task summary:</p>
<ul>
    <li>Unassigned: {{ summary.UNASSIGNED }}</li>
    <li>In progress: {{ summary.IN_PROGRESS }}</li>
    <li>Completed: {{ summary.DONE }}</li>
    <li>Archived: {{ summary.ARCHIVED }}</li>
</ul>
```

Our example uses the keys of the dictionary to access the summary dictionary returned by the template tag.

The filters are the way to go when you need a simpler value transformation. Let's create a custom filter to see the difference.

For our tasks management system, we are requested to display the percentage of completed tasks in an Epic or Sprint. Let's create a custom filter to show this information by following these steps to create your filter.

Now, let's create a new file called **templatetags/tasks_filters.py** and add the following contents:

```
from django import template
from django.db.models import Count, Case, When, FloatField

register = template.Library()

@register.filter
def percent_complete(tasks):
    if tasks.exists():
        # Aggregate count of all tasks and count of completed tasks
        aggregation = tasks.aggregate(
            total=Count("id"),
        done=Count(Case(When(status="DONE", then=1)))
        )

        # Calculate the percentage
        percent_done = (aggregation["done"] / aggregation["total"]) *
        100
        return percent_done
    else:
        return 0
```

The custom filter takes a single parameter: the tasks from which the percentage is computed. The filter uses the ORM to count the total and the tasks in **DONE**. We use a different decorator this time, which is a `@register.filter`.

For using the filter, you need to use the `load` template tag, as shown in the following example:

```
{% load tasks_filters %}

<h2>{{ epic.name }}</h2>
<p>{{ epic.tasks|percent_complete }}% complete</p>
```

```
<h2>{{ sprint.name }}</h2>

<p>{{ sprint.tasks|percent_complete }}% complete</p>
```

Crucially, our custom filter assumes that neither the epic nor the sprint will contain an overwhelming number of tasks. Otherwise, the filter could be very slow. Given our domain problem, it sounds reasonable that an epic or sprint will not contain hundreds of tasks each.

This section, dedicated to "**Debugging Django Templates**", delves deeper into template optimization before applying any caching or optimization strategies.

Using Static Files in Django Templates: CSS, JavaScript, Images

Managing static files in Django is straightforward. Static files, such as CSS, JavaScript, and images, remain unchanged during the application's runtime since it's not so common to dynamically generate them.

For using the static files in your templates, you can use the template tag **{% static 'css/styles.css' %}**, where the second argument is the path to the file. The template tag generates the URL that points to the specific static file.

Django offers a built-in mechanism to modify the storage system used for static files. By default, the framework uses **StaticFilesStorage,** which uses the filesystem to store and serve the files. This can be changed via the **STORAGES** setting.

Django offers two methods to handle static files when using the development server. The first way is to have the **DEBUG** settings set to True. When the setting is enabled, the development server will service the files from the locations you specify in your **STATICFILES_DIRS** setting. When the DEBUG setting is set to False, the development server will not serve the static files.

Later, we will see how to serve the files in production. First, we need to configure some settings to use static files:

First, set **STATIC_URL** and **STATIC_ROOT** in settings.py. **STATIC_URL** is the URL for static files, and **STATIC_ROOT** is the absolute path to the directory where **collectstatic** will collect static files for deployment. The **collectstatic** command in Django is used to gather all static files from each of your applications into a single location, defined by the **STATIC_ROOT** setting.

```
# settings.py

STATIC_URL = "/static/"

STATIC_ROOT = os.path.join(BASE_DIR, "staticfiles")
```

We need to set the **STATICFILES_DIRS**, a list where Django will search for the static files aside from each "**static**" directory of every installed application.

```
STATICFILES_DIRS = [

    (os.path.join(BASE_DIR, "tasks/static"),

]
```

With this setting, we are ready to execute the management command "**collectstatic**":

```
python manage.py collectstatic
```

You can use the static files by using the template tag "**static**". Here are some examples:

```
{% load static %}

<img src="{% static 'images/myimage.jpg' %}" alt="My image">

<link href="{% static 'css/styles.css' %}" rel="stylesheet">

<script src="{% static 'js/main.js' %}"></script>
```

The first example shows how to use the static template tag to show an image, the HTML tag **img** can be used anywhere inside your body.

Let's include a logo in the header template of our project:

```
{% load static %}


<header class="d-flex justify-content-between align-items-center p-3">

   <!-- Left side -->

   <div class="d-flex align-items-center">

      <!-- Logo -->

      <img src="{% static 'images/logo.png' %}" alt="Task Manager"
      width="50" class="mr-3">


      <a href="{% url 'tasks:task-home' %}" class="btn btn-secondary
      mr-2" role="button">Home</a>
```

```
        <a href="{% url 'tasks:task-create' %}" class="btn btn-primary"
        role="button">Create</a>

    </div>


    <!-- Right side -->

    <div class="d-flex">

        <input type="text" class="form-control" id="search"
        placeholder="Search">

        <button type="button" class="btn btn-success ml-2">Search</button>

    </div>

</header>
```

Next step is to execute the collect static command:

```
poetry shell

python manage.py collectstatic
```

You should see the new logo in the header, as shown in *Figure 6.2*:

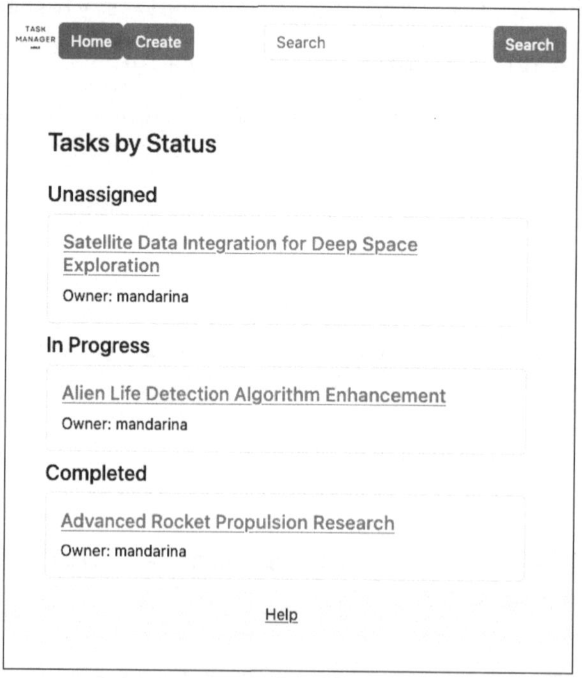

Figure 6.2: *Task manager home page with the new logo*

For including CSS, the HTML "**`link`**" tag can be used in the head of the HTML. A similar approach can be done for including **`JavaScript`** files using the HTML **`script`** tag.

Django's development server serves static files in an inefficient and insecure manner. It's not advisable to use the development server in a production environment. Using the setting makes using a different storage backend for static files possible. Different storages allow you to serve static files from cloud providers or a content delivery network (CDN).

Info: A Content Delivery Network (CDN) consists of a globally distributed network of servers that collaboratively deliver internet content swiftly.

CDNs are also particularly useful for static assets like CSS, JavaScript files, and images. When using a CDN for serving CSS, JavaScript, and others, the website's load times can be reduced since the CDN will be closer to the client, leading to faster load times.

Numerous cloud providers present various storage solutions. One of the most used ones is AWS S3. The Django framework does not come with a storage solution for S3, but many third-party libraries allow the use of S3. For our production setup, we've opted for django-storages, a reputable and well-maintained library.

First, add the dependency using poetry:

```
poetry add django-storages
```

Then, we will need to update our INSTALLED_APPS and add the storages application:

```
# settings.py

INSTALLED_APPS = [

    "django.contrib.admin",

    "django.contrib.auth",

    "django.contrib.contenttypes",

    "django.contrib.sessions",

    "django.contrib.messages",

    "django.contrib.staticfiles",

    "tasks",
```

```
    "storages",
]
```

Since we are using Django 4.2, we need to set up the new **STORAGES** settings:

```
#settings.py

STORAGES = {"staticfiles": {"BACKEND": "storages.backends.s3boto3.
S3StaticStorage"}}
```

Finally, we need to set the access key ID and access key for AWS authentication:

```
# settings.py

AWS_S3_ACCESS_KEY_ID = os.getenv("AWS_S3_ACCESS_KEY_ID")

AWS_S3_SECRET_ACCESS_KEY = os.getenv("AWS_S3_SECRET_ACCESS_KEY")
```

Once we have all these settings configured, we are ready to execute collect static to upload the static files to the S3 bucket:

```
python manage.py collectstatic
```

If you browse your project, you will see that your S3 bucket provides the URLs of your static content.

Django Template Context Processors

Django creates a context each time it renders a template. The view provides the context, which is then gathered using context processors. The template context processor is a way to include data available globally to all the templates. Simply put, a context processor is a Python function that yields a dictionary.

Django comes with several built-in context processors; you can change them in the settings.py configuration file of the project.

Our project has four context processors configured:

```
TEMPLATES = [
    {
        "BACKEND": "django.template.backends.django.DjangoTemplates",
        "DIRS": [
            BASE_DIR / "templates",
        ],
```

```
        "APP_DIRS": True,
        "OPTIONS": {
            "context_processors": [
                "django.template.context_processors.debug",
                "django.template.context_processors.request",
                "django.contrib.auth.context_processors.auth",
                "django.contrib.messages.context_processors.messages",
            ],
        },
    },
]
```

Let's review what each of the context processors does:

- **django.template.context_processors.debug**: If the DEBUG setting is True, this adds a debug flag to the context.
- **django.template.context_processors.request**: Adds the request object.
- **django.contrib.auth.context_processors.auth**: Adds the user and perms objects, representing the currently logged-in user and their permissions.
- **django.contrib.messages.context_processors.messages**: Adds messages for the Django messages framework.

You can also create your custom context processor. Before crafting a custom context processor, find out its global necessity; if not, merely embed it in your view.

Using a context processor can be an elegant way to manage feature flags, especially if the visibility of a feature depends on the user and needs to be determined for every rendered template.

First, create a **context_processors.py** file in the tasks application directory. Inside that file, let's add the context processor function for the feature flag:

```
from django.contrib.auth.models import Group


def feature_flags(request):
```

```
    user = request.user
    flags = {
        "is_priority_feature_enabled": False,
    }
    # Ensure the user is authenticated before checking groups
    if user.is_authenticated:
            flags["is_priority_feature_enabled"] = user.groups.filter(
                name="Task Prioritization Beta Testers"
            ).exists()

    return flags
```

Every template's context will be augmented with the variable **`is_priority_feature_enabled`** through the context processor.

Then, you will need to add the new context processor to your project **settings.py**:

```
TEMPLATES = [
    {
        ...
        "OPTIONS": {
            "context_processors": [
                ...
                "tasks.context_processors.feature_flags",
            ],
        },
    },
]
```

When using the feature flag in your template, treat it as a variable:

```
{% if is_priority_feature_enabled %}
```

```
    <!-- Render UI elements related to task prioritization -->
{% else %}
    <!-- Show a teaser: "Stay tuned for our upcoming feature: Task
    Prioritization!" -->
{% endif %}
```

Remember to be cautious when adding a new context processor; it will be accessible globally and the context processor should avoid heavy processing. If you need to access the database, consider using a cache.

Here is an example of our previous context processor using a cache:

```
from django.core.cache import cache


def feature_flags(request):
    user = request.user
    flags = {
        "is_priority_feature_enabled": False,
    }

    # Ensure the user is authenticated before checking groups
    if user.is_authenticated:
            # Using the user's id to create a unique cache key
            cache_key = f"user_{user.id}_is_priority_feature"
            # Try to get the value from the cache
            is_priority_feature = cache.get(cache_key)

            if is_priority_feature is None:  # If cache miss
                is_priority_feature = user.groups.filter(name="Task
                Prioritization Beta Testers").exists()
            # Store the result in the cache for, say, 5 minutes (300
            seconds)
```

```
        cache.set(cache_key, is_priority_feature, 300)

    flags["is_priority_feature_enabled"] = is_priority_feature

return flags
```

Ensuring each user has a unique cache key is vital. This prevents two users, accessing the context processor simultaneously, from retrieving each other's cached data. If user group details change over time, you might have to invalidate that user's cache to fetch the latest values.

While this example illustrates Django's caching framework simply, cache usage can often be more intricate than shown here.

Debugging Django Templates

While debugging templates, the template tag **`{% debug %}`** proves invaluable. Placing the debug template tag in your template outputs a textual depiction of all accessible context variables.

If you want to use the debug template tag, add it to your template at the location where you want to display the context variables:

```
<pre>{% debug %}</pre>
```

We advise employing the pre-HTML tag; it retains formatting, enhancing readability within the browser.

In a development environment, this template tag becomes helpful for troubleshooting issues. As a piece of advice, always avoid using the **`{% debug %}`** template tag in a production environment to prevent potential security vulnerabilities and inadvertent exposure of sensitive data.

Optimizing Template Rendering

As your application grows in complexity and scale, the need to optimize template rendering intensifies. Here is a checklist of common optimization you can do to your project.

Minimize Database Queries

Often, the primary bottleneck in your application is the database. Here are some tips to tackle them:

- **Use `select_related` and `prefetch_related`**: When dealing with `ForeignKey` or `OneToOneField`, `select_related` fetches related objects in a single query. When dealing with reverse `ForeignKey` or `ManyToMany` fields, consider using `prefetch_related`. There are some situations where the `select_related` can lead to worse performance since the join query could be more expensive that query each table.
- **Avoid using len(queryset)**: Instead, use `queryset.count()` to get the number of items in a `queryset` without evaluating it. Note that is the query was already evaluated you may prefer to use len instead of count.
- **Limit QuerySets**: If you only need a few items, use [:n] slicing. For example, `Article.objects.all()[:5]` only fetches five articles.

Keep templates simple

If you follow good practices, all your business logic should live in the service layer. Ensure your templates remain focused purely on presentation. Utilize `{% extends %}` and `{% block %}` tags for code reuse in templates, helping prevent redundant code.

Use caching

You can use the cache template tag to do fragment caching. Use `{% cache %}` to cache stable sections of a template. This is especially useful when dealing with a part of your template that is expensive to calculate.

Optimize Static Content

Multiple Django packages are available to enhance static content performance. django-compressor offers on-the-fly compression for CSS and JavaScript files. Installing 'compressor' is simple and optimizes CSS and JavaScript files.

For images, you can use `django-imagekit`, which processes and optimizes images. You can also generate thumbnails and convert images to different formats.

As a general rule, keep your custom template tags and filter usage to a minimum and avoid large looping structures.

Securing Django Templates

Many developers emphasize backend security but often overlook the security of templates. Securing your templates is just as crucial as fortifying your backend. Here are some methods for securing your templates:

Don't turn off autoescape

Django auto-escapes all the content by default, which will protect against Cross-Site Scripting (XSS) attacks. However, you can disable **`autoescape`** in the template or employ the **`'safe'`** filter.

Only use **`|safe`** or **`{% autoescape off %}`** when you're confident about the safety of the content. Always validate and sanitize the content before marking it as safe.

Be careful with template caching

For fragment caching, always use unique caching keys per user or context to prevent data exposure. Using the wrong keys for caching could expose information between users.

Custom Template Tags and Filters: Validate Input

If not validated and handled appropriately, custom template tags and filters in Django might lead to vulnerabilities.

Consider an example of a filter to convert markdown to HTML:

```
import markdown


@register.filter(name="markdown_to_html")

def markdown_to_html(content):

    return markdown.markdown(content)
```

And in your template:

```
<div class="post-content">

    {{ post.content|markdown_to_html|safe }}

</div>
```

Now a malicious user could use the following markdown to attack our website:

```
**This is bold text**


<script>

    // Malicious script here

    alert('Hacked!');
```

```
</script>
```

When our filter **markdown_to_html** processes the malicious payload, it will convert the bold text to HTML, but it will leave the script tag untouched. As the **'safe'** filter is applied in the template, executing this script would result in an XSS attack.

You can solve this vulnerability by sanitizing the content from the user:

```
@register.filter(name='markdown_to_html')

def markdown_to_html(content):

    return markdown.markdown(content, output_format='html5',
extensions=["escape_html"])
```

Using the **escape_html** extension will escape any HTML in the markdown preventing the script execution.

In *Chapter 8, User Authentication and Authorization in Django*, we will use the Content Security Policy header to provide additional protection against attacks.

Staying updated with Django's latest releases is important for your application's security and stability. By ensuring that your project is always running on the latest version, you protect against malicious attacks.

Conclusion

The template engine represents the "V" in Django's MVT architecture, serving as a foundational concept to learn for mastery over the framework. By mastering the workings of the template context and Django's tags and filters, you're well-equipped to craft a safe and efficient web application.

The static template tag lets you incorporate static content through the template engine. Leveraging third-party packages to compress and minify static content can significantly enhance your web application's load time.

With the template engine, you can use inheritance and embed other templates, ensuring yours remains consistent and maintainable. You can also extend the template engine by developing template tags, filters, and context processors. Finally, we learned how to optimize and follow best security practices to keep our project secure and fast.

In the next chapter, *Chapter 7, Forms in Django*, we will uncover the intricacies of handling forms in Django, a crucial aspect of user interaction in any web application

Questions

1. Is it recommended to mix DTL and Jinja2 in a Django project? Why or why not?
2. What are filters in the Django template language, and how are they used?
3. How does the `{% url %}` tag function in Django templates?
4. Why is it a best practice to keep heavy logic out of templates?
5. What are the limitations or drawbacks of using the include tag in Django templates?
6. What is the primary difference between a Django template tag and a filter?
7. Why is it important to include an **__init__.py** file in the **'templatetags'** directory?
8. How does a Content Delivery Network (CDN) improve website performance for static assets?
9. Why is the development server of Django not suitable for serving static files in a production environment?
10. Why should you be cautious when adding a new context processor?
11. What does Django auto-escape protect against?
12. How can you potentially expose data between users with fragment caching?

Exercises

1. Write a custom template tag called **`task_priority_summary`**, which takes a sprint as input and returns a summary count of tasks based on their priority levels (for example, High, Medium, Low). Note: you will need to make a migration for this exercise!
2. Considering the importance of template security, write a template snippet that securely displays user comments that have been converted from markdown to HTML.
3. Design and implement the views for both the **`Sprint`** and **`Epic`** models. Create the associated templates to display their respective data in a user-friendly manner.

CHAPTER 7
Forms in Django

Introduction

In web application development, capturing and validating data is essential. As we will see through this chapter, Django offers an object-oriented approach to managing HTML forms. To start, we will understand how HTML forms operate without using Django. Subsequently, we'll delve into the framework's capabilities by creating our first Django Form.

Integrating Django Forms with templates makes your application more elegant and maintainable. The framework offers numerous tools to simplify a developer's tasks. We'll explore these features to enhance our ability to capture user input.

We'll implement different views to get a clearer picture of form submission handling and the presentation of errors.

By the chapter's end, we'll see advanced strategies, like using a token to prevent double submissions.

Structure

In this chapter, we will cover the following topics:

- Understanding Django Forms
- Creating Your First Django Form
- Rendering Forms in Templates
- Handling Form Submission in Views
- Working with Form Fields
- File and Image Upload Field
- Data Validation with Django Forms
- Displaying Form Errors
- Advanced Form Handling: `ModelForms` and `Formsets`
- Preventing Double Submission with Forms

Understanding Django Forms

Using forms allows us to capture user input in web applications. The form can contain various input elements, like text fields, checkboxes, radio buttons, and more.

The elements `form`, `input`, `label`, `select`, and `textarea` are commonly used in HTML forms. The form element contains all the inputs and label elements. The form has two essential attributes: action and method. Action is the URL where the form's data is sent and the method refers to the HTTP method to use, which could be `POST` or `GET`. While these are crucial for basic form functionality, other attributes like `'enctype'` may be necessary depending on specific form requirements, such as file uploads.

Input elements have three essential attributes: type, name and value. The type determines which input to display: text, email, password, checkbox, radio, or submit. The name attribute specifies the name for the data sent when the form is submitted and the value contains the optional initial value of the input.

Here is an example of a raw HTML form to create a new Task object without using Django forms:

```
<form action="/tasks/new/" method="POST">
    <label for="title">Title:</label><br>
    <input type="text" id="title" name="title" required><br>

    <label for="description">Description:</label><br>
    <textarea id="description" name="description"></textarea><br>

    <label for="status">Status:</label><br>
    <select id="status" name="status">
        <option value="UNASSIGNED">Unassigned</option>
        <option value="IN_PROGRESS">In Progress</option>
        <option value="DONE">Completed</option>
        <option value="ARCHIVED">Archived</option>
    </select><br>

    <input type="submit" value="Create Task">
</form>
```

The action attribute of the form utilizes the URL from the view we discussed in *Chapter 5: Django Views and URL Handling*. Since the view supports the POST method for creation, the attribute **`method`** is set to POST.

The input for the title is required, so we are using the `required` in the input.

The description uses `textarea` because the description could be arbitrarily big, and this type of field is ideal for the description.

Then, we select the status of the task with all the possible options to choose from.

Finally, we have the submit button.

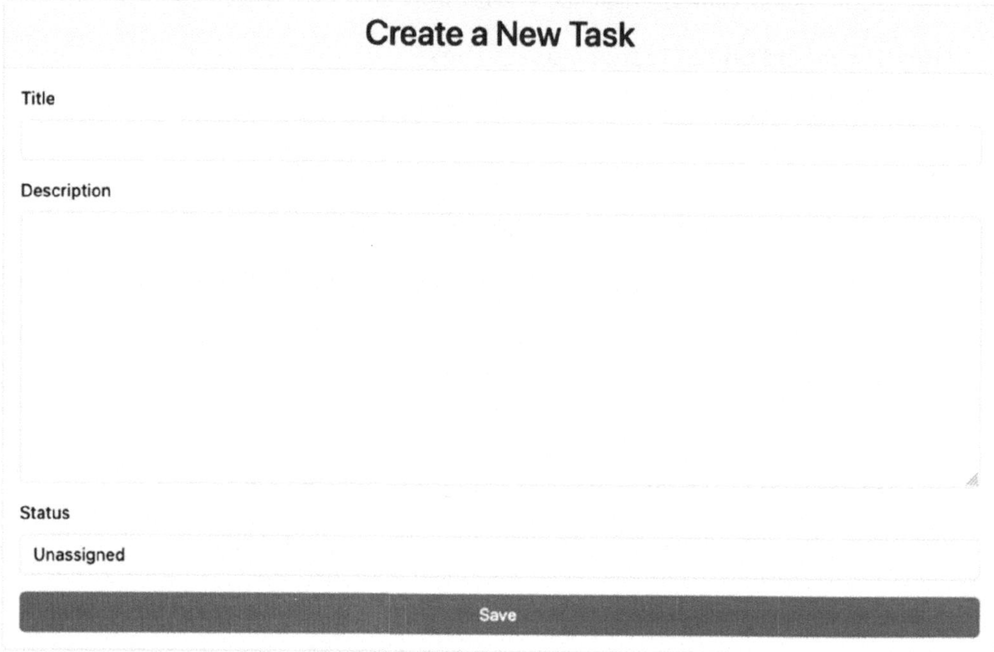

Figure 7.1: *The task creation form*

Some pitfalls exist when employing raw HTML forms with Django. One of them is the maintainability of the HTML. If we want to add a new status, we are forced to change the HTML too. Also, if we want to display errors, the current HTML form will be minimal. The same happens with complex validations. Using raw HTML forms could also bring some security issues, and handling complex fields like datetime or foreign keys could be challenging. The following raw HTML form has no protection against Cross-Site Request Forgery (CSRF).

The framework provides a feature to make our lives easier when handling forms. Django forms are powerful, which allows us to simplify form handling. Django Forms will render the HTML form for you, which will reuse form markup across multiple pages. Django forms create an object-oriented representation of the HTML form, which helps to create an excellent bridge between the HTML world and the Python object-oriented world. Django forms also have a great way of handling form validation to specify conditions to ensure the input data meets the requirements.

There are several types of forms in the framework. Let's review four fundamental types:

- **`Form`**: This is the basic form class in Django. You can use it when no model is associated with the form, like a search or login form.
- **`ModelForm`**: This form is an extension of the Form but has additional support to create forms based on a model. **`ModelForm`** will inspect the model, create the appropriate input types, and use validations using model attributes. For example, if the Task model specifies that the title is required, **`ModelForm`** will create a title input with the required type of text.
- **`FormSet`**: This class is used when it is required to work with multiple forms on one page.
- **`ModelFormSet`**: Equivalent to the **`FormSet`** but allows to create multiple instances of **`ModelForm`** instead.

Let's review what happens when we use Django forms. When a user submits a form on a web page, a POST request is sent to the server. A Django view will process this request and this view will capture the request in an argument.

Typically, the view initializes an instance of the form, passing in the POST payload:

```
form = TaskForm(request.POST)
```

Note: If you're new to Django, you might wonder where **`TaskForm`** comes from. The **`TaskForm`** is a Django Form class we will define later in this chapter. When we say form = **`TaskForm(request.POST)`**, we initialize this Django Form class with the POST data received from the user's form submission.

The next step is to validate the form using the **`is_valid`** method. This method performs a series of validation checks on the provided payload.

```
if form.is_valid():

    ...
```

The **`is_valid`** method returns Python's built-in boolean types True or False. It returns true when the payload is valid; otherwise, it returns false.

When using ModelForm, an additional method save will persist the model to the database when the data is valid.

Creating Your First Django Form

In our task management project, we must design a form that allows users to generate a new task. The form should validate all the fields.

We will start by creating our Form class. Given that our needs revolve around the task model and its creation, **ModelForm** is our go-to:

```
from django import forms


from .models import Task


class TaskForm(forms.ModelForm):

   class Meta:

          model = Task

          fields = ["title", "description", "status"]
```

Place this **TaskForm** class in a file named forms.py within your tasks application directory, following the Django convention for better organization and readability.

The **Meta** inner class serves as the configuration center for your form in Django. Here, the **model** attribute specifies which Django model the form is linked to. The **fields** attribute is a list of model fields you want to include in the form for display and validation. Note that this list should only contain attributes that are part of the specified model.

In the upcoming sections, we will integrate this **TaskForm** class into our application's views to handle task creation and updates. Specifically, we'll use our views, **TaskCreateView** and **TaskUpdateView**.

Rendering Forms in Templates

Numerous methods exist for rendering forms in templates. To control the CSS classes, utilize template tags and iterate through form fields, adjusting the HTML entities as necessary.

To enhance our form's appearance, we'll employ the **django-widget-tweaks** package. While Django provides a robust system for form rendering, certain customizations, especially those related to CSS and layout, can be cumbersome.

The **django-widget-tweaks** package simplifies this, making template improvements more straightforward.

Let's install and configure it:

```
poetry shell

poetry add django-widget-tweaks
```

Then open your taskmanager/settings.py and add **widget_tweaks** to the **INSTALLED_APPS** list.

```
INSTALLED_APPS = [

    …

    "widget_tweaks",

]
```

Let's see an example of the task creation form template. Create a new file in templates/tasks/task_form.html:

```
{% extends "tasks/base.html" %}

{% load widget_tweaks %}


{% block content %}

<div class="d-flex justify-content-center align-items-center vh-100">

   <div class="w-50">

      <div class="card">

         <div class="card-header">

            <h2 class="text-center">Create a New Task</h2>

         </div>

         <div class="card-body">

            <form method="post" action="{% if task.pk %}{% url
            'tasks:task-update' task.pk %}{% else %}{% url 'tasks:task-
            create' %}{% endif %}">


               {% csrf_token %}
```

```
                    {% for field in form %}
                        <div class="mb-3">
                            <label for="{{ field.id_for_label }}"
                            class="form-label">{{ field.label }}</label>
                            {% if field.errors %}
                                <div class="alert alert-danger">
                                    {{ field.errors }}
                                </div>
                            {% endif %}
                            {{ field|add_class:"form-control" }}
                        </div>
                    {% endfor %}
                    <button type="submit" class="btn btn-primary
                    w-100">Save</button>
                </form>
            </div>
        </div>
    </div>
</div>
{% endblock %}
```

To use widget tweaks in the template, we include the line **`{% load widget_tweaks %}`** to load the necessary template tags.

The **`csrf_token`** template tag adds a hidden input type field to the form. This field is used to prevent the vulnerability of Cross-Site Request Forgery (CSRF). Django, often regarded for its "batteries-included" approach, has many security measures to protect web applications. CSRF protection is just one of many security protections.

The form uses the **`task-create`** or the **`task-update`** action URL from the task creation or update view. These views were created in *Chapter 5: Django Views and URL Handling*. The generic view **`TaskCreateView`** allows us to change the form class using the attribute **form_class**. Then, we render all the form fields with a loop iteration of the form. Inside the loop, we render the label, the errors (if any) and the field itself.

For form submission, we use a submit button.

Here is the new **TaskCreateView** using the new form:

```
from django.urls import reverse_lazy

from django.views.generic.edit import CreateView


class TaskCreateView(CreateView):

    model = Task

    template_name = "tasks/task_form.html"

    form_class = TaskForm


    def get_success_url(self):

            return reverse_lazy("tasks:task-detail", kwargs={"pk": self.
            object.id})
```

It's essential to note that we omitted the 'fields' attribute because using both **form_class** and **fields** can lead to unexpected behavior.

Info: In a CSRF attack, an authenticated user's browser is manipulated by a malicious website, email, or program to perform undesired actions on our web application.

Without CSRF protection, the malicious application could submit a form that deletes the sprint without the user's consent.

The protection adds a unique token as a hidden input value. When the form is submitted to the server, the CSRF middleware checks the form token against the token stored in the user's session or cookie-based approach. If the tokens match, the form is submitted. Otherwise, the server will return 403 Forbidden.

Browsers implement additional security measures to block malicious apps from accessing session tokens. The CSRF token is stored in a cookie that is **httpOnly**, making it inaccessible by JavaScript.

Handling Form Submission in Views

In *Chapter 5, Django Views and URL Handling*, we created a class-based view, **TaskCreateView**, which can process form submissions easily. The class inherits from the generic view **CreateView**. The **CreateView** class inherits behavior from the **ModelFormMixin**, which allows the process and validation of a Django Form for the model **Task**.

The framework also provides a generic class-based view for handling forms that aren't tied to a specific model; this is suitable for general-purpose usage. The task management project now requires handling a contact form that sends an email and it does not store anything in the database. We cannot use **CreateView** because we don't have an email model.

We need first to create a contact form in our file **tasks/forms.py**. This time, we will inherit from **Form**:

```
from django import forms


class ContactForm(forms.Form):

    from_email = forms.EmailField(required=True)

    subject = forms.CharField(required=True)

    message = forms.CharField(widget=forms.Textarea, required=True)
```

The form has three fields, and all of them are required.

Each field has a designated type. We use the **Textarea** widget for the **message** field, enabling users to input their message in a spacious textbox.

Now our form view handles the **ContactForm**, open **tasks/views.py** and add the new view:

```
from django.views.generic import FormView

from django.urls import reverse_lazy

from tasks.forms import ContactForm

from tasks import services


class ContactFormView(FormView):
```

```
    template_name = "tasks/contact_form.html"

    form_class = ContactForm

    success_url = reverse_lazy("tasks:contact-success")


    def form_valid(self, form):

            subject = form.cleaned_data.get("subject")

            message = form.cleaned_data.get("message")

            from_email = form.cleaned_data.get("from_email")

            services.send_contact_email(subject, message, from_email,
            ["your-email@example.com"])

            return super().form_valid(form)
```

The **ContactFormView** uses specific attributes to set up the class-based view. The **template_name** is to specify the filename of the form template. The **form_class** is set to the new **ContactForm** we previously created and the **success_url** is the URL that the view will redirect the user to when the form was submitted successfully.

The view will validate the form based on the request's payload for each request. The view will call the method **form_valid** if the payload is valid. The method has one parameter, which is the instance of the form. From the parameter "form" we extract the data of the form using the **cleaned_data** attribute. Recall our guideline: views shouldn't contain business logic. Thus, **form_valid** should invoke the service layer instead. In our case, we will call our notification service layer **send_contact_email** function.

Let's add the send contact email service to the **tasks/services.py** file:

```
from django.core.mail import send_mail


def send_contact_email(subject: str, message: str, from_email: str, to_
email: str) -> None:

    send_mail(subject, message, from_email, [to_email])
```

To make **send_mail** functional, you'll need to set up the email configurations in the Django project's settings file **projectmanager/settings.py**

```
import os
```

```
if DEBUG:
    # Using the console backend will simply print the emails to the console
    EMAIL_BACKEND = "django.core.mail.backends.console.EmailBackend"
else:
    EMAIL_BACKEND = "django.core.mail.backends.smtp.EmailBackend"
    EMAIL_HOST = os.getenv("EMAIL_HOST", "mailhog")
    EMAIL_PORT = int(os.getenv("EMAIL_PORT", "1025"))
    EMAIL_USE_TLS = os.getenv("EMAIL_USE_TLS", "False") == "True"
    EMAIL_HOST_USER = os.getenv("EMAIL_HOST_USER", "default@example.com")
    EMAIL_HOST_PASSWORD = os.getenv("EMAIL_HOST_PASSWORD",
"defaultpassword")
```

We also need to create a new contact form template. Place this template in the templates/tasks/ directory and name it **contact_form.html**.

```
{% extends "tasks/base.html" %}
{% load widget_tweaks %}

{% block content %}
<div class="d-flex justify-content-center align-items-center vh-100">
    <div class="w-50">
        <div class="card">
            <div class="card-header">
                <h2 class="text-center">Contact Us!</h2>
            </div>
            <div class="card-body">
                <form method="post" action="{% url 'tasks:contact' %}">
                    {% csrf_token %}
                    {% for field in form %}
                        <div class="mb-3">
```

```
                        <label for="{{ field.id_for_label }}"
                        class="form-label">{{ field.label }}</label>
                        {% if field.errors %}
                            <div class="alert alert-danger">
                                {{ field.errors }}
                            </div>
                        {% endif %}
                        {{ field|add_class:"form-control" }}
                    </div>
                {% endfor %}
                <button type="submit" class="btn btn-primary
                w-100">Send</button>
            </form>
        </div>
    </div>
</div>
</div>
{% endblock %}
```

We need to add the URLs we are going to use for the contact form and edit the tasks/urls.py:

```
from django.urls import path
from .views import ContactFormView
from django.views.generic import TemplateView

urlpatterns = [
    path("contact/", ContactFormView.as_view(), name="contact"),
    path(
        "contact-success/",
```

```
        TemplateView.as_view(template_name="contact_success.html"),
        name="contact-success",
    ),
    ...
]
```

The **templates/tasks/contact_success.html** template just shows a simple message to the user:

```
{% extends "base.html" %}

{% block content %}
  <div class="container">
    <h1>Contact Message Sent!</h1>
    <p>Thank you for reaching out! We have received your message and
    will respond as soon as possible.</p>
    <a href="{% url 'home' %}">Return Home</a>
  </div>
{% endblock %}
```

Let's add a link to the contact form in our footer **templates/tasks/_footer.html**:

```
{% load url %}
<footer class="footer mt-auto py-3 bg-light text-center">
   <div class="container">
      <a href="{% url 'tasks:help' %}" class="text-dark">Help</a> |
      <a href="{% url 'tasks:contact' %}" class="text-dark">Contact</a>
   </div>
</footer>
```

Testing the contact form should output the email in the terminal since the **DEBUG** setting is set to True in our development environment:

```
[12/Sep/2023 19:15:26] "GET /contact/ HTTP/1.1" 200 3511
```

```
Content-Type: text/plain; charset="utf-8"

MIME-Version: 1.0

Content-Transfer-Encoding: 7bit

Subject: Celebration Time!

From: happynews@example.com

To: ['your-email@example.com']

Date: Tue, 12 Sep 2023 19:17:03 -0000

Message-ID: <169453542365.11010.6693373536973317817@mandarinas-mbp.home>

Hello! I'm excited to announce that I've just achieved a significant milestone in my project.

It wouldn't have been possible without the support and encouragement of this beautiful community.

Thank you for being a part of this journey. Let's celebrate together!

-------------------------------------------------------------------------------

[12/Sep/2023 19:17:03] "POST /contact/ HTTP/1.1" 302 0

[12/Sep/2023 19:17:03] "GET /contact-success/ HTTP/1.1" 200 2073
```

Note: If you want to test the emails locally, you can extend the docker-compose configuration to use the `MailHog` SMTP service.

services:

```
 …
  mailhog:
    image: mailhog/mailhog
    ports:
      - "8025:8025" # Web UI
      - "1025:1025" # SMTP server
```

MailHog is an email testing tool with a fully featured web UI out of the box. MailHog starts an SMTP server that accepts all emails and displays them in the web interface.

In our GitHub repository, you can check how MailHog is configured with the task management project to test emails.

Leveraging **FormView** or **CreateView** for form handling is optimal. These views are designed for this purpose, leading to concise and straightforward code.

However, we also have the option to handle the form using function-based views. We will see an example of handling the **ContactForm**:

```
from django.shortcuts import render, redirect, reverse

from .forms import ContactForm

from .services import send_contact_email


def contact_form_view(request):

    if request.method == 'POST':

        form = ContactForm(request.POST)

        if form.is_valid():

            subject = form.cleaned_data.get('subject')

            message = form.cleaned_data.get('message')

            from_email = form.cleaned_data.get('from_email')


            send_contact_email(subject, message, from_email, 'your-
            email@example.com')


            return redirect(reverse('contact-success'))

    else:

        form = ContactForm()


    return render(request, 'contact_form.html', {'form': form})
```

The view first checks for the request method to be POST, otherwise for a GET it renders an empty form. Then, it initializes the **`ContactForm`** using the request payload stored in the **`request.POST`** dictionary. If the form is valid, we can extract the data from the **`clean_data`** attribute of the form and call our service layer.

Finally, we redirect the user to the contact-success view.

Working with Form Fields

Django offers a variety of field types to process the different data input needs in web forms. While the **`ModelForm`** class auto-generates form fields from the associated model attributes, you may need to define form fields if you are not using **`ModelForm`** explicitly. As shown with **`ContactForm`**, you can explicitly declare fields to customize form behavior.

We enumerate some frequently utilized fields Django offers:

- **`CharField`**: One of the most common form fields used to handle text input. You can limit the maximum length of input using the **`max_length`** attribute.
- **`TextField`**: A text field for arbitrarily large amounts of text.
- **`IntegerField`**: This field is for integer input.
- **`DecimalField`**: A field for handling decimal numbers. It's mandatory to specify **`max_digits`** and **`decimal_places`** attributes.
- **`BooleanField`**: A field for handling boolean values.
- **`ChoiceField`**: This field presents the user with a list of choices. You provide the choices by using a list of tuples.
- **`DateField`**: A field for collecting dates. It uses a widget attribute that can be set to **`SelectDateWidget`** to provide a date-picker interface.
- **`EmailField`**: A field that checks if the provided input is a valid email address.
- **`FileField`**: A field for handling file upload. It must be used in conjunction with Django's file storage API.
- **`ImageField`**: Similar to **`FileField`**, but validates that the uploaded object is a valid image. Requires Pillow to be installed.

We already learned how to render fields by using iteration on the form (**`{% for field in form %}`**) and then using the variable to render the field (**`{{ field }}`**). However, the framework provides other ways to render the fields.

Here is an alternative way to render the fields:

```
<form method="post">

    {% csrf_token %}

    {{ form.as_p }}

    <button type="submit">Submit</button>

</form>
```

In this new template, we are not doing the iteration and manually rendering the fields, but we use the method "**as_p**". The form supports at least four types of rendering:

- **{{ form.as_div }}** Input elements will be wrapped between divs.
- **{{ form.as_table }}** Fields will be rendered to a table
- **{{ form.as_p }}** Input elements will be wrapped between p tags.
- **{{ form.as_ul }}** Inputs will be rendered using the HTML unordered list.

Sometimes, you will need more control over rendering the fields. In that case, you will need to use the iteration.

Custom form fields

There are instances where Django might not have the specific field we require for our form. For those scenarios, it is possible to create our field class.

To implement a custom form field in Django, you typically would override the following methods of the **django.forms.Field** class:

- **to_python(self, value)**: This method converts the value into the correct Python datatype. For example, if you have a custom field that deals with numeric data, you would use this method to ensure that the data is converted into a Python integer or float.
- **validate(self, value)**: This method runs field-specific validation rules. You could raise the **ValidationError** from here if the validation fails.
- **clean(self, value)**: This method is used to provide the **cleaned** data, which is the result of calling **to_python()** and **validate()**. You usually don't need to override this unless you need to change its behavior fundamentally.

- **bound_data(self, data, initial)**: This returns the value that should be shown for this field when rendering it with the specified initial data and the submitted data. This method is typically used for fields where the user's input is not necessarily the same as the output.
- **prepare_value(self, value)**: Converts Python objects to query string values.
- **widget_attrs(self, widget)**: This adds any HTML attributes needed for your widget based on the field.

Suppose you want to create a form that accepts a list of email addresses in a comma-separated format. While Django doesn't provide this field type out of the box, you can easily create a custom field to fulfill this need. Here, we show how to implement this custom field and use it in a Django model form.

Create a new file in the tasks application, fields.py:

```
from django import forms

from django.core.validators import EmailValidator


email_validator = EmailValidator(message="One or more email addresses are
not valid")


class EmailsListField(forms.CharField):

    def to_python(self, value):

            "Normalize data to a list of strings."

            # Return an empty list if no input was given.

            If not value:

                return []

            return [email.strip() for email in value.split(',')]


    def validate(self, value):

            "Check if value consists only of valid emails."

            Super().validate(value)

            for email in value:
```

```
            email_validator(email)
```

The class implements two methods, the **to_python** and validate. The method **to_python** converts the comma-separated string to a list of strings. The list comprehension also cleans up the string by removing white spaces.

The validation method uses the **forms.EmailValidator** and if one of those strings is not an email, a **ValidationError** will be raised.

We are requested to add a watcher list to our Task model. This new requirement aligns with our custom **EmailsListField**.

The current Task model does not support the watcher's email list, forcing us to change the schema. Since there could be more than one watcher, we will use a separate related model, the **SubscribedEmail**. Open the file tasks/models.py and add the new model:

```
class SubscribedEmail(models.Model):

    email = models.EmailField()

    task = models.ForeignKey(Task, on_delete=models.CASCADE, related_
    name="watchers")
```

Using a related model allows us to keep the Task schema unchanged; this approach is normalized.

Let's create the migration and migrate our development environment:

```
poetry shell

python manage.py makemigrations

python manage.py migrate
```

Now we will update our **TaskForm** to incorporate emails by using the new custom field, **EmailsListField**. This modified form will be used in the view that handles task creation and updates, edit the file **tasks/forms.py**, and change the **TaskForm** class to use the new field:

```
from django import forms

from tasks.fields import EmailsListField


from .models import SubscribedEmail, Task
```

```
class TaskForm(forms.ModelForm):
    watchers = EmailsListField(required=False)

    class Meta:
            model = Task
            fields = ["title", "description", "status", "watchers"]

    def __init__(self, *args, **kwargs):
            super(TaskForm, self).__init__(*args, **kwargs)
            # Check if an instance is provided and populate watchers field
            if self.instance and self.instance.pk:
                self.fields['watchers'].initial = ', '.join(email.email
                for email in self.instance.watchers.all())

    def save(self, commit=True):
            # First, save the Task instance
            task = super().save(commit)

            # If commit is True, save the associated emails
            if commit:
                # First, remove the old emails associated with this task
                task.watchers.all().delete()

            # Add the new emails to the Email model
            for email_str in self.cleaned_data["watchers"]:
                    SubscribedEmail.objects.create(email=email_str,
                    task=task)

        return task
```

The form now uses the new **`EmailListField`** for the watchers' relationship. It also implements the **`__init__`** and the **`save`** methods. The **`__init__`** is required when the form is used for editing a **Task**, and it will populate the watcher's emails.

The **`save`** method is implemented to save the **`Task`** first, delete all the watchers, and then save the new ones.

We'll now modify the form template to incorporate the newly added watcher list, open the file **templates/tasks/task_detail.html** and update the template:

```
{% extends "tasks/base.html" %}


{% block content %}

<div class="vh-100 d-flex justify-content-center align-items-center">

    <div class="container text-center">

        <h1 class="mb-4 ">{{ task.title }}</h1>

        <div class="card">

            <div class="card-body">

                <h2 class="card-title">Description</h2>

                <p class="card-text">{{ task.description }}</p>


                <!-- Emails list -->

                <h3>Watchers</h3>

                <ul class="list-unstyled">

                    {% for watcher in task.watchers.all %}

                    <li>{{ watcher.email }}</li>

                    {% endfor %}

                </ul>

            </div>

        </div>

        <div class="mt-4 d-inline-block">

            <a href="{% url 'tasks:task-update' task.id %}" class="btn
```

```
        btn-primary me-2">Edit</a>

        <a href="{% url 'tasks:task-delete' task.id %}" class="btn
        btn-danger me-2">Delete</a>

        <a href="{% url 'tasks:task-list' %}" class="btn btn-
        secondary">Back to List</a>

      </div>

    </div>

</div>

{% endblock %}
```

If a task has associated watchers, their email addresses will be displayed in a list. This is achieved using the **`{% for watcher in the task.watchers.all %}`** loop, which iterates over the related Email model instances to render each watcher's email address.

File and Image Upload Field

To improve our project management, we will extend it to support file and image uploads for the **`Task`** model. We must change our models and settings before using the form file and image upload fields.

Let's add new attributes to our Task model:

```
class Task(models.Model):

    ...

    file_upload = models.FileField(upload_to="tasks/files/", null=True,
blank=True)

    image_upload = models.ImageField(upload_to="tasks/images/", null=True,
blank=True)
```

We need to create the migrations and execute them:

```
poetry add Pillow  # Pillow is required for the ImageField

poetry shell

python manage.py makemigrations

python manage.py migrate
```

Open the taskmanager/settings.py to set the MEDIA_ROOT and MEDIA_URL, this defines the absolute filesystem path to the directory for storing uploaded files and their URL base.

```
MEDIA_ROOT = os.path.join(BASE_DIR, "media/")

MEDIA_URL = "/media/"
```

Note: **`MEDIA_ROOT`** and **`MEDIA_URL`** are settings in Django that specify how media files are handled. These settings are crucial for file uploads, image uploads, and any other user-generated static content that needs to be served.

`MEDIA_ROOT`: This is an absolute filesystem path to the directory where all uploaded media files will be stored.

`MEDIA_URL`: This is the base URL used for serving the media files stored in **`MEDIA_ROOT`**. When you need to reference or link to the saved media files in your templates or views, Django will use MEDIA_URL as the base to construct the URL for those files.

To be able to use these fields in the Task create or upload view, we need to add the fields to the form:

```
class TaskForm(forms.ModelForm):

    ...

    class Meta:

        model = Task

        fields = ["title", "description", "status", "watchers", "file_upload", "image_upload"]

    ...
```

Django will automatically generate the necessary form fields for file and image upload. This automatic generation also applies to the admin interface.

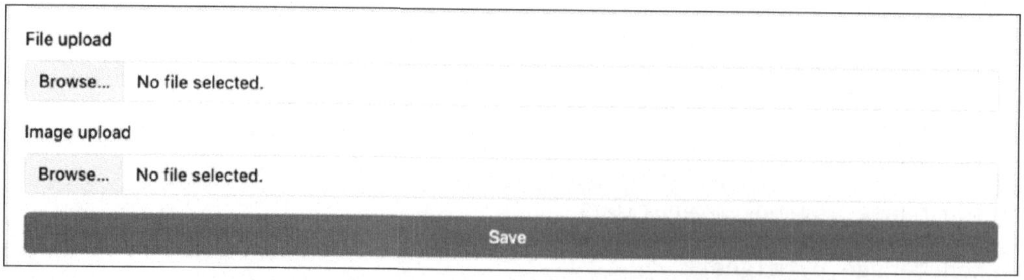

Figure 7.2: *Django form with file and image upload fields*

Since we are using the development server, let's add a way to serve media files, open the **projectmanagement/urls.py** and add the following conditional URL:

```
from django.conf import settings

from django.conf.urls.static import static


urlpatterns = [

    ...

]

if settings.DEBUG:

    urlpatterns += static(settings.MEDIA_URL, document_root=settings.
    MEDIA_ROOT)
```

The preceding code allows serving the uploaded media using the development server. This view is only available when the DEBUG setting is set to true. In *Chapter 11: Deploying Django Applications with Gunicorn and Docker*, we will use a cloud provider to upload and serve our uploaded files and media.

Note: It's important to note that serving media files using Django's built-in development server, as shown in this guide, is only intended for development purposes. The DEBUG setting should never be set to True in a production environment, as it exposes various security vulnerabilities.

If we want to see a file download link and an image preview, we need to modify our **templates/tasks/task_details.html** template.

Just before the actions buttons, add the following template code:

```
{% if task.file_upload %}

    <a href="{{ task.file_upload.url }}" download>Download File</a>

{% endif %}


{% if task.image_upload %}

    <div>

        <img src="{{ task.image_upload.url }}" alt="Task Image"
        style="max-width: 300px;">
```

```
    </div>
{% endif %}
```

Data Validation with Django Forms

Django forms simplify the task of data validation, offering a wide array of tools to both validate and sanitize data. Django Forms performs validation on each field type. For example, **EmailField** checks if the given data is a valid email format.

Validators

When the field type check is insufficient and additional constraints have to be added, it is possible to use validators. Form fields allow a list of validators:

```
from django import forms
from django.core.validators import MaxValueValidator


class TaskForm(forms.Form):
    priority = forms.IntegerField(validators=[MaxValueValidator(100)])
```

In the preceding code, we are using the **MaxValueValidator** that checks if the priority of the task is less than 100.

The framework provides a variety of validators. Here is a list of some of the most useful ones:

- **EmailValidator**: Validates that a value is a valid email address.
- **URLValidator**: Validates that a value is a valid URL.
- **RegexValidator**: Validates a value based on a provided regular expression.
- **MinLengthValidator**: Validates that a value has at least a certain length.
- **MaxLengthValidator**: Validates that a value doesn't exceed a certain length.
- **MinValueValidator**: Validates that a value is at least a specified minimum.
- **MaxValueValidator**: Validates that a value doesn't exceed a specified maximum.
- **FileExtensionValidator**: Validates that a file has a specific extension.

Clean methods

The form also has what is called cleaning methods. There are two types per attribute and a general cleaning. The cleaning methods are part of the validation process and are called automatically when the **`is_valid`** method is called.

For each field, it is possible to implement a method **`clean_<fieldname>()`** and you can perform validation against the attribute. If your form has the attribute email, you can implement the **`clean_email`** method to make additional validation against this email attribute:

```
def clean_email(self) -> str:

    email = self.cleaned_data.get("email")

    email = email.strip()

    validate_email(email)

    return email
```

The method associated with the clean attribute gives back the sanitized value specific to that field. In the example, we strip the white spaces from the email. We also validate the email str using a **`validate_email`** function that raises **`ValidationError`** if the email is invalid. Finally, we return the email string.

The general **`clean`** method should return a dictionary containing all the cleaned data.

```
def clean(self) -> dict:

    cleaned_data = super().clean()

    # perform validations or cleanups

    return cleaned_data
```

You can employ the generic clean method when there's a need to validate multiple fields sharing a validation logic simultaneously.

Clean methods should raise **`forms.ValidationError`** when there is invalid data.

When the **`is_valid`** method returns false, the form will contain errors that can be accessed via the attribute **`errors`**. These errors are a dictionary structure with field names as keys and a list of messages as values.

ModelForm Validation

With **ModelForm**, you get extra validation for free, derived from the associated model's constraints. For instance, if a model's char field has **max_length=100**, the associated form field will inherit this constraint.

However, you can still use **clean_<fieldname>()** and **clean()** methods for additional validation logic.

Displaying Form Errors

Whenever a form gets submitted to the server, Django verifies the submitted form data. Effective form validation ensures that users input data correctly. By displaying concise error messages, you assist users in recognizing mistakes. A user encountering an unexplained form rejection may abandon the task entirely, potentially losing conversions, sign-ups, or any other desired action.

Note: From a user experience perspective, how errors are communicated can have a significant impact. Errors should not simply highlight mistakes; they should do so in a way that feels constructive rather than punitive. Therefore, while implementing form validation in Django, you may want to customize error messages to align with this approach.

Each form field comes with its own set of validation rules. For example, the **EmailField** requires a string that is a valid email. When it is invalid, the form allows access to the errors via the **errors** attribute of the form instance. The **errors** attribute is a dictionary holding fields that did not meet the validation criteria.

In our template, the **errors** attribute displays the validation issues. However, it can be customized for a better user experience.

```
<form method="post">

  {% csrf_token %}


  {% for field in form %}

    <div class="form-group mb-3">

      <label for="{{ field.id_for_label }}" class="form-label">{{
      field.label }}</label>
```

```
        {{ field|add_class:"form-control" }}
        {% if field.errors %}
        <div class="alert alert-danger mt-2">
          {% for error in field.errors %}
          <p class="mb-0"><strong>{{ error }}</strong></p>
          {% endfor %}
        </div>
        {% endif %}
      </div>
    {% endfor %}

  {% if form.non_field_errors %}
    <div class="alert alert-danger">
      <ul>
        {% for error in form.non_field_errors %}
       <li>{{ error }}</li>
        {% endfor %}
      </ul>
    </div>
  {% endif %}

  <button type="submit" class="btn btn-primary">Submit</button>
</form>
```

For simplicity, the example code iterates over form fields to render them. You could also use built-in methods like **as_p** for a simpler output, but further appearance customization can be done by iterating the fields as shown. The template employs a conditional to check for the presence of any errors. When there are errors, it shows all the errors inside a div with CSS classes to alert the user about the error after processing the form.

Each error message is displayed inside an HTML unordered list by iterating over the form's **errors** attribute or **non_field_errors** attribute, as applicable. It's important to note that a single field could encompass multiple errors, necessitating the iteration through all of them.

In Django forms, the **errors** and **non_field_errors** attributes play a crucial role in form validation and user feedback. The **errors** attribute is a dictionary that holds the validation errors for each field in the form. Each key-value pair in the dictionary corresponds to a form field and its associated list of error messages. On the other hand, the **non_field_errors** attribute holds errors that are not associated with a specific field but are form-wide issues, such as conflicting field values or missing required combinations.

Advanced Form Handling: ModelFormsSets and Formsets

Django offers tools like **ModelFormSets** and **FormSets** to handle multiple objects simultaneously.

In our task management application, users need the capability to edit the details of multiple tasks within an epic all at once. A form can represent each task, and a **FormSet** enables simultaneous display and processing.

In the Django framework, both **FormSet** and **ModelFormSet** allow developers to work with multiple forms collectively, making it ideal for scenarios where batch processing or editing is required. A **FormSet** is a layer of abstraction that permits you to manage and validate multiple forms simultaneously, irrespective of any specific database model. On the other hand, **ModelFormSet** is intrinsically tied to a specific Django model. It provides an interface to create, update, or delete multiple model instances.

While a **ModelFormSet** is similar to a **FormSet**, its unique association with a Django model makes it different.

Here is an example of how to use **ModelFormSet** with the Task model:

```
# tasks/forms.py

EpicFormSet = modelformset_factory(Task, form=TaskForm, extra=0)
```

We set the **extra** parameter to zero in the **modelformset_factory** for this **EpicFormSet**, ensuring we only modify existing tasks without adding new ones to the epic. Using extra with 1 or more will force the user to create a new task every time the form gets submitted. Using zero ensures that users can only modify existing tasks within an epic and are not prompted to add new ones.

We will opt for a function-based view because **FormSet**s are more straightforward to manipulate within this view.

```
from django.shortcuts import render, redirect

from .models import Task

from .forms import EpicFormSet


def manage_epic_tasks(request, epic_pk):

    epic = services.get_epic_by_id(epic_pk)

    if not epic:

        raise Http404("Epic does not exist")

    if request.method == "POST":

        formset = EpicFormSet(request.POST, queryset=services.get_
        tasks_for_epic(epic))

        if formset.is_valid():

            tasks = formset.save(commit=False)

            services.save_tasks_for_epic(epic, tasks)

            formset.save_m2m()  # handle many-to-many relations if
            there are any

            return redirect('tasks:task-list')

    else:

        formset = EpicFormSet(queryset=services.get_tasks_for_epic(epic))


    return render(request, 'tasks/manage_epic.html', {'formset': formset,
    'epic': epic})
```

The **manage_epic_tasks** view employs the **epic_pk** parameter as an integral part of its functionality. If the epic isn't found using this parameter, Django raises a 404 error. If the method is POST, the code first validates the form. When the form is valid, it retrieves the tasks but doesn't immediately commit the changes. Using the services, we save all the tasks for the epic. Django will not automatically save the many-to-many data. After manually handling and saving the primary instance, you should call **save_m2m()** to ensure the many-to-many relationships are properly saved.

Our new services will be:

```
from .models import Epic, Task


def get_epic_by_id(epic_id: int) -> Epic | None:
    return Epic.objects.filter(pk=epic_id).first()


def get_tasks_for_epic(epic: Epic) -> list[Task]:
    return Task.objects.filter(epics=epic)


def save_tasks_for_epic(epic: Epic, tasks: list[Task]) -> None:
    for task in tasks:
        task.save()
        task.epics.add(epic)
```

The new services perform basic operations and there is no custom business logic for now.

- **get_epic_by_id**: gets the Epic object by pk
- **get_tasks_for_epic**: returns all the tasks for an epic
- **save_tasks_for_epic**: saves all the tasks and adds them to the epic

For **FormSet** and **ModelFormSet** the template is slightly different:

```
{% extends "tasks/base.html" %}
{% load widget_tweaks %}

{% block content %}
<div class="container mt-5">
    <h1>Epic: {{epic.name}}</h1>
  <form method="post">
```

```
{% csrf_token %}
{{ formset.management_form }}

<div class="row">
   {% for form in formset %}
   <div class="col-md-6 mb-3">
      <div class="card">
         <div class="card-body">
                {% for field in form %}
                <div class="mb-3">
                   <label for="{{ field.id_for_label }}"
                   class="form-label">{{ field.label }}</label>
                   {{ field|add_class:"form-control" }}
                   {% if field.errors %}
                   <div class="alert alert-danger mt-2">
                      {% for error in field.errors %}
                      <p class="mb-0">{{ error }}</p>
                      {% endfor %}
                   </div>
                   {% endif %}
                </div>
                {% endfor %}
         </div>
      </div>
   </div>
   {% endfor %}
</div>
```

```
        <div class="mt-3">
            <button type="submit" class="btn btn-primary">Save</button>
        </div>
    </form>
</div>
{% endblock %}
```

Pay attention to `formset.management_form`. It's a specialized form in all `FormSets`, containing their management data. Including this in your template is essential, or Django will need help to process the `FormSet` correctly.

Don't forget to add the new URL pattern to the tasks tasks/urls.py file:

```
path("epic/<int:epic_pk>/", manage_epic_tasks, name="task-batch-create"),
```

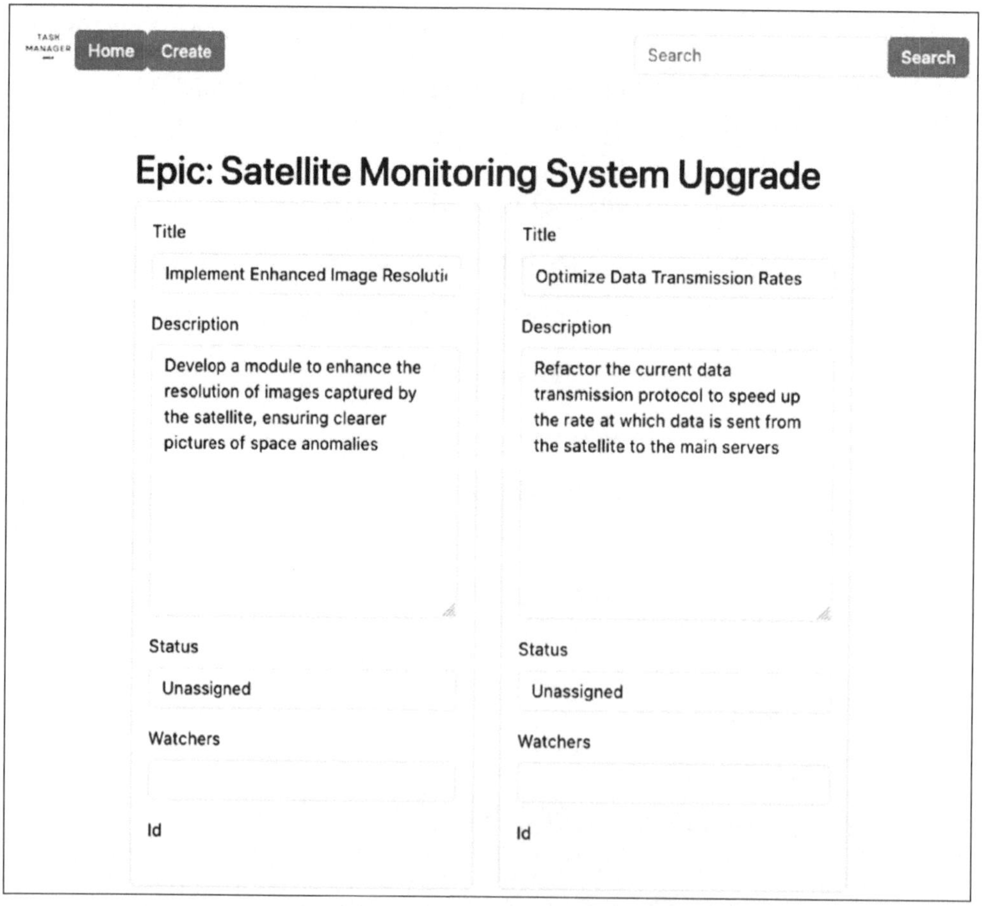

Figure 7.3: *ModelFormSet is used to edit all the tasks for an epic*

Preventing Double Submission in Forms

Sometimes, it's expected for Django Forms to allow users to submit data multiple times. Still, there are scenarios where we want to prevent double submission. For example, preventing double submissions when processing reservations or payments is critical.

Note: Allowing users to make multiple form submissions might seem harmless initially. However, from a user experience perspective, this can lead to confusion and unintended consequences. For instance, if users unknowingly submit a payment form twice, they might be charged twice, leading to unnecessary stress and potential disputes.

There are various methods to prevent double submission. We are going to focus on two possible solutions. The first approach, commonly implemented, is to simply disable the form's submit button using JavaScript. The second solution is more complex and uses an ID to keep track of the submitted forms.

We will change the **TaskForm** to add the JavaScript solution:

```
{% block content %}

<div class="d-flex justify-content-center align-items-center vh-100">

   <div class="w-50">

      <div class="card">

         <div class="card-header">

            <h2 class="text-center">Create a New Task</h2>

         </div>

         <div class="card-body">

            <form id="taskForm" method="post" action="{% if task.pk
            %}{% url 'tasks:task-update' task.pk %}{% else %}{% url
            'tasks:task-create' %}{% endif %}">

...

{% endblock %}

{% block extra_javascript %}
```

```
<script>

    document.getElementById('taskForm').addEventListener('submit',
    function(){

        this.querySelector('button[type="submit"]').disabled = true;

    });

</script>

{% endblock %}
```

The template will stay almost the same, on the content block we will only add the id attribute to the form. This will allow us to disable the form submit button using JavaScript.

Next, we'll expand on the **extra_javascript** block from *Chapter 6, Using The Django Template Engine*. The script will listen to the form submit and disable the button to prevent multiple clicks.

While this frontend solution enhances user experience, there is still the possibility of multiple form submissions, which can be bypassed by determined users. Restrictions on the frontend side can always be bypassed and for a more robust solution, we need to implement a restriction on the backend side.

The backend solution uses a unique token associated with the form. This token is universally unique and will be stored in a hidden field of the form.

The form now will have a UUID field:

```
class TaskForm(forms.ModelForm):

    uuid = forms.UUIDField(required=False, widget=forms.HiddenInput())

    watchers = EmailsListField(required=False)


    class Meta:

        model = Task

        fields = ["title", "description", "status", "watchers"]


    def __init__(self, *args, **kwargs):

        super(TaskForm, self).__init__(*args, **kwargs)
```

```
        # Check if an instance is provided and populate watchers field
        if self.instance and self.instance.pk:
            self.fields["watchers"].initial = ', '.join(email.email for
            email in self.instance.watchers.all())
        self.fields["uuid"].initial = uuid.uuid4()

    def clean_uuid(self):
        uuid_value = self.cleaned_data.get("uuid")

        with transaction.atomic():
            # Try to record the form submission by UUID
            try:
                FormSubmission.objects.create(uuid=uuid_value)
            except IntegrityError:
              # The UUID already exists, so the form was already submitted
                raise ValidationError("This form has already been
                submitted.")
        return uuid_value

    def save(self, commit=True):
        # First, save the Task instance
        task = super().save(commit)

        # If commit is True, save the associated emails
        if commit:
            # First, remove the old emails associated with this task
            task.watchers.all().delete()

            # Add the new emails to the Email model
```

```
            for email_str in self.cleaned_data["watchers"]:

                Email.objects.create(email=email_str, task=task)


        return task
```

The **FormSubmission** model is simple and unrelated to business. We only store the UUID as a unique value to prevent duplicates.

We have not implemented this in the service layer since our form handles the prevention of double submissions directly, and our business logic does not dictate it.

The **__init__** method generates a new UUID for each form creation. The form now includes a hidden UUID as an input, with the UUID as a value.

When the form is validated, it will automatically call the **clean_<attribute_name>** methods. The **clean_uuid** method saves the UUID using the create method of the object manager. If the form was already submitted, the unique constraint in the database will prevent the creation of the FormSubmission object and prevent the double submission. This approach hinges on the principle that UUID generation yields a unique value with every call.

Note: The Universally Unique Identifier (UUID) is a 128-bit number used to identify information uniquely.

The probability of creating two identical UUIDs is extremely low and it works well in distributed systems.

UUID is written as a sequence of lower-case hexadecimal digits in five groups separated by hyphens, in the form 8-4-4-4-12 for 32 digits. Here's an example of a UUID: c6b3b76c-f700-4d55-8a48-50fae11f9e26

Let me present you the model to store the form UUIDs:

```
from django.db import models

class FormSubmission(models.Model):

    uuid = models.UUIDField(unique=True)
```

We need to create the migrations and migrate the database again:

```
poetry shell

python manage.py makemigrations
```

```
python manage.py migrate
```

If you want to avoid creating a new model due to database overhead, you can handle duplication with Django's caching mechanism. Naively using the caching could bring race conditions, so we have to use atomic operations with the caching solution carefully.

Note: A race condition occurs in a multi-threaded or distributed system when two or more operations must execute in the correct sequence, but the program does not guarantee the sequence. Typically, race conditions manifest when checking for a record's existence in the database. If a context switch occurs at this point–before confirming non-existence–other threads might create the record. Once the initial thread regains control, it operates under the assumption that the record doesn't exist, even though it might have been created during the context switch.

Redis is an open-source, high-performance, in-memory data structure store that can be used as a caching backend. Redis has a command similar to the **`SELECT … FOR UPDATE`**, which is the SETNX. The syntax of the SETNX command is the SETNX key value, which will set the key with the value if the key does not exist. No operation is performed when the key already exists.

First, we need to install the **`django-redis`** third-party package:

```
poetry add django-redis
```

Now let's add **`redis`** to our docker-compose configuration:

```
services:

  ...

  redis:

    image: redis:latest

    ports:

      - "6379:6379"

    volumes:

      - redis_data:/data

volumes:

  postgres_data:
```

```
  redis_data:
```

The **redis** server will have a mapped port to localhost at 6379. We also added a volume for the Redis container, which is optional for our use case.

Next, open the project settings **taskmanager/settings.py** and set the backend to **RedisCache** and the location to use the redis provided by docker:

```
CACHES = {
        "default": {
        "BACKEND": "django_redis.cache.RedisCache",
        "LOCATION": "redis://127.0.0.1:6379/1",
        "OPTIONS": {
                "CLIENT_CLASS": "django_redis.client.DefaultClient",
        }
        }
}
```

Next is the code of our form to use redis:

```
class TaskForm(forms.ModelForm):
    ...

    def clean_uuid(self):
            uuid_value = str(self.cleaned_data.get("uuid"))

            was_set = cache.set(uuid_value, "submitted", nx=True)
            if not was_set:
                # If 'was_set' is False, the UUID already exists in the
                cache.
              # This indicates a duplicate form submission.
                raise ValidationError("This form has already been
                submitted.")
        return uuid_value
```

The form implementation is the same except for the **clean_uuid**, which uses the Django-cache framework. We use the **set** method of the cache and the **nx** parameter to true. This will use the Redis SETNX command. The **set** method will return false if the value was not previously set. Otherwise, it will return true. When the **set** returns true, we raise a **ValidationError**.

Setting this UUID can consume a significant amount of memory over time. To prevent the problem of memory usage, we can set a timeout to the **set** call. Using this timeout, we can also allow re-submission of the form, so we must be careful with the value we set it to. Using a small timeout will potentially allow resubmission to happen.

Using Redis for form uniqueness offers performance advantages due to its in-memory nature, ensuring fast read and write operations compared to traditional databases. Redis's atomic operations, like SETNX, effectively handle race conditions, making the system more robust. Additionally, Redis can automatically expire old form tokens with its TTL feature, reducing manual overhead. These qualities make Redis particularly well-suited for high-concurrency, real-time applications where quick data access is critical.

Note: In the chapter_6 branch on the project repository https://github.com/llazzaro/web_applications_django.git, you will find two classes for the **TaskForm**, one using the database (**TaskFormWithModel**) and the other one using redis (**TaskFormWithRedis**). By default, the task view uses the Redis form (**TaskFormWithRedis**), but you can easily change the form class via the **form_class** attribute.

Conclusion

Using Django's form system is indispensable. It provides an abstraction that allows you to validate the data your users send to your web application. Django offers several ready-to-use generic views designed to work with forms.

Forms in Django are highly customizable; using templates to alter their appearance and modifying fields for specific validations are just a couple of possibilities.

Django's built-in file and image fields offer a reliable way to handle attachments in our Task model.

Form sets in Django enable batch creation and editing of objects; for instance, they proved invaluable when crafting a view to modify Tasks linked to an Epic.

While client-side validation can enhance the user experience, backend restrictions are needed to ensure data integrity. Both frontend and backend approaches are essential for a robust form submission process to tackle different layers of potential issues.

By employing UUIDs, we've developed a robust mechanism using forms to prevent duplicate submissions.

In the next chapter, we will add authentication and authorization to our task management project using the framework security features.

Questions

1. How do Django Forms alleviate the drawbacks of using raw HTML forms?
2. How does the Django framework use the "Meta" inner class in form classes?
3. Explain the role of CSRF protection in Django forms.
4. How do Django's different form field types, like `CharField`, `IntegerField`, and `EmailField`, handle data input?
5. When might you use `FormView` instead of `CreateView` for handling form submissions?
6. What are cleaning methods in Django forms and when are they invoked?
7. What should the cleaning methods raise when they encounter invalid data?
8. How can Django's forms be customized for a better user experience?
9. What is the use of `modelformset_factory` in Django?
10. How can double submission in forms be prevented in Django? Provide two methods.

Exercises

1. Using Django Forms, create a `ModelForm` for a model "Sprint" which has attributes title (required), content, and author. Make sure the author is the authenticated user creating the blog post.
2. Create a custom Django form field that accepts a phone number and validates that it's in the correct format (that is, exactly 10 digits). The form should raise a `ValidationError` if the format is incorrect.
3. Implement a `ModelFormSet` for the Sprint model. Add the capability to edit multiple objects simultaneously and save them to the database.

Chapter 8
User Authentication and Authorization in Django

Introduction

Until now, our task manager project lacks authentication and authorization. This missing functionality renders our project unusable for everyday use.

This chapter will introduce essential concepts of authentication and authorization that are crucial for securing web applications. The Django middleware system is vital to providing authorization and authentication to our web application. We will learn how it works and how to customize it.

We will enhance our task management project by incorporating authorization features, including registration, login, and logout views. After establishing authentication, we will focus on implementing authorization mechanisms to our views.

Modifying Django's user model will allow our task manager to serve multiple customers or tenants.

As we conclude this chapter, we will evaluate security practices that are useful to review before launching any project to production.

Structure

In this chapter, we will cover the following topics:

- Understanding Django's Authentication System
- Introduction to Django's Middleware
- Understanding Django Middleware
- User Registration with Django's User Model
- Authenticating Users: Login and Logout
- Managing User Sessions
- Password Management in Django: Hashing and Password Reset
- User Authorization: Permissions and Groups
- Protecting Views with Login Required Decorators
- Multi-tenant authentication with Custom Django's User Model
- Security Best Practices in Django

Understanding Django's Authentication System

The HTTP protocol is stateless, meaning that each request to the server is treated as an isolated event. The protocol requires a mechanism to manage state continuity across multiple requests. The server creates cookies, which is a way to store information on the client side. Using these cookies, we can identify an authenticated user using a session identifier.

To understand Django's authentication system, there are two essential concepts: authentication and authorization.

Authentication is the process of verifying the identity of a user or entity. Authentication answers the question, "Are you who you say you are?"

Authorization occurs after authentication and determines what an authenticated user is allowed to do. Authorization answers, "Are you allowed to access or do?"

When a user uses username and password credentials to log in, we term this as authentication. Authorization is when the server checks for the proper permissions to allow the operation the user wants to perform. For example, an authenticated user with the role Editor who wants to delete a Task will get an authorization error. Many APIs use tokens, such as JSON Web Token (JWT) or

OAuth tokens, for authentication and authorization. We will see more about tokens in *Chapter* 9, *Django Ninja and* APIs.

There are specific HTTP response status codes, 401 and 403, respectively, for denied authentication and authorization.

The Django framework provides features that work with HTTP authorization and authentication, which we will see throughout the chapter.

Introduction to Django's Middleware

Before diving deep into the authentication system, it's essential to understand middleware first.

Consider middleware as layers inserted before processing each view or after a view has returned a response.

These middlewares are configured under the `MIDDLEWARE` section in the **taskmanager/settings.py** file. `MIDDLEWARE` configuration is a list, and the framework will execute each middleware in the order of this list for requests, but then in the reverse order for the response of processing.

Middleware can modify requests or responses, add security, enable redirects, or embed valuable data for views. Middleware can also raise exceptions when some conditions are unmet, making them ideal for checking authentication and authorization.

Now, let's suppose the scenario where the user navigates to the Task view and makes an HTTP request to the server.

The server received the request and will go through a chain of middleware. The default `MIDDLEWARE` configuration looks like the following one:

```
MIDDLEWARE = [

    "django.middleware.security.SecurityMiddleware",

    "django.contrib.sessions.middleware.SessionMiddleware",

    "django.middleware.common.CommonMiddleware",

    "django.middleware.csrf.CsrfViewMiddleware",

    "django.contrib.auth.middleware.AuthenticationMiddleware",

    "django.contrib.messages.middleware.MessageMiddleware",
```

```
    "django.middleware.clickjacking.XFrameOptionsMiddleware",
]
```

Each layer may evaluate the request as the request traverses this middleware chain. If a layer detects an issue, it can halt further processing, returning the relevant status code.

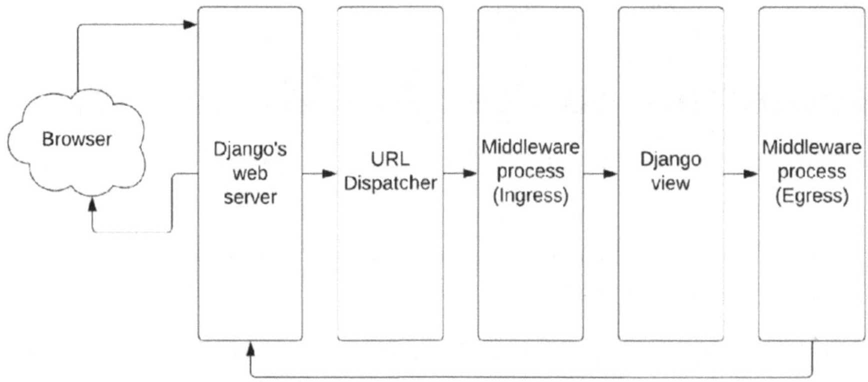

Figure 8.1: *Journey of an HTTP Request Through Django's Architecture*

The **SecurityMiddleware** checks for generic security configurations, like secure SSL redirects. We will deeply review the best security practices by the chapter's end.

Once the **SecurityMiddleware** checks are successful, the framework will continue with the next middleware in the list, the **SessionMiddleware**. The **SessionMiddleware** provides a way to store data in the session, making this data available in the request object.

CommonMiddleware handles redirects based on URL trailing slashes. Additionally, it uses the PREPEND_WWW setting and appends a content-length header.

Django protects against Cross-site request forgery using the middleware **CsrfViewMiddleware**. This middleware checks if the requests are safe based on the token verification. This middleware uses the token we set in forms, covered in the previous chapter, when we added **{% csrf_token %}**.

When **AuthenticationMiddleware** is enabled in the settings, it associates the corresponding user, if any, with the request object. If the user is authenticated, it will use the session store to locate the user. If the user is not authenticated, it will assign an instance of AnonymousUser.

The Django framework allows showing onetime informational messages to the users. The middleware **MessageMiddleware** stores these messages in the request.

Lastly, **`XFrameOptionsMiddleware`** protects against clickjacking by setting the X-Frame-Options header, dictating if browsers can render a page within tags like **`<frame>`**, **`<iframe>`**, **`<embed>`**, or **`<object>`**.

Info: **`Clickjacking`** is a malicious technique where an attacker tricks a user into clicking something different from what the user perceives. Clickjacking can lead to unintended actions on a different application without the user's consent.

When using the X-Frame-Options, the browser will allow or not to render a page inside an **`<iframe>`**.

Understanding Django Middleware

The framework makes it very easy to create your custom middleware. You will need to create a new class and implement some methods.

We'll create a middleware in Django to measure request render times, helping us address any efficiency issues.

Create a new file **tasks/middlewares.py** with the following code:

```
import time

import logging


logger = logging.getLogger(__name__)


class RequestTimeMiddleware:

    def __init__(self, get_response):

        self.get_response = get_response


    def __call__(self, request):

        # Start the timer when a request is received

        start_time = time.time()


        # Process the request and get the response

        response = self.get_response(request)
```

```
        # Calculate the time taken to process the request

        duration = time.time() - start_time


        # Log the time taken

        logger.info(f"Request to {request.path} took {duration:.2f}
        seconds.")


        return response
```

The class defines **__init__** and **__call__** methods, where **__init__** receives the **get_response** function to obtain the response later.

In Python, the **__call__** method allows class instances to be callable, meaning they can be invoked using parentheses, like functions.

The **__call__** method records the current time, gets the response, and then calculates the duration it took to process **get_response**. For logging, we use an f-string, a formatted string literal. The brackets allow the value of a variable to be inserted into the string. This syntax also allows the format's specification using a colon and some configuration. In the preceding example, we use **.2f** to format the value as a floating-point number with exactly two decimal places.

Finally, the code returns the response for the next middleware or view.

You can now add the **RequestTimeMiddleware** to the `MIDDLEWARE` setting in the **settings.py** file:

```
MIDDLEWARE = [

    "tasks.middlewares.RequestTimeMiddleware",

    …

    ]
```

Your custom middleware is ready to use! Note that the new middleware is placed at the beginning of the list. It will be the first to be called on an incoming request and the last to be called on the given response object.

If you want to manipulate the response, you can easily add data after calling the **get_response**. If you want to add a new header, here is an example:

```
def __call__(self, request):
```

```
    response = self.get_response(request)

    response["X-Custom-Header"] = "This is a custom header value"

    return response
```

User Registration with Django's User Model

We need to provide a way to allow users to register for our task management project. The Django framework has a built-in authentication system that provides views for logging in, logging out, and making password changes and resets. Django doesn't provide a built-in view specifically for user registration, so we must define ours.

For setting up the authentication application, we need to verify that the following framework application was added to the **INSTALLED_APPS**:

```
INSTALLED_APPS = [

    # ...

    'django.contrib.auth',

    'django.contrib.contenttypes',

    'django.contrib.sessions',

    # ...

]
```

Verify that **AuthenticationMiddleware** and **SessionMiddleware** have been added to your **MIDDLEWARE** setting.

To follow best practices, we will place anything related to authentication into a new application called accounts.

```
poetry shell

python manage.py startapp accounts
```

Open the project settings.py and add the newly created application to the **INSTALLED_APPS**.

```
INSTALLED_APPS = [

    ...
```

```
    "accounts",
]
```

We are ready to create our registration view in the **accounts/views.py**.

Our registration view will use the `UserCreationForm` provided by the framework, and we'll handle the user registration flow using this form.

```
from django.shortcuts import render, redirect
from django.contrib.auth.forms import UserCreationForm
from django.contrib import messages


def register(request):
    if request.method == "POST":
        form = UserCreationForm(request.POST)
        if form.is_valid():
            form.save()
            username = form.cleaned_data.get("username")
            messages.success(request, f"Account created for {username}!")
            return redirect("login")  # Redirect to the login page or
            any other page you want
    else:
        form = UserCreationForm()
    return render(request, "accounts/register.html", {"form": form})
```

Our view will first check for the method type. If the request is a POST, we use the `request.POST` payload to instantiate the `UserCreationForm`. When the form is valid, the form is saved, causing the user to be created.

We then use the message framework to add a notification to let the user know that the account was created successfully and redirect the user to the login page.

When the request is of type GET, we render the form using the register.html template.

We still need to create our registration template. Let's create a new directory in the templates directory, called **accounts**. In this new directory **accounts**, let's create the register.html file with the following contents:

```
{% extends "tasks/base.html" %}


{% block content %}

<div class="container">

    <div class="row justify-content-center">

        <div class="col-md-6">

            <h2 class="mb-4">Register</h2>

            <form method="post" class="border p-4 rounded">

                {% csrf_token %}

                {% for field in form %}

                <div class="mb-3">

                    <label for="{{ field.id_for_label }}" class="form-
                    label">{{ field.label }}</label>

                    {{ field }}

                    {% if field.help_text %}

                    <small class="form-text text-muted">{{ field.help_text
                    }}</small>

                    {% endif %}

                    {% for error in field.errors %}

                    <div class="text-danger">{{ error }}</div>

                    {% endfor %}

                </div>

                {% endfor %}

                <button type="submit" class="btn btn-primary">Register</
                button>

            </form>
```

```
        </div>
    </div>
</div>
{% endblock %}
```

The template is straightforward. It uses the block content to render the registration form with the CSRF token.

We need to set up our URLs. Let's create the URL patterns in our newly created accounts application, open **accounts/urls.py** and add the register view path:

```
from django.urls import path
from . import views

app_name = "accounts"
urlpatterns = [
    path("register/", views.register, name="register"),
]
```

Finally, we need to add our accounts application URLs to our project URLs, open the project taskmanager/urls.py and add the accounts URLs:

```
from django.contrib import admin
from django.urls import include, path

urlpatterns = [
     path("admin/", admin.site.urls),
     path("accounts/", include("accounts.urls")),
     path("", include("tasks.urls")),
]
```

Now navigate to http://localhost:8000/accounts/register and you should see the registration form:

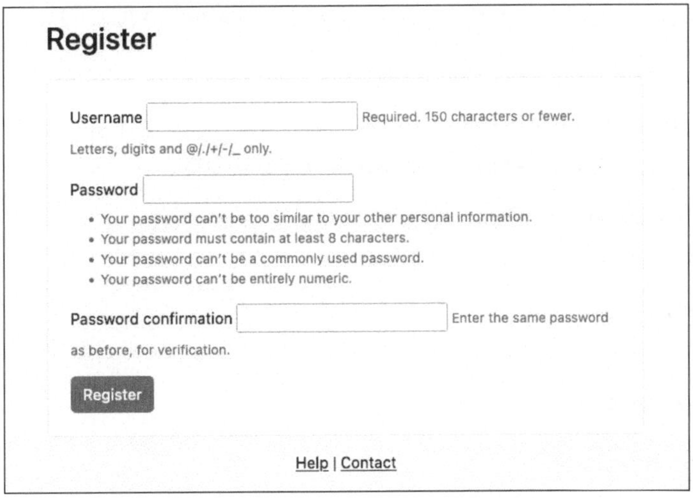

Figure 8.2: *Task manager registration form*

Note: Some third-party packages offer registration out of the box, saving you time when developing the registration flow. You can check the well-known Django-registration (https://github.com/ubernostrum/django-registration), which will provide an out-of-the-box solution that integrates with the framework's authentication system.

Authenticating Users: Login and Logout

Luckily, the framework provides login and logout views. We need to set up the URLs and the templates for it.

Open the **accounts/urls.py** and add two new paths:

```
from django.urls import path

from django.contrib.auth.views import LoginView, LogoutView

from . import views


app_name = "accounts"

urlpatterns = [

    path("register/", views.register, name="register"),

    path("login/", LoginView.as_view(template_name="accounts/login.
    html"), name="login"),
```

```
    path("logout/", LogoutView.as_view(), name="logout"),
]
```

Our login template will extend the base as always and use the content block. Create a new file in **templates/accounts/login.html**:

```
{% extends 'tasks/base.html' %}


{% load static %}


{% block content %}
<div class="container">
  <div class="row justify-content-center">
    <div class="col-md-6">
      <div class="card mt-5">
        <div class="card-body">
          <h2 class="text-center">Login</h2>
          <form method="post" class="mt-3">
            {% csrf_token %}

            <div class="mb-3">
              <label for="{{ form.username.id_for_label }}" class="form-
              label">Username</label>
              <input type="text" class="form-control" id="{{ form.
              username.id_for_label }}" name="{{ form.username.name }}">
            </div>


            <div class="mb-3">
              <label for="{{ form.password.id_for_label }}" class="form-
              label">Password</label>
              <input type="password" class="form-control" id="{{ form.
```

```
password.id_for_label }}" name="{{ form.password.name }}">
          </div>

          <div class="d-grid gap-2">
           <button type="submit" class="btn btn-primary">Login</button>
          </div>
         </form>
        </div>
       </div>
      </div>
     </div>
    </div>
{% endblock %}
```

As we have seen in *Chapter 6, Using the Django Template Engine*, the template renders the Django form with some customization to make it look nicer.

You can access the login page at the URL http://localhost:8000/accounts/login:

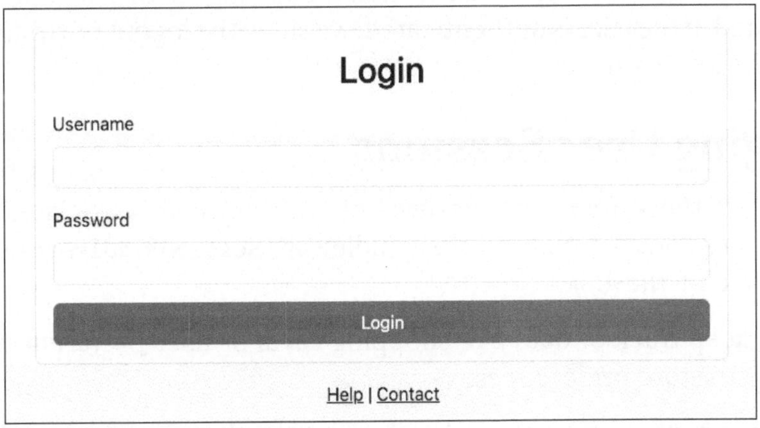

Figure 8.3: *The Login Form*

The logout view we added in the **urlpatterns** will redirect the user to a URL. You can specify the destination URL using the `LOGOUT_REDIRECT_URL` and `LOGIN_REDIRECT_URL` settings in the **taskmanager/settings.py**.

```
LOGIN_REDIRECT_URL = "tasks:task-home"

LOGOUT_REDIRECT_URL = "accounts:login"
```

In the following sections, we will add protections to the views. Users who are not authenticated will be redirected to the login page.

To allow our users easy access to the login and logout functionalities, let's update the header to show a login link when the user is not authenticated and a logout link otherwise. Open the **templates/tasks/_header.html** and update it with the new authentication links:

```
<!-- Login/Logout links →

{% if user.is_authenticated %}

   <a href="{% url 'accounts:logout' %}" class="btn btn-danger
   ml-2" role="button">Logout</a>

{% else %}

   <a href="{% url 'accounts:login' %}" class="btn btn-info ml-2"
   role="button">Login</a>

{% endif %}
```

The template context processor **django.contrib.auth.context_processors.auth** adds the user variable to the context, allowing us to check if the user is authenticated. If the user is authenticated, we show the logout button; otherwise, we show the log-in one.

Managing User Sessions

Django allows the storage and retrieval of arbitrary data associated with each site visitor. Sessions are built on the middleware **SessionMiddleware** so that you can use it out-of-the-box.

Usually, to keep track of data like shopping carts or user preferences, sessions are the way to store preferences.

The framework has different backends to store the session data. By default, Django uses the database backend, which uses the configured database.

When you use the database backend and execute the migrate command, it will create the table **django_session**. The **django_session** table is where all the sessions will be stored.

You can explore the table using the psql command:

```
docker-compose exec -u postgres db psql

postgres=# \c mydatabase

mydatabase=# \d+ django_session

Table "public.django_session"

|  Column |          Type          |

 -----------+------------------------+

session_key  | character varying(40)    |

session_data | text                     |

expire_date  | timestamp with time zone |


Indexes:

   "django_session_pkey" PRIMARY KEY, btree (session_key)

   "django_session_expire_date_a5c62663" btree (expire_date)

   "django_session_session_key_c0390e0f_like" btree (session_key varchar_
   pattern_ops)

Access method: heap
```

We executed the **psql** command inside the database container. Then we switched to the taskmanager database **mydatabase**. Using **\d+** we can show the table schema with the indexes.

If you are just starting with your project, using the database backend is the most common and appropriate choice. If you face scalability issues, switching to a different backend could be required to meet the application demands.

If you start to have a high volume of concurrent users, you may need to switch to the cached session backend. You can change the backend to cached by setting `SESSION_ENGINE` in the settings.py file:

```
SESSION_ENGINE = "django.contrib.sessions.backends.cache"
```

The cache backend will reduce latency and database usage.

Using the cache backend has some drawbacks. First, you have another service to maintain in your infrastructure and another potential point of failure. Caches are volatile and any reset of the cache service could potentially lose the data.

There is another session backend that uses the cache and database together. This is the **cached_db** backend. The **cache_db** backend primarily utilizes caching. When the framework needs to get the session data, it will go first to the cache; if not found, it will go to the database. When the framework needs to store the session data, it will always write to the database. This backend will reduce the latency, but it will not reduce the database usage on the writing part. This backend could be used as a transition to the cache backend.

The framework also provides a file backend to store the session in the file system. This file backend is rare since it has many unwanted drawbacks. The most critical problem with the file backend is that it only allows you to scale the application with one server quickly. Using the file backend is also a terrible idea if you are planning to deploy the application to the Kubernetes cluster since the cluster could restart or kill the container at any moment, and this will produce lost sessions without using volumes.

If you are using file backend and you have multiple instances of the server on different servers or containers, the user always has to use the same server or it will lose the session. Session data will be stored in the filesystem; if those files don't have the appropriate permission, this will be a security risk. There are scenarios where the file backend could be helpful, but for most common scenarios, the database is the most appropriate backend.

Following the principle that your local environment should be as similar as possible to the production environment, using the same session backend as in production is recommended.

Session customization

The session has many settings. Let's review some of them:

When dealing with an application that handles sensitive data, consider setting a shorter session timeout to log out the user and reduce the potential risk of unauthorized access.

```
SESSION_COOKIE_AGE = 1200  # 20 minutes in seconds. This is the default.
```

Clean up the cookies when the user closes the browser:

```
SESSION_EXPIRE_AT_BROWSER_CLOSE = True
```

If you're using cookie-based sessions or sending the session ID in a cookie, it's a good idea to use secure cookies in production:

```
SESSION_COOKIE_SECURE = True
```

Session usage

You can access the session data via the request object.

Here are some examples of usage:

```
# Access to the user_profile_color value

request.session["user_profile_color"]

# You can also set values as a dictionary

# When you set a session value in Django, you modify an in-memory dictionary. The session data is written to the backend storage at the end of the request-response cycle by the SessionMiddleware, optimizing for efficiency and performance.

request.session["user_profile_color"] = "red"

# You can also get the keys

request.session.keys()

# clear will delete the session data, but it will NOT delete the cookie

request.session.clear()

# flush will delete the session data and the cookie

request.session.flush()

# You can also set the expiry and get it

request.session.set_expiry(100)

request.session.get_expiry_date()

# cycle_key Destroys current session data and creates a new session

# with a new session key.

# This is useful for avoiding session fixation attacks.

request.session.cycle_key()
```

Session good practices

Django sessions are not meant to store extensive data. If you need to store large amounts of information, consider using caching or database models.

Never store sensitive information like passwords or credit card numbers in session. For sensitive data, you should use other secure mechanisms.

When using database-backed sessions, expired sessions can accumulate over time. Use Django's **`clearsessions`** management command regularly to clean out old data and ensure your database remains efficient.

Password Management in Django: Change and Password Reset

Django has built-in views for password management. We can easily handle the password change and reset flows using these views.

We need to change our **accounts/urls.py** and settings to use password management views. Let's start first with the password change views, open the **accounts/urls.py** and add the new paths:

```
from django.urls import path

from django.contrib.auth.views import LoginView, LogoutView,
PasswordChangeView, PasswordChangeDoneView

from django.urls import reverse_lazy


urlpatterns = [

    # ...

    path("password_change/", auth_views.PasswordChangeView.as_
    view(success_url=reverse_lazy("accounts:password_change_done"),
    template_name="accounts/password_change_form.html"), name="password_
    change"),

    path("password_change/done/", auth_views.PasswordChangeDoneView.
    as_view(template_name="accounts/password_change_done.html"),
    name="password_change_done"),

]
```

We have added two new paths in our URL patterns using the framework's class-based views. Using the **template_name** we can set up the template we want to use for rendering the form and show a successful message when the password is changed.

The next step is to define our templates. Here is the code for **templates/accounts/password_change.html**:

```
{% extends "tasks/base.html" %}

{% load widget_tweaks %}


{% block content %}

  <div class="container my-5">

   <div class="row">

   <div class="col-lg-6 offset-lg-3">

       <div class="card">

       <div class="card-body">

           <h2 class="card-title">Change Password</h2>

           <form method="post" class="mt-4">

               {% csrf_token %}

               <div class="mb-3">

               <!-- Assuming you have fields like 'old_password', 'new_
               password', 'confirm_new_password' in your form -->

               <label for="{{ form.old_password.id_for_label }}"
               class="form-label">Old Password</label>

               {{ form.old_password|add_class:"form-control" }}

               </div>

               <div class="mb-3">

               <label for="{{ form.new_password.id_for_label }}"
               class="form-label">New Password</label>

               {{ form.new_password1|add_class:"form-control" }}
```

```
            </div>

            <div class="mb-3">

            <label for="{{ form.confirm_new_password.id_for_label }}"
            class="form-label">Confirm New Password</label>

            {{ form.new_password2|add_class:"form-control" }}

            </div>

            <button type="submit" class="btn btn-primary">Change
            Password</button>

         </form>

      </div>

      </div>

   </div>

   </div>

  </div>

{% endblock %}
```

As always, we extend our **base.html** template to maintain the look and feel of our project. Then, we use the block content to render the form using the CSRF token.

The password change done template is simple and it will have a link to the login page, open the file **templates/accounts/password_change_done.html:**

```
{% extends "tasks/base.html" %}


{% block content %}

  <div class="container my-5">

   <div class="row">

   <div class="col-lg-6 offset-lg-3">

      <div class="card">

      <div class="card-body text-center">
```

```
        <h2 class="card-title">Password Change Successful</h2>
        <p class="card-text">Your password has been changed
        successfully!</p>
        <a href="{% url 'accounts:login' %}" class="btn btn-
        primary">Login Again</a>
      </div>
      </div>
    </div>
    </div>
  </div>
{% endblock %}
```

Now our users are ready to change their password if they want to. However, if one of our users needs to remember their password, we still need to add this functionality to our project. The reset flow is more complex than the password change since it involves email notifications to verify the user. Let's review the user password reset flow.

1. **User Requests Password Reset:**

   The user goes to a password reset form on the website and enters their email address. When the server receives the request to reset the password, it checks if the email address is associated with an existing user account. If the account exists, it continues to the next step.

2. **Email is Sent:**

   Django generates a unique token and sends an email to the user containing a link to this token. The user receives the email with a password reset link.

3. **User Clicks on Password Reset Link:**

   The user clicks on the link, which leads to a password reset form on the website. Django verifies that the token is valid and hasn't expired.

4. **User Resets Password:**

   The user enters and submits a new password into the form. Django verifies the new password meets the requirements and then updates the user's password in the database. The token becomes invalid after use.

5. **Password Reset Complete:**

   The user is notified that their password has been successfully changed. Django might optionally send a confirmation email to the user, notifying them of the change.

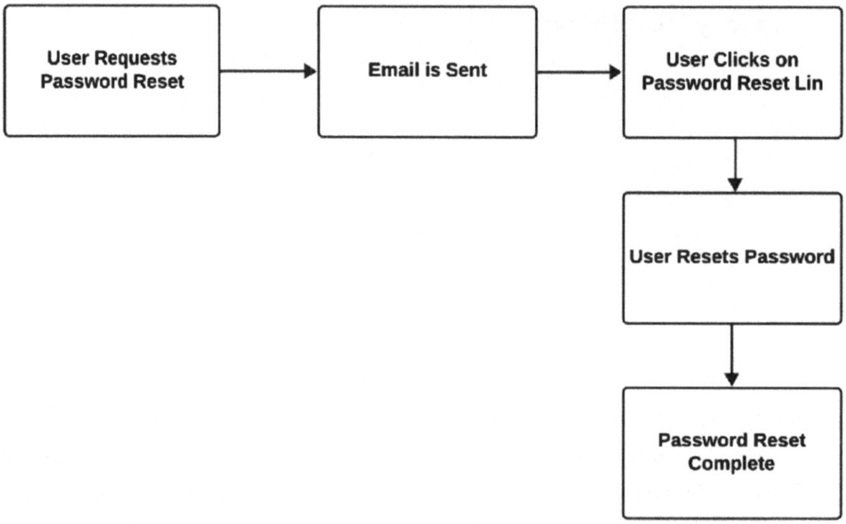

Figure 8.4: *Password reset flow*

Let's add the new URLs to our **accounts/urls.py**:

```
urlpatterns = [

    # ...

    path('password_reset/', PasswordResetView.as_view(email_template_
    name="accounts/custom_password_reset_email.html"), name='password_
    reset'),

    path('password_reset/done/', PasswordResetDoneView.as_view(),
    name='password_reset_done'),

    path('reset/<uidb64>/<token>/', PasswordResetConfirmView.as_view(),
    name='password_reset_confirm'),

    path('reset/done/', PasswordResetCompleteView.as_view(),
    name='password_reset_complete'),

]
```

These four reset password views require us to create four html templates. Still, before creating those templates, we must configure our email backend in our

taskmanager/settings.py.

As with the session backend, Django supports different backends for sending emails. For development, it is expected to use the console backend, which will print the email in the console.

```
EMAIL_BACKEND = 'django.core.mail.backends.console.EmailBackend'
```

For production, you will be required to set up the SMTP configuration in the settings.py:

```
EMAIL_BACKEND = 'django.core.mail.backends.smtp.EmailBackend'

EMAIL_HOST = 'your-smtp-server.com'

EMAIL_PORT = 587

EMAIL_USE_TLS = True

EMAIL_HOST_USER = 'your_email@example.com'

EMAIL_HOST_PASSWORD = 'your_email_password'
```

If you want to use the same backend in both environments, you can use tools like MailHog. MailHog is an open-source tool to test SMTP and has a web interface to inspect emails.

Let's update our docker-compose yaml to add MailHog in the services section:

```
  mailhog:

    image: mailhog/mailhog

    container_name: mailhog

    ports:

      - "1025:1025"  # SMTP server

      - "8025:8025"  # Web UI
```

Restart docker-compose:

```
docker-compose down

docker-compose up -d
```

Now you can navigate to localhost:8025 to open the mailhog web interface.

Finally, set the Django settings to use `mailhog`:

```
EMAIL_BACKEND = "django.core.mail.backends.smtp.EmailBackend"
EMAIL_HOST = "localhost"
EMAIL_PORT = 1025
EMAIL_USE_TLS = False
```

We need to define for each template the password reset flow:

Create a new file in **templates/accounts/password_reset_form.html**

```
{% extends "tasks/base.html" %}

{% block content %}
 <div class="container mt-5">
  <div class="row justify-content-center">
  <div class="col-md-6">
     <div class="card">
     <div class="card-header bg-primary text-white">
        <h2>Reset Password</h2>
     </div>
     <div class="card-body">
        <form method="post">
           {% csrf_token %}
           <div class="mb-3">
           {{ form.email.label_tag }} {{ form.email }}
           {% if form.email.errors %}
              <div class="alert alert-danger mt-2">
                    {{ form.email.errors }}
              </div>
           {% endif %}
           </div>
```

```
            <button type="submit" class="btn btn-primary">Reset
            Password</button>

         </form>

      </div>

      </div>

   </div>

   </div>

  </div>

{% endblock %}
```

The preceding template shows the form with one text input and a button. This form will allow the user to receive an email with a password reset link.

You can use the default email template that comes shipped with the framework or if you want to customize, you can create a new template in **templates/accounts/custom_password_reset_email.html** with the following code:

```
{% autoescape off %}

Hi {{ user.username }},

You're receiving this email because you requested a password reset for
your account.

Please go to the following page and choose a new password:

{{ protocol }}://{{ domain }}{% url 'accounts:password_reset_confirm'
uidb64=uid token=token %}


Thanks for using our site!

{% endautoescape %}
```

The preceding template uses auto escape off to render the special characters correctly in plain text.

Then, it uses the user from the context to create a personalized hello message about the password reset.

The link generation uses protocol and domain from the Sites framework that you can configure from the admin page. The URL template tag generates the URL for the password reset page using the uidb6 and token.

Next, we need to customize the password reset confirm form to ask the user for the new password twice and create a new file in **accounts/templates/password_reset_confirm_form.html**:

```
{% extends "tasks/base.html" %}


{% block content %}

<div class="container mt-5">

    <div class="row justify-content-center">

        <div class="col-md-6">

            <div class="card">

                <div class="card-header bg-primary text-white">

                    <h3>Set New Password</h3>

                </div>

                <div class="card-body">

                    <form method="post">

                            {% csrf_token %}


                            <div class="mb-3">

                                {{ form.new_password1.label_tag }}

                                {{ form.new_password1 }}

                                {% if form.new_password1.errors %}

                                    <div class="alert alert-danger mt-2">

                                        {{ form.new_password1.errors }}

                                    </div>

                                {% endif %}

                            </div>


                            <div class="mb-3">
```

```
                    {{ form.new_password2.label_tag }}
                    {{ form.new_password2 }}
                    {% if form.new_password2.errors %}
                        <div class="alert alert-danger mt-2">
                            {{ form.new_password2.errors }}
                        </div>
                    {% endif %}
                </div>

                <button type="submit" class="btn btn-
                primary">Change Password</button>
            </form>
          </div>
        </div>
      </div>
    </div>
</div>
{% endblock %}
```

The password reset confirm form will ask the user to input the new password twice. A complete password reset message will be shown when the user submits a correct new password twice. For customization of this message create a new file **templates/accounts/password_reset_complete.html** with the following template:

```
{% extends "base.html" %}
{% load static %}

{% block content %}
  <div class="container mt-5">
    <div class="row justify-content-center">
```

```
   <div class="col-md-6">
      <div class="card">
      <div class="card-body text-center">
         <h2 class="card-title">Password Reset Successful</h2>
         <p class="card-text">Your password has been reset
         successfully. You can now log in using your new password.</p>
         <a href="{% url 'accounts:login' %}" class="btn btn-primary
         mt-3">Login</a>
      </div>
      </div>
   </div>
   </div>
  </div>
{% endblock %}
```

The password reset complete template shows a message to the user informing that the operation was completed.

Protecting Views with Login Required Decorators

In *Chapter* 5, *Django Views and* URL *Handling*, we learned that there are two types of views: function-based views (FBV) and class-based views (CBV). Django provides different ways to protect the views depending on the view type.

The Django framework offers a **login_required** decorator specifically for function-based views. When you decorate the FBV with this decorator, the framework will check whether the user is authenticated before executing the view code. The decorator evaluates **request.user**, an attribute added by the **AuthenticationMiddleware**. If the user is not authenticated, it will be redirected to the **LOGIN_URL** set in the settings.py file.

Let's add a decorator to our create task on sprint view:

```
from django.contrib.auth.decorators import login_required
from django.http import HttpRequest, HttpResponseRedirect
```

```
from django.shortcuts import render, redirect

from .services import create_task_and_add_to_sprint


@login_required

def create_task_on_sprint(request: HttpRequest, sprint_id: int) ->
HttpResponseRedirect:

    if request.method == "POST":

        task_data: Dict[str, str] = {

            'title': request.POST.get("title", "Untitled"),

            'description': request.POST.get("description", ""),

            'status': request.POST.get("status", "UNASSIGNED"),

        }

        task = create_task_and_add_to_sprint(task_data, sprint_id,
        request.user)

        return redirect("task-detail", task_id=task.id)
```

Users must now authenticate to create a task or else face redirection to the login page.

We can employ the login_required decorator or inherit from **`LoginRequiredMixin`** for class-based views.

In *Chapter 5, Django Views and URL Handling*, we created several class-based views, `TaskListView`, `TaskDetailView`, `TaskCreateView`, `TaskUpdateView` and `TaskDeleteView`. The simplest way to authenticate the views is to inherit from the `LoginRequiredMixin`:

```
from django.contrib.auth.mixins import LoginRequiredMixin

from django.views.generic import ListView


class TaskListView(LoginRequiredMixin, ListView):

   model = Task

   template_name = 'task_list.html'

   context_object_name = 'tasks'
```

With this, our task list view gains protection, enforcing user authentication effectively. It's important to put the **LoginRequiredMixin** before the ListView.

There is an alternative way using the **login_required** decorator:

```
from django.utils.decorators import method_decorator

from django.contrib.auth.decorators import login_required

from django.views.generic import ListView


@method_decorator(login_required, name='dispatch')

class TaskListView(ListView):

    model = Task

    template_name = 'task_list.html'

    context_object_name = 'tasks'
```

Now our views are protected and the framework will enforce authentication. It's important to remember that the framework will not protect our views by default. If you don't inherit from `LoginRequiredMixin` or use the `login_required` decorator, our views are public and accessible to everyone.

In the next *Chapter, Django Ninja and APIs*, we will review how to force authentication to our API endpoints by default.

The ContactFormView will remain accessible without authentication to allow unrestricted contact access.

User Authorization: Permissions and Groups

Permissions offer granular access control, determining who has the authority to create, update, or delete objects. Groups facilitate the bundling of various permissions into one set.

In *Chapter* 4, *Django Models and PostgreSQL*, we saw how to check for permission in the admin and used the data migration to configure our project groups. Now, we will see how to use those groups and permission in the views.

Let's recap the groups we created:

- **Creator**: Can create new tasks and view tasks. This group will have the `add_task` permission.
- **Editor**: Has permission to view and edit tasks. This group will have the `change_task` permission.
- **Admin**: Has permissions to `create`, `view` and `delete`. This group has all the permissions enabled.

For function-based views, the decorator '**`permission_required`**' can be employed. We need to specify the permission we want to provide as a parameter.

```
from django.http import HttpRequest, HttpResponseRedirect

from django.shortcuts import render, redirect

from .services import create_task_and_add_to_sprint

from django.contrib.auth.decorators import permission_required


@permission_required("tasks.add_task")

def create_task_on_sprint(request: HttpRequest, sprint_id: int) ->
HttpResponseRedirect:

    if request.method == "POST":

            task_data: Dict[str, str] = {

            "title": request.POST["title"],

            "description": request.POST.get("description', ""),

            "status": request.POST.get("status", "UNASSIGNED"),

            }

            task = create_task_and_add_to_sprint(task_data, sprint_id,
            request.user)

            return redirect('task-detail', task_id=task.id)
```

Our view now uses the **`permission_required`** to check for the permission **`add_tasks`**; the permission's prefix is the application name. There is no need to use the **`login_required`** since the **`permission_required`** includes authentication checking.

Additionally, the decorator features two optional parameters, **login_url** and **raise_exception**.

The `login_url` can specify an alternative URL for the login page when the user is not authenticated.

With **raise_exception=True**, the view will raise a **PermissionDenied** exception if the user lacks permission rather than returning a 403 Forbidden response. You can catch this exception and handle it as needed.

You can define custom permission at the model level using the Meta class:

```
from django.db import models

from django.contrib.auth.models import User


class Task(models.Model):

    # ...

    class Meta:

        permissions = [

            ("custom_task", "Custom Task Permission"),

        ]
```

The task model is now endowed with a new permission named **custom_task**. When adding custom permission, you will need to execute the makemigrations and then execute the migrate command. This will create the new permission in the database.

We can set the required permissions using the mixin **PermissionRequiredMixin** and the **permission_required** attribute

```
from django.contrib.auth.mixins import PermissionRequiredMixin

from django.views.generic import ListView


class TaskListView(PermissionRequiredMixin, ListView):

    permission_required = "tasks.view_task"

    model = Task
```

```
    template_name = 'task_list.html'

    context_object_name = 'tasks'
```

Similarly to the LoginRequiredMixin, we used the PermissionRequiredMixin. This mixin allows us to check for the permission set in the permission_required. The permission format is the same as with FBV "**model.permission_name**".

The **`permission_required`** allows you to specify more than one permission using a tuple or list. When using multiple permissions, the user must have all of them to access the view. As with the decorator, we can also use **`login_url`** and **`raise_exception`**:

```
from django.contrib.auth.mixins import PermissionRequiredMixin

from django.views.generic import ListView


class TaskListView(PermissionRequiredMixin, ListView):

    permission_required = ("tasks.view_task", "tasks.custom_task")

    model = Task

    template_name = 'task_list.html'

    context_object_name = 'tasks'

    login_url = '/login/'

    raise_exception = True
```

In *Chapter 4, Django Models and PostgreSQL*, the owner attribute was set to null=True when we created the Task model. It was set to allow null values since, at the design time, we weren't allowed to set the creator to the logged-in user. Now that we have our authentication, we can set the creator.

Let's modify our model to not allow null values in the creator attribute:

```
class Task(models.Model):

    ...

    owner = models.ForeignKey(

        User, related_name="owned_tasks", on_delete=models.CASCADE,
        null=False

    )
```

Now we need to create the migrations and update our database schema:

```
poetry shell

python manage.py makemigrations

python manage.py migrate
```

While it's not necessary to make the creator non-nullable, its absence could lead to instances without a defined creator, an undesirable outcome as every task should be associated with a creator.

Now we need to modify the `TaskCreateView` to set the creator:

```
class TaskCreateView(LoginRequiredMixin, CreateView):

    …

    def form_valid(self, form):

        # Set the creator to the currently logged in user

        form.instance.creator = self.request.user

        return super().form_valid(form)
```

In the preceding code, we added a new method form_valid to the class view `TaskCreateView`. This method overrides the **`form_valid`** and sets the task's creator to the logged-in user before calling super **`form_valid`**.

The framework allows a more granular way to handle the permissions for scenarios that require a more specific check.

In the class-based view, you can override the method **`has_permission`** to make more complex permission checks. Here is an example of how to override it:

```
from django.views.generic.edit import UpdateView

from django.shortcuts import get_object_or_404

from .models import Task


class TaskUpdateView(PermissionRequiredMixin, LoginRequiredMixin,
UpdateView):

   model = Task

   form_class = TaskForm
```

```
template_name = 'task_edit.html'

permission_required = ('tasks.change_task',)


def has_permission(self):

        # First, check if the user has the general permission to edit
        tasks

        has_general_permission = super().has_permission()

        if not has_general_permission:

            # Then check if the user is either the

            return False

        # Then check if the user is either the

        # creator or the owner of this task

        task_id = self.kwargs.get('pk')

        task = get_object_or_404(Task, id=task_id)

        is_creator_or_owner = task.creator == self.request.user or
        task.owner == self.request.user

        # Return True only if both conditions are met

        return has_general_permission and is_creator_or_owner
```

The **has_permission** method verifies the task's existence, as the request might carry invalid data. If the task does not exist, a 404 response will be returned. Then, using the task creator or owner, it will check against the logged-in user. Finally, it will allow the logged-in user to update the task, whether it is the creator or the owner.

As you can see, the framework provides robust authentication and authorization features to create complex permission scenarios that allow a high degree of customization. However, with great power comes great responsibility: without careful planning and structuring, this system can quickly turn into a tangled web of "permission spaghetti." To avoid confusion and maintain clarity, it's crucial to implement a well-organized permission structure.

Multi-tenant authentication with Custom Django's User Model

Sometimes, the user class provided by the framework needs some customization to support different use cases. The framework provides ways to customize and change the user model to a different one.

Before opting for a different user class, let's consider an alternative that is often beneficial when additional attributes are needed for the user model.

The simplest way is to create a UserProfile class with a reference to the user using a one-to-one relationship and with the extended attributes required by the business.

Here is a user profile class example:

```
from django.contrib.auth.models import User

from django.db import models


class UserProfile(models.Model):

   user = models.OneToOneField(User, on_delete=models.CASCADE)

   biography = models.TextField()

   photo = models.ImageField(upload_to='user_photos/')
```

The `UserProfile` model has a one-to-one relationship with the user class and has two fields required by the business: the biography and the photo. Consider this profile approach, as it obviates the need to customize the authentication backend. The user profile class should be placed in the **accounts/models.py** of our project.

Imagine you have a business requirement and are building a SaaS application where different organizations can register and have separate users, roles and permissions. Every organization (tenant) needs a distinct namespace to avoid username or email address conflicts with others.

For a multi-tenant scenario, we need to create a custom user model. Let's add a new user model in our file **accounts/models.py**:

```
from django.contrib.auth.models import AbstractUser

from django.contrib.auth.models import BaseUserManager
```

```
from django.db import models

class Organization(models.Model):
    name = models.CharField(max_length=255)

class CustomUserManager(BaseUserManager):
    def create_user(self, username, email, password=None, **extra_fields):
        if not email:
            raise ValueError('The Email field must be set')
        email = self.normalize_email(email)
        user = self.model(username=username, email=email, **extra_fields)
        user.set_password(password)
        user.save(using=self._db)
        return user

    def create_superuser(self, username, email=None, password=None,
    **extra_fields):
        extra_fields.setdefault('is_staff', True)
        extra_fields.setdefault('is_superuser', True)

        if extra_fields.get('is_staff') is not True:
            raise ValueError('Superuser must have is_staff=True.')
        if extra_fields.get('is_superuser') is not True:
            raise ValueError('Superuser must have is_superuser=True.')

        extra_fields.setdefault('organization_id', 1)

        return self.create_user(username, email, password, **extra_fields)

class TaskManagerUser(AbstractUser):
    organization = models.ForeignKey(Organization, on_delete=models.
    CASCADE)
```

```
    username = models.CharField(max_length=255)
    email = models.EmailField()

    objects = CustomUserManager()
    class Meta:
        unique_together = (
                        ('organization', 'username'),
                        ('organization', 'email'),
        )
```

We have introduced the Organization class that is related to the new **TaskManagerUser**. Using the organization, username and organization, email we can set a **unique_together** to guarantee no duplicate user will be created.

As always, we change our model. It's imperative to create and execute migrations.

```
poetry shell
python manage.py makemigrations
python manage.py migrate
```

Our last step is to change the configuration of the project to use the new user model, open the settings.py to set the **AUTH_USER_MODEL**:

```
AUTH_USER_MODEL = "accounts.TaskManagerUser"
```

You should be prudent when using the option for a custom user model. There are some drawbacks to using a custom user model. Transitioning the `AUTH_USER_MODEL` is a complex process, especially for projects in production with an existing user base. Doing this will require a migration and can introduce complexities. Transitioning a project using a custom user model with several users is considered a bad practice. Ensure you use a custom user object from the beginning of the project. It will be tough to change it later. Always try to find an alternative solution before customizing the user model.

Despite these changes, our login page won't utilize the organization ID until we employ a custom authentication backend for organization validation.

Create a new file in **accounts/backends.py** with the following content:

```
from django.contrib.auth.backends import ModelBackend
```

```
from django.contrib.auth import get_user_model

from django.db.models import Q


class OrganizationUsernameOrEmailBackend(ModelBackend):

    def authenticate(self, request, username=None, password=None,
    organization_id=None, **kwargs):

            UserModel = get_user_model()


            if organization_id is None:

                return None


            user = UserModel.objects.filter(

                (Q(username__iexact=username) | Q(email__
                iexact=username)) &

                Q(organization_id=organization_id)

            ).first()


            if user and user.check_password(password):

             return user


    def get_user(self, user_id):

            UserModel = get_user_model()

            try:

               return UserModel.objects.get(pk=user_id)

            except UserModel.DoesNotExist:

               return None
```

Then update your project settings, open the file **taskmanager/settings.py** and change the authentication backend to the new one:

```
AUTHENTICATION_BACKENDS = [
```

```
    "accounts.backends.OrganizationUsernameOrEmailBackend",
]
```

We need to pass the new organization ID to the backend, for this, we need to update the login form, open the file **accounts/forms.py** and add a new clean method to the form:

```
class CustomAuthenticationForm(AuthenticationForm):
    organization_id = forms.IntegerField(
            required=True,
            widget=forms.TextInput(attrs={'autofocus': True})
    )

    def clean(self):
        username = self.cleaned_data.get('username')
        password = self.cleaned_data.get('password')
        organization_id = self.cleaned_data.get('organization_id')

        if username and password and organization_id:
            self.user_cache = authenticate(
                self.request,
                username=username,
                password=password,
                organization_id=organization_id
            )

            if self.user_cache is None:
                raise forms.ValidationError(
                    "Invalid username, password, or organization ID.",
                    code='invalid_login',
                )
```

```
            return self.cleaned_data
```

The clean method extracts the username, password, and **organization_id** from the form's validated data. If the values are not None, it will call the frameworks to authenticate, which will call our new backend since we changed it on the **settings.py**.

A ValidationError is raised by the clean method if it doesn't return a user.

Now we are going to create the authentication form. Create a new file in **accounts/forms.py** with the new authentication form:

```
from django import forms

from django.contrib.auth.forms import AuthenticationForm


class CustomAuthenticationForm(AuthenticationForm):

    organization_id = forms.IntegerField(

        required=True,

        widget=forms.TextInput(attrs={'autofocus': True})

    )
```

Override the LoginView to use the new form, edit the file **accounts/views.py** and add the new `CustomLoginView`:

```
from django.contrib.auth.views import LoginView

from .forms import CustomAuthenticationForm


class CustomLoginView(LoginView):

    authentication_form = CustomAuthenticationForm
```

Update the URL patterns to use the new view:

```
urlpatterns = [

    path('login/', CustomLoginView.as_view(), name='login'),

    # ... your other url patterns

]
```

Up to this point, we will ask the user for the username, email and organization id.

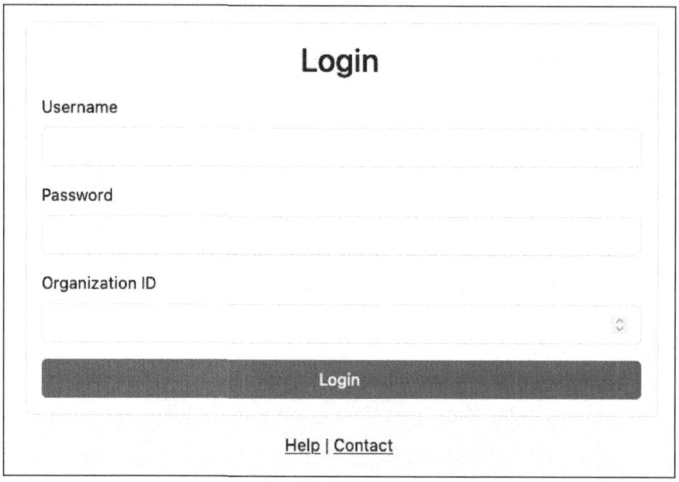

Figure 8.5: *The new multi-tenant login*

Security Best Practices in Django

As a bonus, we will review the best settings to keep your Django project as secure as possible. A completely secure system is challenging, and inherent security bugs or misconfigurations exist in every framework or project.

Next, we present a list of the most common settings you should always check. Use this list as a preflight checklist before going to production.

Update all your libraries and frameworks

Always update your libraries and keep Django with the latest hotfix upgraded. While updating to the latest Django version isn't mandatory, applying the newest hotfix to your project is crucial. Many tools can check your poetry files to ensure you are not deploying any insecure version. You can easily integrate these tools with your continuous integration. Some of these tools are Safety, bandit, pyup.io, and Snyk, but many more tools can help spot any trivial security issue in your project.

Project Settings Hardening

Now we will focus mainly on the **setting.py** of your project.

Turn off Debug in production

```
DEBUG = False
```

Setting the `DEBUG` to False is a mandatory setting for production. When `DEBUG` is enabled, any error page could leak information to malicious users.

Use Secure Cookies

```
SESSION_COOKIE_SECURE = True

CSRF_COOKIE_SECURE = True
```

By ensuring cookies are transmitted exclusively over HTTPS. These settings mitigate the risk of Man-in-the-Middle (MitM) attacks.

HTTP Strict Transport Security (HSTS)

```
SECURE_HSTS_SECONDS = 31536000  # Equivalent to 1-year

SECURE_HSTS_INCLUDE_SUBDOMAINS = True

SECURE_HSTS_PRELOAD = True
```

HSTS ensures that your site is accessed only over HTTPS. The `INCLUDE_SUBDOMAINS` option ensures that all subdomains are `HTTPS-only`, and `PRELOAD` allows the domain to be included in browser preload lists.

Content Security Policy (CSP)

To enable this setting you will need to install django-csp

```
poetry shell

poetry add django-csp
```

Now open the **settings.py** and add the **`CSPMiddleware`**:

```
MIDDLEWARE = [

    # ...

    'csp.middleware.CSPMiddleware',

    # ...

]
```

```
CSP_IMG_SRC = ("'self'", "img.com",)

CSP_SCRIPT_SRC = ("'self'", "scripts.com",)
```

Implementing a Content Security Policy (CSP) is instrumental in thwarting various content injection vulnerabilities, including cross-site scripting (XSS).

X-Content-Type-Options

```
SECURE_CONTENT_TYPE_NOSNIFF = True
```

This setting prevents the browser from guessing the MIME type, which could lead to security vulnerabilities.

X-XSS-Protection

```
SECURE_BROWSER_XSS_FILTER = True
```

This header helps protect against cross-site scripting (XSS) attacks.

Secure Referrer Policy

```
SECURE_REFERRER_POLICY = 'strict-origin-when-cross-origin'
```

This setting controls the Referrer header in links from your site, limiting the amount of information leaked to other sites.

Use Secure Password Hashing Algorithms

```
PASSWORD_HASHERS = [

    'django.contrib.auth.hashers.Argon2PasswordHasher',

    'django.contrib.auth.hashers.PBKDF2PasswordHasher',

    # ...

]
```

Django allows for the use of multiple password hashing algorithms. `Argon2` is usually recommended as it is considered among the most secure.

Limit Access to Admin

```
# Use a non-standard URL for the admin

# For example, change from /admin/ to /Luridness7880/
```

```
ADMIN_URL = 'Luridness7880/'
```

Changing the URL for the Django admin interface can make it harder for attackers to find and target it.

Keep SECRET_KEY Secret

The `SECRET_KEY` should never be hardcoded in settings.py for production. Instead, use environment variables or a separate configuration file to store it.

Set ALLOWED_HOSTS

```
ALLOWED_HOSTS = ['www.example.com']
```

This setting is a security measure to prevent HTTP Host header attacks. Only set it to domains that should serve your application.

Conclusion

Few use cases don't require authentication and authorization. For most of them, identifying the users is a prerequisite for the feature you will need to develop.

Mastering and understanding authentication is basic knowledge for building web applications. Without authentication, there is no way to protect your user's privacy or data.

We have created the authentication of our task management project using the framework tools, minimizing our work. The framework provides enough flexibility to customize how authentication pages look.

We developed a rich authorization schema for our application using permission and groups. We have enough granularity to allow different roles to perform and limit specific actions.

We created a multi-tenant task management authentication by customizing the user model.

Finally, we reviewed a list of best security practices for your project that can be used as a preflight checklist. With all this knowledge, you are now equipped to develop secure and efficient web applications that prioritize user privacy and data protection.

In the next chapter, we will see what it means to Restful API and how to build one using Django Ninja.

Questions

1. What does it mean that the HTTP protocol is stateless?
2. What are the HTTP status codes 401 and 403 used for?
3. What role does middleware play in Django's architecture?
4. How does a user typically acquire a session ID in a web application?
5. How are sessions in Django related to middleware?
6. How does Django store and manage user session data by default?
7. What are the drawbacks of using the file backend for session data storage in Django?
8. Can you describe the steps involved in the password reset flow in Django?
9. What security measures are implemented in Django's password reset flow to ensure user authenticity?
10. How are permissions and groups used in Django for user authorization?
11. How can permissions be customized to create more specific authorization scenarios in class-based views?
12. How can Django's user model be customized to accommodate additional attributes or functionalities?
13. How is a custom authentication backend implemented and utilized in Django for additional authentication criteria?

Exercises

1. Update the project authentication views to support multitenant. Example: Update registration and password reset.
2. Customize the registration email template to replace Django's default template.
3. Update a Django project's settings to enhance security, including secure cookies, HSTS, and content security policy.

Chapter 9
Django Ninja and APIs

Introduction

Application Programming Interface (API) allows two or more computer programs to communicate with each other. Designing an API from the beginning is essential because changing it becomes challenging once an API is made public. API design-first approach is a process that will allow us to gather quick feedback before any implementation is done, thus saving us time.

Django Ninja was introduced as a modern, fast, easy-to-use, and intuitive framework for building APIs on top of Django. Inspired by Flask and FastAPI, Django Ninja integrates select features and conveniences of these frameworks into the Django ecosystem.

This chapter guides you through extending our Task Management project with a secure, RESTful API. We will follow API design first to craft a shallow API specification that yields mock data. We will use the Django ninja schemas to generate OpenAPI Specifications (OAS). OpenAPI Specifications (OAS) provide a standard, language-agnostic interface to RESTful APIs, allowing both humans and computers to discover and understand the capabilities of a service without accessing its source code or extensive documentation. The initial API will return mock data, allowing us to save time and have quicker feedback. We finally iterated the solution to make it functional, adding authentication and permission checking.

Structure

In this chapter, we will cover the following topics:

- Introduction to API design
- API Design-first approach
- HTTP Response status codes
- Introduction to Django Ninja
- Setting Up Django Ninja in Your Project
- Building Your First API with Django Ninja
- Request and Response Models with Pydantic
- API Documentation
- Understanding HTTP Methods in Django Ninja
- API Pagination
- Working with Path Parameters and Query Parameters
- Validation and Error Handling in Django Ninja
- Authenticating API Users
- Securing APIs: Permissions and Throttling
- Versioning Your API

Introduction to API design

Roy Fielding introduced the concept of Representational State Transfer (REST) in his doctoral dissertation titled "*Architectural Styles and the Design of Network-based Software Architectures*". REST is an architectural style for designing network applications.

Roy, in his dissertation, does not strictly tie REST to HTTP. The dissertation describes REST as an architectural style with constraints and principles for designing distributed systems.

We are separating the architectural style from HTTP because adhering to REST's principles allows the creation of APIs without relying on HTTP. You can implement a REST API with other technologies.

Most real-world RESTful systems are implemented over HTTP, given the alignment between REST principles and HTTP semantics. In the dissertation, Fielding uses HTTP to illustrate how REST can be applied.

The six principles are as follows:

- **Stateless**: The server should not store anything about the client's state between requests. Each request is independent and must contain all the information the server needs.
- **Client-Server Architecture**: The client and server are different entities. The client is responsible for the user interface and the server is for the backend and data storage.
- **Layered System**: The API can be composed of multiple layers. The client cannot tell whether it is connected directly to the end server or with intermediary layers.
- **Cacheability**: Responses can be labeled as cacheable. If a response is cacheable, the client cache can reuse it for equivalent responses in the future.
- **Uniform Interface**: All components interact through a consistent interface, simplifying the architecture and improving visibility and portability
- **Code on demand** (optional): The server can return code to extend the client functionality. This could potentially expose a security vulnerability and its use has to be carefully considered.

There are other misconceptions related to REST; two prevalent ones are that REST requires JSON or was meant for CRUD operations. REST is not limited to CRUD. RESTful services can offer other operations beyond basic CRUD, and not every RESTful service needs to implement all CRUD operations.

JSON is a popular choice of data interchange due to its lightweight nature and ease of use. RESTful services can return binary data, like MessagePack or Protocol Buffers. Some other services can return CSV, images, or even XML if you are unlucky.

The principles are sufficiently generic, allowing you to opt for technology that suits your needs or adapt to emerging technologies.

Designing an API involves following these principles and choosing the right technologies to solve the problems. This chapter will focus on JSON and some CRUD operations since we plan to give this API to external users to operate on our project management tool.

API Design-first approach

The API design-first approach is a process for building APIs where the design of the API is prioritized before any coding takes place. Adopting an API-first strategy enhances team and user communication, offering valuable early feedback before coding occurs.

A simplified API design-first process could look like this:

1. **Design**: We design the API using a tool or document.
2. **Review**: Stakeholders or clients can review our design by reading the document or using a mock.
3. **Build**: After sufficient iteration between design and review, we implement the API.
4. **Validation**: The API is ready. We iterate by adding non-breaking changes, new features, or fixing bugs.

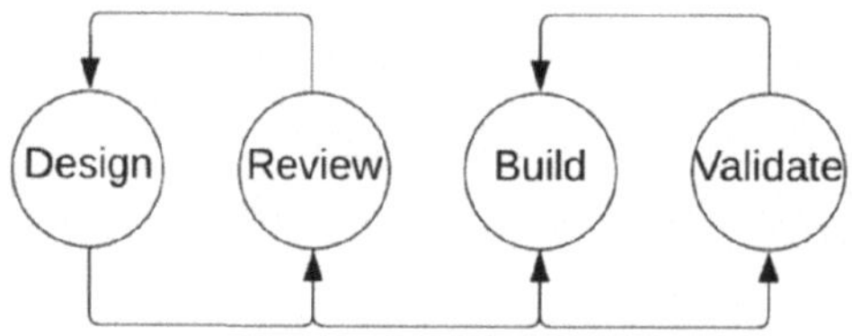

Figure 9.1: API *first-approach process simplified*

This chapter guides you through crafting a specification using a shallow API that returns mock data. We will use the Django ninja schemas to generate open API documentation. The initial API will return mock data, allowing us to save time and have quicker feedback.

Note: While various approaches exist for specification work, this book employs Django-ninja for generating OpenAPI specifications. In the market, several tools exist to create your open API, even when no service is created.

In the context of our book, we already have a Django project and choose to use Ninja. However, in another project, the technology had yet to be decided. The first API design will allow you to start the design even when no decision is made regarding project technology.

Here is a list of tools to create open API schemas:

- OpenAPI-GUI
- Apicurio

- Stoplight
- Swagger tools

There are more tools in the market. The previous list shows the most popular ones.

Typically, API development starts internally, culminating in the final API realization. Ignoring best practices often leads to APIs leaking internal abstractions, compromising usability and clarity.

As an example of a leaky abstraction, we could expose the Epic attribute **`completion_status`** of type float:

```
completion_status = models.FloatField(default=0.0)
```

By exposing this attribute via the API, our users must learn what its ambiguous representation means. Is it a percentage (0-100) or a fraction (0-1)? Furthermore, this value must be updated whenever tasks under that epic change status, risking inconsistency if not handled correctly.

If the team working on the project does not follow an API design first approach, thinking about how to use the API, you risk exposing internal representation that you don't need or want to expose.

Idempotence in the context of APIs means that making the same call multiple times results in the same outcome as making it once. This property is essential to ensure reliability and consistency in API interactions. For example, HTTP methods like GET and PUT are typically idempotent. Executing a GET request multiple times to retrieve data won't change the underlying data, and repeatedly updating (PUT) the same data to a specific URL will leave the data unchanged after the first request. In contrast, non-idempotent methods like POST can result in different outcomes when called multiple times.

Ensuring backward compatibility is essential when designing API. There are different strategies. We will use URI versioning in this chapter.

HTTP Response status codes

HTTP has response status codes, which are used to provide information on the result of the operation on the server. Adhering to the appropriate use of status codes not only aids users but also aligns with established community standards.

Here is a summary of the most common ones used in RESTful APIs:

2xx (Success)

- 200 OK: The request was successful, and the result is returned in the response.
- 201 Created: Indicates a new resource has been created, returning its URI in the response.

3xx (Redirection)

- 301 Moved Permanently: The URL of the requested resource has been changed permanently.
- 302 Found (Previously "Moved Temporarily"): Indicates that the requested resource resides temporarily under a different URI.

4xx (Client Errors)

- 400 Bad Request: The request was invalid or cannot be processed by the server.
- 401 Unauthorized: The client must authenticate to gain permission to access the requested resource.
- 403 Forbidden: The client does not have access rights to the content.
- 404 Not Found: The server cannot find the requested resource.
- 405 Method Not Allowed: The HTTP method is not supported for the requested resource.
- 429 Too Many Requests: The user has sent too many requests in a given amount of time

5xx (Server Errors)

- 500 Internal Server Error: The server encountered an error and could not fulfill the request.
- 502 Bad Gateway: While acting as a gateway, the server received an invalid response from the upstream server.
- 503 Service Unavailable: The server is not ready to handle the request. It could be due to being overloaded or under maintenance.

In our API's development, status codes will be integral for implementing views communicating precise response statuses.

Introduction to Django Ninja

Django Ninja is a third-party library for building APIs in Django applications. One of its main features is the utilization of Python's type hints, which accelerates the development process. Type hints improve code readability, enable better IDE support with auto-completion and error checking, and facilitate easier refactoring. These benefits lead to enhanced developer productivity and more maintainable code. The integration of pydantic and async support enhances its performance speed. Django Ninja integrates well with existing Django projects, allowing developers to add it to the projects and straightforwardly build an API.

Another web framework that recently gained much traction, FastAPI, highly influenced the framework.

Note: Pydantic serves as both a data validation and settings management library. Utilizing type annotations, the library validates data types and enables the addition of constraints. It is used with data structures like dictionaries, JSON and similar formats. Classes inheriting from Pydantic BaseModel are referred to as Pydantic models. The library can also be used for serialization and it supports custom validators.

Django Ninja automatically generates interactive API documentation, making it easy for developers to test and understand the API endpoints, as in the follow-up sections.

Setting Up Django Ninja in Your Project

Begin by installing **`django-ninja`** via poetry with the command:

```
poetry add django-ninja
```

Django Ninja doesn't require inclusion in the **`INSTALLED_APPS`** setting of your Django project to function correctly or to serve the OpenAPI/Swagger UI documentation.

Migrations are unnecessary – there's nothing to migrate!

Building Your first API with Django Ninja

With our project set up, it's time to introduce an API.

We first incorporate a router into the API utilizing the **`add_router`** method. A router allows you to divide your API into multiple logical sections. Employing a router contributes to a well-structured, easily maintainable codebase.

Let's add the new file to the tasks application, called **tasks/api/tasks.py**:

```
from ninja import Router


router = Router()


@router.get("/")

def list_tasks(request):

   return {"results": [

          {"id": 1, "title": "test title"},

   ]}
```

This additional file introduces a fresh API endpoint, using the GET method to retrieve tasks. We first instantiate a new Router object, serving as a container for handling various API routes. The `@router.get('/')` decorator establishes a new API endpoint accessible via the GET method at the router's root path ('/').

This endpoint currently returns a static JSON response containing a list of tasks. Each task is a dictionary with an *id* and *title*. In a real-world application, this will be dynamic, fetching data from a database or another data source. Using the service layer and schemas, we will implement this in the following sections.

Next, create a new file named **tasksmanager/api.py** within the tasks manager project. Populate it with the following content:

```
from ninja import NinjaAPI

from tasks.api import router as tasks_router


api = NinjaAPI()

api.add_router("/tasks/", tasks_router)
```

Now, let's breakdown the key elements:

`api = NinjaAPI()` creates a new instance of the NinjaAPI class. It's the foundation of our API, where we will attach our routes and configure settings. We have no starting point or structure to build our API without this instance.

`api.add_router("/tasks/", tasks_router)` associates the **`tasks_router`** with the API, mounting it at the **`/tasks/`** path. Each router can be thought of as a collection of related endpoints, and by attaching it to a path, we're defining where these endpoints can be accessed.

Next, we must incorporate the API into our project, open the **tasksmanager/urls.py** and add the API to the **`urlpatterns`**:

```
from django.contrib import admin

from django.urls import include, path


from tasksmanager.api import api


urlpatterns = [

   path("admin/", admin.site.urls),

   path("api/v1", api.urls),

   path("", include("tasks.urls")),

]
```

This code adds the newly created API into the Django project's URL configuration. The `path("api", api.urls)` specifically adds all the API's routes under the `"api"` prefix, establishing a clear and organized URL structure.

In the follow-up sections, we will learn how to use API versioning. API versioning is critical to adding new features or breaking changes to our API.

With the new API in place, let's test its functionality using curl:

```
 $ curl -s http://localhost:8000/api/tasks/ | python -m json.tool

{"results": [

   {

          "id": 1,

          "title": "test title"

   }

]}
```

This curl command tests the API's functionality by requesting the specified endpoint and using `python -m json.tool` for a pretty-printed output. It's essential to verify that the API is responding as expected.

Congratulations on your first API! We still need a lot of work; our API needs schemas and we need to remove the hardcoded results. We will refine this solution using schemas in the following section.

Request and Response Models with Pydantic

Django Ninja uses schemas to validate, serialize, and document what is going in and out of the API. Ninja schema is based on Pydantic and adds a layer that wraps Pydantic for smoother integration with Django.

Two primary schema types exist: **`in`** and **`out`**. As a convention, the schema used for input will use the postfix "In" and the schema for output or responses will have the postfix "Out".

An added advantage of schemas is their employment of type annotations, used for validation and serialization. Instantiating the schema or calling a validation method is unnecessary.

Let's define our schemas in the new file **tasks/schemas.py**:

```
from ninja import Schema


class TaskSchemaIn(Schema):

   title: str

   description: str


class CreateSchemaOut(Schema):

   id: int
```

These schemas will be used for the creation endpoint to validate and serialize the Task object for both input and output.

Our new creation API endpoint will be:

```
@router.post("/", response=CreateSchemaOut)

def create_task(request: HttpRequest, task_in: TaskSchemaIn):
```

```
    return CreateSchemaOut(id=1)
```

Our creation view code is lean and straightforward thanks of the usage of schemas. It instantiates a `CreateSchemaOut` using id 1.

We can test our API using curl to create a new task:

```
$ curl -X POST -s http://localhost:8000/api/tasks/ -d '{"title": "Alien
Life Detection Algorithm Enhancement", "description": "Improve the
existing algorithm used for detecting alien life. "}'
```

The response is expected to be a dictionary containing the **`id`** of the newly created Task object.

```
{"id": 1}
```

Django Ninja also supports model schemas. The concept is similar to the model views we saw in *Chapter 5, Django Views and URL Handling*. A **`ModelSchema`** is a class that will generate schemas based on your models.

Let's use **`ModelSchema`** instead of Schema for our **`TaskSchemaIn`**:

```
from ninja import ModelSchema

from .models import Task


class TaskSchemaIn(ModelSchema):

    class Config:

        model = Task

        model_fields = ["title", "description"]

        model_fields_optional = ["status"]


class TaskSchemaOut(ModelSchema):

   owner: UserSchema | None = Field(None)


   class Config:

          model = Task

          model_fields = ["title", "description"]
```

Instead of using Meta, ninja uses Config like Pydantic. In the code above, we specify the model Task and the attributes we want in the schema. `ModelSchema` has several configs to use in the schemas. We also used `model_fields_optional`, which is a way to make some schema attributes optional. Using the optional configuration, we can create a Task with an initial status. `ModelSchema` will use model types to validate and serialize data.

Response schemas transform models into the output format and contribute to generating OpenAPI documentation. The response schemas will limit the information that your API will return. This is very important to prevent any information leak.

Let's also update our `lists_tasks` view to use the new schemas:

```
@router.get('/', response=list[TaskSchemaOut])
def list_tasks(request):
    return [TaskSchemaOut(title="Mock Task", description="Task description")]
```

Testing it with curl with return a list of one task as expected:

```
$ curl -X GET -s http://localhost:8000/api/tasks/
{"items": [{"title": "Mock Task", "description": "Task description", "owner": null}], "count": 1}
```

API Documentation

With Python's type annotations and the schemas defined in your API endpoints, Django Ninja generates API documentation automatically. Ninja hosts the documentation at the /doc URL; access it directly via http://localhost:8000/api/v1/docs:

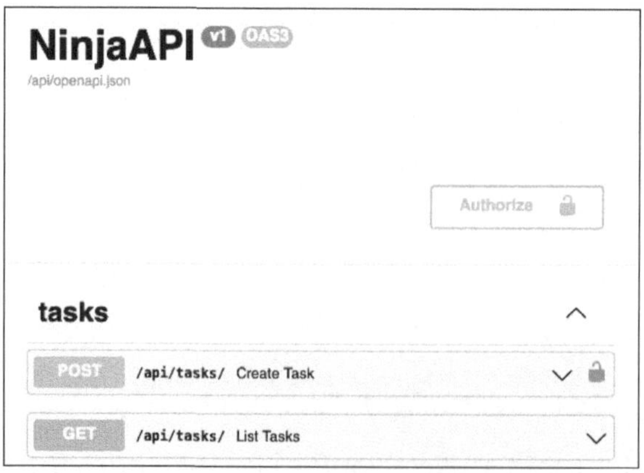

Figure 9.2: *OpenAPI generated documentation*

Enhancing API documentation is achievable by incorporating descriptions, examples, and additional annotations to both routes and schemas. Rich documentation is essential to improve API usability.

Let's review some of our previous schemas and API routes.

```
from ninja import Router, Schema, Field


class TaskSchemaIn(Schema):

    title: str = Field(..., example="Enhanced Satellite Data Analysis")

    description: str = Field(..., example="Develop a comprehensive
    analytical model to process")


    class Config:

            description = "Schema for creating a new task"


class CreateSchemaOut(Schema):

    id: int = Field(..., example=1)


    class Config:

            description = "Schema for the created object output"
```

We can also specify tags to the router or individual endpoints via a decorator.

Let's assign the tag `"task"` to the task router, open task/api/tasks.py and set the tags:

```
router = Router(tags=["tasks"])
```

Now our API will be grouped under the `"tasks"` tag instead of the `"default"` tag.

Up to this point, we have a shallow API that has documentation. We can deliver this API to gather feedback from our stakeholders, clients, or users. We can also use this specification to build the API client once everyone agrees on the API contract.

Understanding HTTP Methods in Django Ninja

In *Chapter 5, Django Views and URL Handling*, we learned how HTTP protocol works and implemented some Django views using different HTTP methods. Next, we will apply similar concepts to our API.

In many RESTful web services, HTTP methods map to CRUD operations somewhat straightforwardly, as shown in *Table 9.1*:

Action	HTTP Method	URL
Create	POST	http://localhost:8000/api/v1/tasks
Read (list)	GET	http://localhost:8000/api/v1/tasks
Read (object)	GET	http://localhost:8000/api/v1/tasks/{id}
Update	PUT or PATCH	http://localhost:8000/api/v1/tasks/{id}
Delete	DELETE	http://localhost:8000/api/v1/tasks/{id}

Table 9.1: *CRUD operations mapping to REST API for Tasks*

The mapping is straightforward and the URL paths are intuitive. In the URL path, *tasks* denote the resource accessed. The object ID is included in the URL and used for resource identification.

Let's construct our CRUD API views using the Ninja framework. We are going to leave some hardcoded data as a holder for now. Open the file **tasks/api/tasks.py** and add the new endpoints:

```
from http import HTTPStatus

from django.http import HttpRequest, HttpResponse

from ninja import Router


router = Router()


@router.post("/", response={201: CreateSchemaOut})

def create_task(request: HttpRequest, task_in: TaskSchemaIn):

    creator = request.user
```

```
    return services.create_task(creator, **task_in.dict())


@router.get("/", response=list[TaskSchemaOut])
def list_tasks(request):
    return services.list_tasks()
@router.get("/{int:task_id}", response=TaskSchemaOut)
def get_task(request: HttpRequest, task_id: int):
    task = services.get_task(task_id)
    if task is None:
            raise Http404("Task not found.")

    return task


@router.put("/{int:task_id}")
def update_task(request: HttpRequest, task_id: int, task_data:
TaskSchemaIn):
    services.update_task(task_id=task_id, **task_data.dict())
    return HttpResponse(status=HTTPStatus.NO_CONTENT)


@router.delete("/{int:task_id}")
def delete_task(request: HttpRequest, task_id: int):
services.delete_task(task_id=task_id)
    return HttpResponse(status=HTTPStatus.NO_CONTENT)
```

We have established five API endpoints implementing CRUD operations.

Let's review each endpoint's code.

- **`create_task`**: Extracts the currently authenticated user from the request (**`request.user`**) and utilizes the **`services.create_task`** function to create a task with the given input data. The creator of the task is set to the currently authenticated user. Returns the created task's details with a status code of 201 Created. The output data format will be according to **CreateSchemaOut**.

- **list_tasks**: Calls the **services.list_tasks** function to retrieve all tasks. Returns a list of tasks where each task is structured as per the **TaskSchemaOut**.
- **get_task**: Uses the **services.get_task** function to retrieve the task details for the provided **task_id**. If the task is not found, it raises an Http404 error. Returns the task details structured as per **TaskSchemaOut**.
- **update_task**: Uses the **services.update_task** function to update the task with the provided input data. Returns a 204 No Content status code, indicating that the update was successful but no content is being returned.
- **delete_task**: Calls the **services.delete_task** function to delete the task with the provided **task_id**. Returns a 204 No Content status code, indicating that the deletion was successful but no content is being returned.

The backend logic is abstracted into a services layer in all these endpoints, as we did in *Chapter 5, Django Views and URL Handling*. The service layer contains the core logic for interacting with the database or data storage.

Let's use the curl command to test our endpoints:

Create a new task using the post:

```
$ curl -X POST -s http://localhost:8000/api/tasks/ -d '{"title": "Alien Life Detection Algorithm Enhancement", "description": "Improve the existing algorithm used for detecting alien life. "}'

{
    "id": 5
}
```

We can proceed with updating the task using the PUT method:

```
$ curl -X PUT -s http://localhost:8000/api/tasks/5 -d '{"title": "Alien Life Detection Algorithm", "description": "New description"}'
```

For deleting the Task let's use the **DELETE** method:

```
$ curl -X DELETE -s -w "%{http_code}\n" http://localhost:8000/api/tasks/5
```

With the curl command, we can specify the HTTP method via the parameter **-X <method>**. As expected, our endpoint returned an empty response.

According to HTTP standards, returning a 201 Created status code is more appropriate when a new resource is created on the server. This provides clear feedback that the resource was successfully created, aligning with RESTful API best practices.

API Pagination

If our database has thousands of tasks, the API's response could be voluminous and potentially slow. To solve this issue, we can introduce pagination to our API. Fortunately, Ninja features a pagination decorator that allows us to paginate the results.

```
from ninja.pagination import paginate

from tasks.services import tasks as services


@router.get("/", response=list[TaskSchemaOut])

@paginate

def list_tasks(request):

   return services.list_tasks()
```

The API now has the pagination functionality by adding the paginate decorator. This is possible thanks to our service layer function `list_tasks` returns a **`QuerySet`** that the paginate decorator will use for getting the correct results.

The default setting limits the output to 100 items. You can change it by using the **`NINJA_PAGINATION_PER_PAGE`** in your **`taskmanmager/settings.py`** file. The pagination allows setting the limit and offset by using the URL parameters limit and offset:

http://localhost:8000/api/v1/tasks/?limit=2&offset=4

The framework also provides pagination by page number. You can change it with the setting **`NINJA_PAGINATION_CLASS`** set to the **`PageNumberPagination`**.

If the pagination schema offered by Ninja doesn't align with your requirements, you can craft a custom one. In that case, you can also create a custom pagination schema by implementing a class that overrides the Input and Output schema classes.

Create a new file in the tasks/pagination.py with the new pagination class:

```
from ninja.pagination import paginate, PaginationBase

from ninja import Schema


class TaskManagerPagination(PaginationBase):

   # only `skip` param, defaults to 5 per page

   class Input(Schema):

         skip_records: int


   class Output(Schema):

         items: list[Any]

         count: int

         page_size: int


   def paginate_queryset(self, queryset, pagination: Input, **params):

         skip_records = pagination.skip_records

         return {

            "data": queryset[skip_records: skip_records + 5],

         "count": queryset.count(),

         "page_size": 5,

         }
```

Next, modify the **taskmanager/settings.py** file to incorporate the newly created class:

```
NINJA_PAGINATION_CLASS=TaskManagerPagination
```

Working with Path Parameters and Query Parameters

This section explains Path Parameters and Query Parameters:

Path parameters

Since the introduction of the API for the task model, we already used path parameters for the `task_id` with type annotations. The framework will also check for a valid integer when using type annotation in the ninja API views. When the type of the path parameter does not match the type annotation, the API will return a 404 status code.

We can also use the ninja path parameter with Django path converters, as we saw in *Chapter 5: Django Views and URL Handling.*

```
@router.get("/{int:task_id}", response=TaskSchemaOut)

def get_task(request: HttpRequest, task_id: int):

    task = services.get_task(task_id)

    if task is None:

            raise Http404("Task not found.")


    return task
```

We only had to change the router string path to the new one using the path converters to specify the int: `/{int:task_id}`. The outcome is a 404 (not found) response from our endpoint if the path parameter type isn't an integer.

```
curl -I http://localhost:8000/api/v1/tasks/invalid_id
```

And the curl output displays a 404 status code:

```
HTTP/1.1 404 Not Found
```

Ninja also supports using schema for more complex path parameters. Let's add an API that retrieves archived tasks based on a specific date. We will start by adding a new view in **tasks/api/tasks.py**:

```
from ninja import Path

from ninja.pagination import paginate
```

```
from tasks.schemas import PathDate


@router.get("/archive/{year}/{month}/{day}",
response=list[TaskSchemaOut])
@paginate
def archived_tasks(request, created_at: PathDate = Path(...)):
    return services.search_tasks(created_at=created_at.value(),
    status=TaskStatus.ARCHIVED.value)
```

The router decorator registers the function below it as a **GET** endpoint in the Django Ninja framework. The URL pattern "**/archive/{year}/{month}/{day}**" t expects three path parameters: year, month, and day to specify a particular date. The **PathDate = Path(...)** is a type-annotated function parameter.

The function calls a **search_tasks** of the service layer, passing the **created_at** and the status. **TaskStatus.ARCHIVED.value** specifies that the tasks to be fetched should have a status of **ARCHIVED**.

PathDate is a schema defined like this:

```
import datetime
from ninja import Schema


class PathDate(Schema):
    year: int
    month: int
    day: int

    def value(self):
            return datetime.date(self.year, self.month, self.day)
```

The schema defines type int for the year, month and day. The value method returns a date object from Python's built-in datetime module. When called, it constructs a date object using the schema instance's year, month, and day attributes.

We are now using the parameters in the **search_tasks** service. We must filter the results by changing the service layer implementation at **tasks/services/tasks.py**:

```
from datetime import date

from tasks.enums import TaskStatus


def search_tasks(

    created_at: date,

    status: TaskStatus,

) -> list[Task]:

    tasks = Task.objects.filter(created_at__date=created_at,
    status=status).order_by("status", "created_at")

    return tasks
```

The new service will filter tasks based on `created_at` and status. We use a double underscore with `created_at__date` to filter by date, excluding the time. Without **`__date`**, the query would attempt to match both the date and time, making the search criteria more restrictive

Let's test the new API with curl:

```
$ curl http://localhost:8000/api/tasks/archive/2023/09/11
```



```
{"items": [{"id": 15, "title": "Mars Weather Data Aggregation Tool",
"description": "Develop a tool to aggregate and visualize daily weather
data from the Perseverance rover on Mars.", "owner": {"id": 1, "username":
"mandarina"}, "creator": {"id": 1, "username": "mandarina"}, "status":
"ARCHIVED"}], "count": 1}
```

Note: Remember you can always check the GitHub repository with all the book code. It is recommended that you write the code along with the chapters, but if you have doubts or want to test the project management, you can always check out the chapter branch.

Query parameters

For implementing the query parameters, we will add some filters to the task list endpoint.

We will add the status filter. This is an interesting case since the Task model has only four valid choices to filter on the status. We will use Ninja to validate the query parameter. We have to change our Task model to use an Enum.

Create a new file in **tasks/enums.py** with the following content:

```
from enum import Enum


class TaskStatus(str, Enum):

    UNASSIGNED = "UNASSIGNED"

    IN_PROGRESS = "IN_PROGRESS"

    DONE = "DONE"

    ARCHIVED = "ARCHIVED"
```

We introduced a new `Enum` class using the standard module `enum`. The `enum` module in Python supports creating enumerations, a set of symbolic names bound to unique constant values.

Now, we can change our Task model to use the new `enum`:

```
class Task(models.Model):

    STATUS_CHOICES = [(status.value, status.name.replace('_', '
    ').title()) for status in TaskStatus]


    ...

    status = models.CharField(

        max_length=20,

        choices=STATUS_CHOICES,

        default=TaskStatus.UNASSIGNED.value,

    )

        ...
```

There is no need to make migrations since our schema didn't change. We just changed the code to use the new `enum`.

A search service will support the search API as well. Since we are finding a pattern to search, we will use the same service we use for `archived_tasks` API, but we will use the status filter instead.

The new list API code will be straightforward:

```
@router.get("/", response=list[TaskSchemaOut])

@paginate

def list_tasks(request: HttpRequest, filters: TaskFilterSchema =
Query(...)):

    return services.list_tasks(**filters.dict())
```

Ninja can encapsulate the filters into a **FilterSchema** class. Using the FilterSchema will allow us to simplify the code of our service layer and it will extend the search API.

We also want to filter by title. To allow this, we create the **TaskFilterSchema** with the attributes:

```
class TaskFilterSchema(FilterSchema):

    title: str | None

    status: TaskStatus | None
```

Now, by using the **TaskFilterSchema**, we can add more query parameters on the search API endpoint.

The search API will also validate the query parameters. If we try to search using the wrong status, it will return a nice error message:

```
$ curl -s http://localhost:8000/api/tasks/\?status\=AAA | python -m json.
tool

{

    "detail": [

        {

            "loc": [

                "query",

                "status"

            ],

            "msg": "value is not a valid enumeration member; permitted:
            'UNASSIGNED', 'IN_PROGRESS', 'DONE', 'ARCHIVED'",
```

```
            "type": "type_error.enum",
            "ctx": {
                "enum_values": [
                    "UNASSIGNED",
                    "IN_PROGRESS",
                    "DONE",
                    "ARCHIVED"
                ]
            }
        }
    ]
}
```


The error message provided by the endpoint gives lots of information about the error and the API user will quickly know how to solve the problem due to a wrong status used in the query parameter.

Validation and Error Handling in Django Ninja

In this section, we will learn how to manage validation and error in Django Ninja.

Validations

Django Ninja uses the Pydantic library for validation, attributed to its robustness and flexibility in validating request data.

We used schemas in the previous section for validation. Let's revisit the **`PathDate` `schema`** to add more detailed validations.

```
from ninja import Field, Schema

class PathDate(Schema):

    year: int = Field(..., ge=1)  # Year must be greater than or equal
    to 1.
```

```
    month: int = Field(..., ge=1, le=12)  # Month must be between 1 and
    12.

    day: int = Field(..., ge=1, le=31)  # Day must be between 1 and 31.


    def value(self):

        return datetime.date(self.year, self.month, self.day)
```

The schema attributes now use the ninja Field, allowing for simple validations on individual date components. In the code above, we use greater or equal (ge) and less or equal (le) to ensure the numbers for the year, month, and day are within valid numerical ranges. However, this does not guarantee the overall date's validity (for example, April 31st is not a valid date). Therefore, an additional validation step is required to confirm the actual date's validity, as demonstrated later with a custom validator.

We can still validate using a more complex logic by using the validator decorator

```
@model_validator(mode='after')

def validate_date(self) -> "PathDate":

    try:

        return datetime.date(self.year, self.month, self.day)

    except ValueError:

        raise ValueError(f"The date {self.year}-{self.month}-{self.day}
        is not valid.")
```

This code defines a model validator in Python, executed after the primary validation, that checks if the combination of year, month, and day fields in a PathDate object forms a valid date, raising a **`ValueError`** if the date is invalid.

Error handling

Ninja has built-in support for handling different types of errors and allows you to define custom error handling.

Ninja returns an error response with an appropriate status code and detailed error information for prevalent errors. The most common HTTP status codes with built-in support include 400 Bad Reuqest, 404 Not Found, and 422 Unprocessable Entity.

Still, sometimes we want to have custom error handling. One way to do it is by raising the **`HttpError`** exception.

```
from ninja import Router, HttpError

router = Router()


@router.get("/error")

def generate_error(request):

    raise HttpError(status_code=400, detail="Custom error message")
```

If you want you can register exception handlers for specific exceptions. The typical case is when we try to fetch an object from the database that does not exist, raising the **`ObjectDoesNotExist`**. When Django raises **`ObjectDoesNotExist`**, Ninja will return a 500 error. A functional customization will be to return 404 with a custom message.

Open the file **taskmanager/api.py** and register the new exception handler for **`ObjectDoesNotExists`**:

```
from django.core.exceptions import ObjectDoesNotExist


@api.exception_handler(ObjectDoesNotExist)

def on_object_does_not_exist(request, exc):

    return api.create_response(

        request,

        {"message": "Object not found."},

        status=404,

    )
```

Now, if any of our APIs raise the **`ObjectDoesNotExist`** exception, the response will be 404 with the message **`Object not found`**.

It is also possible to change the error response of the built-in errors by adding an exception handler for specific Django exceptions:

- **`Exception`**
- **`Http404`**

- **HttpError**
- **ValidationError**
- **AuthenticationError**

By using the **exception_handler** decorator with the exceptions listed previously, you can customize the built-in error responses in your application. For instance, you can provide a more informative error message or change the status code. An example implementation might involve decorating a function with **@exception_handler(Http404)** and defining the custom response you wish to return for a 404 error.

Authenticating API Users

In this section, we will explore two methods of adding authentication to our API endpoints. Initially, we will begin with token-based authentication. Subsequently, we will implement a more advanced approach using JWT (JSON Web Tokens).

Token-Based Authentication

API token-based authentication uses a token issued by the server after the user's credentials are authenticated. This token is then used in every request to the API, thus eliminating the need to send the username and password.

We must create a model for storing generated tokens to facilitate token-based authentication. Achieve this by opening **accounts/models.py** and adding the **ApiToken** model:

```
import uuid
from django.db import models


class ApiToken(models.Model):
    token = models.UUIDField(default=uuid.uuid4, unique=True)
    user = models.ForeignKey(TaskManagerUser, on_delete=models.CASCADE)

    def __str__(self):
            return str(self.token)
```

This new model stores the key using **uuid** and the user who owns the key. As always, generate the migrations and execute them:

```
poetry shell

python manage.py makemigrations

python manage.py migrate
```

We will incorporate `ApiKeyAuth` into the Ninja API next. Initiate this by creating a new file in **tasks/api/security.py** and adding the new `ApiKeyAuth` class:

```
from ninja.security import HttpBearer

from django.http import HttpRequest

from accounts.models import ApiToken


class  ApiTokenAuth(HttpBearer):

    def authenticate(

        self, request: HttpRequest, token: str

    ) -> str | None:

        if ApiToken.objects.filter(token=token).exists():

            return token

        else:

            return None
```

Here, we're inheriting from `ninja.security.HttpBearer` and overriding the *authenticate* method. This method tries to get an **`ApiToken`** object from the database that matches the provided token. If it succeeds, it returns the token. Otherwise, it returns None, indicating failed authentication.

We must now extend the authentication across all API views, we can achieve this by using the auth parameter within the Ninja decorators. For example, here is the `list_tasks` endpoint protected with token-based authentication:

```
from accounts.api.security import ApiKeyAuth


@router.get("/", response=list[TaskSchemaOut], auth= ApiTokenAuth ())

@paginate

def list_tasks(request):
```

```
    return services.list_tasks()
```

Incorporating authentication into every view can lead to mistakes, such as overlooking the addition of authentication to crucial endpoints. A more efficient approach is to implement global authentication through the NinjaAPI class. To do this, open the file **taskmanager/api.py** and modify it to integrate the new authentication method.

```
from accounts.api.security import  ApiTokenAuth

api_v1 = NinjaAPI(version="v1", auth= ApiTokenAuth ())
```

If we don't want to affect the project globally, we can add authentication at the router level:

```
from accounts.api.security import  ApiTokenAuth

router = Router(auth= ApiTokenAuth ())
```

With our APIs protected, we now need a way to generate the tokens for our users. We will create a new view to generate and display this token.

On our account's application, create a new file for the service layer **accounts/services.py** and populate it with the following contents:

```
def generate_token(user: AbstractUser) -> str:

    token, _ = ApiToken.objects.get_or_create(user=user)

    return str(token.token)
```

The function **generate_token** gets or creates a new UUID token by using the Django objects manager method **get_or_create**.

Let's now create a view to display the token to the user:

```
from django.contrib.auth.decorators import login_required

from django.shortcuts import redirect, render


@login_required

def token_generation_view(request):

    token = generate_token(request.user)

    return render(request, "accounts/token_display.html", {"token":
    token})
```

Then we need to add the new view to the accounts/urls.py:

```
urlpatterns = [

    …

    path("show-api-token/", views.token_generation_view, name="api-
    token"),

]
```

We still need to create the new template to display the token in the **templates/accounts/token_display.html**:

```
{% extends 'tasks/base.html' %}


{% load static %}


{% block content %}

<!DOCTYPE html>

<html lang="en">

<head>

   <meta charset="UTF-8">

   <meta name="viewport" content="width=device-width, initial-scale=1.0">

   <title>API Token</title>

</head>

<body class="bg-light">

   <div class="container py-5">

       <div class="row justify-content-center">

           <div class="col-md-8">

               <div class="card">

                   <div class="card-header">

                         <h1 class="card-title">Your API Token</h1>

                   </div>
```

```
                <div class="card-body">
                    {% if token %}
                        <p class="card-text">Your token: <code>{{
                        token }}</code></p>
                    {% else %}
                        <p class="card-text">No token available.</p>
                    {% endif %}
                </div>
            </div>
        </div>
    </div>
  </div>
</body>
</html>
{% endblock %}
```

The template is specifically designed for displaying an API token in a user-friendly manner. Extending from a base template (**tasks/base.html**), it inherits a common structure and styling, ensuring a consistent look across different application parts.

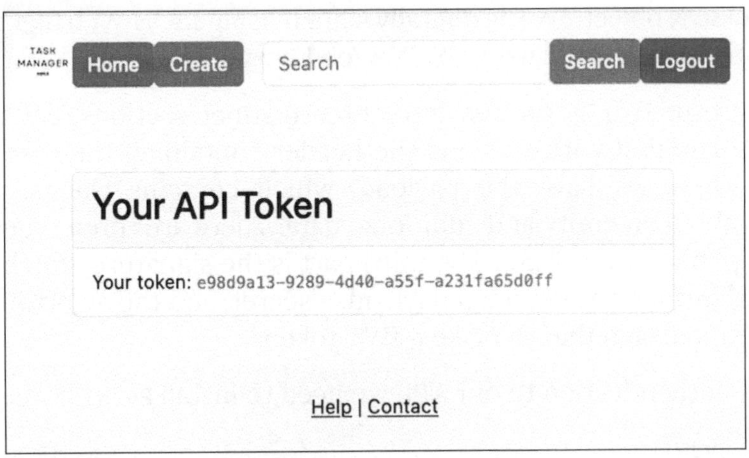

Figure 9.3: *The API token view*

If we now try to request any of our endpoints, we will get an error:

```
$ curl http://localhost:8000/api/tasks/archive/2023/02/12
```

```
{"detail": "Unauthorized"}
```

But including the authorization header will allow us to get the response:

```
curl -H "Authorization: Bearer e98d9a13-9289-4d40-a55f-a231fa65d0ff"
http://localhost:8000/api/tasks/archive/2023/02/14
```

```
{"items": [], "count": 0}
```

It's important to acknowledge that the approaches mentioned thus far are quite basic. For enhanced security, it is advisable to adopt best practices in token management. A key practice is to display the token to the user only once upon its generation, emphasizing the importance of its confidentiality. Moreover, setting an expiration for tokens ensures they remain valid only for a predetermined duration, reducing the risk of unauthorized long-term use. The ability to invalidate tokens provides an additional layer of control, enabling swift response to potential security breaches. Furthermore, tracking the usage of each token can offer valuable insights into their activity, helping to identify and mitigate any irregular or suspicious behavior. Implementing these practices not only strengthens security but also instills a greater sense of trust and reliability in the system.

JSON Web Tokens Authentication

JSON web tokens or JWT is an open standard (RFC 7519 https://tools.ietf.org/html/rfc7519) that defines a compact and secure way to exchange data between parties as a JSON object. JWT is digitally signed using JSON Web Signature (JWS) and can optionally encrypt using JSON Web Encryption (JWE).

The structure of JWT is divided into three distinct sections, each separated by dots ("."). The first part contains the header containing the token type and algorithm. Then, we have the payload, which contains claims. Claims are statements about an entity and additional data. There are three types of claims: registered, public, and private. The third part is the signature. You have to take the encoded header, the encoded payload, a secret, and the algorithm specified in the header and sign that to make a JWT token.

To add JWT authentication to our API, we need to install **`PyJWT`** library first:

```
poetry add PyJWT
```

Then, in our **tasks/api/security.py** file, we will add a new class to create the JWT Authentication:

```
import jwt

from django.conf import settings

from ninja.security import HttpBearer

from django.contrib.auth import get_user_model

from django.contrib.auth.models import User


class JWTAuth(HttpBearer):


    def authenticate(self, request, token):

        try:

            # Decode the JWT token

            payload = jwt.decode(token, settings.JWT_SECRET_KEY,
            algorithms=["HS256"])


            # Get the user information from the token's payload

            user = get_user_model().objects.get(id=payload["id"])

            return user, token

        except Exception as e:

            return None
```

The class inherits from HttpBearer and overrides the authenticate method. The method uses the JWT library to decode the token using the secret. The secret is retrieved from the settings, which uses environment variables to get the JWT secret. If the token can be decoded, the code can access the payload containing the user ID. With the user ID, we retrieve and return the user. If any error occurs, the method returns None, making the authentication fail due to invalid or expired tokens.

Note: It's important to note that we have a hardcoded algorithm and we never parse the algorithm from the token header. Using the algorithm from the header will create a security vulnerability. This vulnerability is called algorithm substitution. For instance, an attacker might change the "alg" field to "none," a valid option according to the JWT specification.

Now we need a function to issue the JWT token given to a user. Open the **accounts/service.py** and add the new function to issue a JWT token:

```
import jwt

from django.conf import settings

from django.contrib.auth.models import AbstractUser

from datetime import datetime, timedelta


def issue_jwt_token(user: AbstractUser) -> str:

    payload = {

        "id": user.id,

        "exp": datetime.utcnow() + timedelta(days=1)  # The token will
        expire in 1 day

    }

    token = jwt.encode(payload, settings.JWT_SECRET_KEY,
    algorithm="HS256")

    return token
```

The function **`issue_jwt_token`** accepts a User that will be used to get the **`id`** and build the payload. The payload also contains the "**`exp`**" key to specify the token's expiration. Finally, we encode the payload using the same secret from the settings. Note that we use the same algorithm HS256.

You must add the new **`JWT_SECRET_KEY`** settings in the **taskmanager/settings.py** and get it from the environment variables:

```
JWT_SECRET_KEY = os.getenv("JWT_SECRET_KEY", "jwt_secret")
```

Now, we can add JWT Token authentication to our endpoints. Let's allow both of the authentication methods by using a list for the auth parameter:

```
api_v1 = NinjaAPI(version="v1", auth=[ApiKeyAuth(), JWTAuth()])
```

And now let's update our token view to include the JWT token:

```
@login_required

def token_generation_view(request):

    token = generate_token(request.user)

    jwt_token = issue_jwt_token(request.user)

    return render(request, "accounts/token_display.html", {"token": token,
"jwt_token": jwt_token})
```

It will be left as an exercise the update of the template to show the new JWT token.

With the new JWT token, we are ready to test our API using curl:

```
curl -H "Authorization: Bearer JWT_TOKEN" http://localhost:8000/api/
tasks/archive/2023/02/14
```

JWT has the advantage of being stateless, reducing server-side database usage. JWT tokens are more complex due to the encoding and decoding. JWT provides a good security level since tokens are optionally encrypted, signed and have an expiry time.

Token-based is simple to implement and understand. The server will need to store the tokens in the database. It is also important to generate secure tokens using good random generators. Tokens don't usually expire, which could be problematic if any token is leaked.

The choice between the two often depends on specific use cases, security considerations, and scalability requirements.

Securing APIs: Permissions and Throttling

Next, we will see how to secure APIs.

Permissions

Ninja provides a way to implement handling permissions. Permissions are utilized to grant or deny access to specific API views in our project using the user's attributes or other criteria.

In *Chapter 9, User Authentication and Authorization in Django*, we defined three security groups: **`Creator`**, **`Editor`**, and **`Admin`**. We will use the same groups to provide access to our APIs.

Open the file **accounts/api/security.py** and add a new permission class to check if the user has a particular permission:

```
from functools import wraps

from django.http import HttpResponseForbidden


def require_permission(permission_name):

    def decorator(func):

          @wraps(func)

          def wrapper(request, *args, **kwargs):

          if not request.user.has_perm(permission_name):

                return HttpResponseForbidden("You don't have the
                required permission!")

          return func(request, *args, **kwargs)

          return wrapper

    return decorator
```

This code introduces the `require_permission` decorator to verify if an authenticated user has specific permission before accessing an endpoint. The decorator accepts a `permission_name` and checks the `request.user` object's permissions using Django's `has_perm` method. If the user lacks the permission, an `HttpResponseForbidden` response is generated. Otherwise, the original function proceeds. This decorator can be applied to any route in the router to ensure authorization checks.

We are now equipped to restrict the task creation via the API exclusively to users who have permission:

```
@router.post("/", response={201: CreateSchemaOut}, auth=ApiKeyAuth())

@require_permission("tasks.add_tasks")

def create_task(request: HttpRequest, task_in: TaskSchemaIn):

    creator = request.user
```

```
    return services.create_task(creator, **task_in.dict())
```

The `create_task` API endpoint now will check for the permission `tasks.add_tasks`.

Throttling

In Django, the **`django-ratelimit`** library utilizes the same backend as Django's caching framework for storing rate limiting information, ensuring consistent and efficient handling of data.

Throttling limits the rate at which clients can request our API. The implementation of rate limiting serves the dual purpose of preventing API abuse and guaranteeing the service's quality.

We will need to install the third-party library **`django-ratelimit`** (https://github.com/jsocol/django-ratelimit):

```
poetry add django-ratelimit
```

Let's add the rate limit to our create task endpoint:

```
@router.post("/", response={201: CreateSchemaOut}, auth=ApiKeyAuth())

@require_permission('tasks.add_tasks')

@ratelimit(key='ip', rate='100/h')

def create_task(request: HttpRequest, task_in: TaskSchemaIn):

    creator = request.user

    return services.create_task(creator, **task_in.dict())
```

By adding the rate-limit decorator using the IP address and with a maximum of 100 requests per hour, the task creation endpoint is now protected against abuse by limiting the number of requests.

Versioning Your API

API needs to evolve and it is required to introduce changes that could break the current API. API versioning is a practice that helps developers introduce non-breaking changes and new features or deprecate the old ones without affecting the existing users. Ninja supports API versioning via a version parameter of the **`NinjaAPI`** object.

Here is an example of API versioning using Ninja:

```
from ninja import NinjaAPI

from . import views_v1, views_v2


# Create an API instance for version 1

api_v1 = NinjaAPI(version="v1")

api_v1.add_router("/tasks", views_v1.router)


# Create an API instance for version 2

api_v2 = NinjaAPI(version="v2")

api_v2.add_router("/tasks", views_v2.router)
```

The code above creates two APIs using different routers. The value of the version specifies the path in the URL for the version.

Conclusion

Adopting an API-first design approach allows us to focus intensely on the problems we need to solve, providing rapid feedback even before we fully develop a solution. Understanding the power of schemas with type annotations in our API will make you save time and implement a robust performant API.

This chapter shows the effectiveness of a service layer; our API efficiently reutilized functionalities established in previous chapters.

We also explored adding authentication and authorization to our endpoints through various methods, including token-based and JWT token strategies.

With all the tools we learned in this chapter, we are now equipped to tackle the construction of complex APIs in any upcoming project.

Django Ninja, a recently popularized project, holds a promising future as the foundational framework for our APIs.

In the next chapter, we will learn how to add tests using pytest to our project. Tests will ensure code quality, detect bugs early and maintain system reliability as the codebase evolves.

Questions

1. What does it mean for a system to be **stateless** in the context of REST?
2. Can REST APIs be implemented without HTTP?
3. What are some challenges of using an API-first approach, and how does it benefit the design process?
4. What is the purpose of using routers in Django Ninja?
5. What are the advantages of using **`ModelSchema`** over Schema in Django Ninja?
6. What is the significance of the URL path in the REST API for Tasks, especially regarding resource identification?
7. Why is returning a 201 status code considered appropriate when creating a new resource in a RESTful API?
8. What is the primary purpose of token-based authentication in an API?
9. How can you protect an API endpoint with token-based authentication in Django using Ninja API decorators?
10. Can you explain the three distinct sections of a JWT?
11. What is the purpose of a refresh token in JWT authentication?
12. In what scenarios would you recommend using JWT over simple token-based authentication?
13. Discuss the security implications of token leakage in both JWT and simple token-based systems.

Exercises

1. Implement an API endpoint to claim a task using the service function **`claim_task`**.
2. Implement all the endpoints to have a complete CRUD operation for the Epic and Sprint models.
3. Add the appropriate permission to API views using the correct groups: Creator, Editor or Admin on all the endpoints.

CHAPTER 10
Testing with pytest

Introduction

Testing is a crucial process that verifies the expected behavior of a software application. Testing involves a variety of practices and methodologies to rigorously evaluate different software parts, from individual functions and integration between components to entire systems.

A multitude of tools are available for testing a Python application. Pytest has become one of the most popular testing frameworks due to its simplicity and ability to handle complex test scenarios.

Pytest supports different test types, including unit tests, integration tests, and more. The framework's capabilities can be augmented using plugins, enhancing its power.

This chapter will guide us through incorporating tests into our project. Initially, we'll begin with straightforward unit test cases; subsequently, integration tests will be added, and ultimately, we will enhance the framework with Behavior-Driven Development (BDD) for scenario writing.

Structure

In this chapter, we will cover the following topics:

- Introduction to testing and pytest
- Installing and setting up pytest for Django
- The Pytest conftest.py file
- Writing your first test with pytest
- Understanding Django test database and pytest fixtures
- Pytest-django fixtures
- Mocking and patching in tests
- Testing Django views
- Testing Django forms
- Test factories
- Testing the API
- Behavior-driven development
- Advanced pytest features: Parametrization, plugins, and configuration

Introduction to testing and pytest

Testing is a crucial component of software development that ensures your code behaves as expected and helps maintain its quality over time. pytest is a robust, feature-rich testing framework for Python that enables developers to write simple and scalable test codes.

Understanding test

Testing involves executing software to verify its results to find errors, bugs, or other issues. The primary goal of testing is to ensure the application's quality, reliability, and proper performance.

Many types of software testing exist. We will focus on some of them:

- Unit testing
- Integration testing
- End-to-end tests

In software testing, there is a concept called the testing pyramid. The testing pyramid concept refers to the distribution of different types of tests within a software project. As shown in *Figure 10.1*, the pyramid's base consists of the unit tests, followed by the integration tests and end-to-end tests.

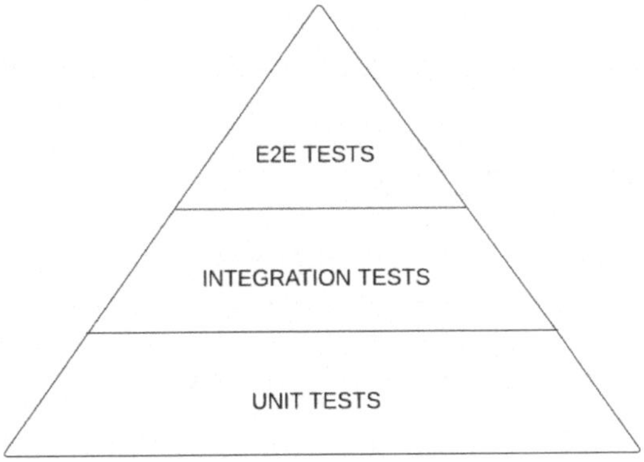

Figure 10.1: *Testing pyramid*

There are many reasons to have the test distribution, like a pyramid. The higher we go in the pyramid, the more complex, slow, and harder it is to maintain tests. At the top of the pyramid, we should have the essential real-user scenarios, while at the bottom, we test isolated and small parts of the software.

Test-driven development

Test-driven development, or TDD, is an approach to building software. In TDD, tests are written before the actual code. Once all the tests are written, the developer follows a process cycle known as Red-Green-Refactor. We start by writing tests that initially fail, then develop the functionality to make these tests pass. Finally, we refactor the code to enhance its structure and efficiency, ensuring a robust and well-designed application. Writing the tests first will make the developer think about how to use the classes, functions, and methods in a usable way. When writing the code first, sometimes we get to the point where our code is hard to use or understand.

In this book, we did not adopt TDD due to its learning curve, which can challenge beginners to grasp the process's final purpose.

Test coverage

In testing, there exist many measures or metrics. Test coverage describes the degree to which the source code of a program is executed when a particular test suite runs. It's a metric that helps developers to understand how much of their code is being tested. This metric can identify parts of a program that have not been tested and could contain potential bugs.

Note: It is crucial to note that the coverage metric can be artificially inflated by writing trivial tests that traverse the code paths without validating the outcomes; therefore, we must use these metrics cautiously, whether intentionally or not. Having 100% test coverage doesn't necessarily guarantee high-quality levels.

Introduction to pytest

Pytest is a popular framework for writing tests in a simple and scalable way. It is known for its simplicity and powerful features.

Let us now examine the features offered by pytest.

Initiating work with pytest is straightforward. Tests are Python functions prefixed with the word **test.**

To illustrate how pytest can be used for testing, let's consider a function that computes the Fibonacci sequence as an example. The Fibonacci sequence is a classic problem demonstrating how different test cases, such as base cases, general cases, and error handling, can be structured.

The Fibonacci sequence is a series of numbers where each number is the sum of the two preceding ones. Typically, the sequence starts with 0 and 1:

```
def fibonacci(n):

    if n <= 0:

        raise ValueError("Fibonacci numbers are defined for n >= 1")

    elif n == 1:

        return 0

    elif n == 2:

        return 1


    a, b = 0, 1

    for _ in range(2, n):

        a, b = b, a + b

    return b
```

The function starts by ensuring the input n is valid, as Fibonacci numbers are defined for n >= 1, and throws a ValueError for non-positive values. The first two Fibonacci numbers return 0 and 1 when n is 1 and 2, respectively. The function then uses an iterative approach to calculate the Fibonacci number for a larger n. It initializes two variables, a and b, with the first two numbers of the sequence (0 and 1) and iteratively updates them in a loop that runs from 2 to n - 1. After completing the loop, the function returns b, which holds the n-th Fibonacci number.

```
def test_base_case():

    assert fibonacci(1) == 0

    assert fibonacci(2) == 1
```

The test **test_base_case** verifies the base cases are computed correctly. The function name starts with test so that pytest detects and executes this function. Pytest uses the assert statement. When the expression evaluated by the assert statement is true, the program continues to execute as normal. However, if the expression is false, an AssertionError exception is raised.

```
def test_fibonacci_general():

    assert fibonacci(5) == 3  # The 5th Fibonacci number is 3
```

In the preceding test, the verification is that the loop accurately calculates the Fibonacci number. During test composition, it is common practice to contemplate branches and coverage to fashion unit tests that verify your code's various components and logic.

```
def test_fibonacci_invalid_input():

    with pytest.raises(ValueError):

        fibonacci(-1)
```

In the last example, we test how the function behaves when the input is outside its valid range. The test uses **pytest.raises** to verify that the execution raises an exception. If the exception is not raised, the test will fail.

To run the tests, we need to execute the command pytest. Pytest will automatically discover tests that are named according to the convention. The convention is test_*.py or *_test.py files, with functions named test_*. In the next section, we will install and configure pytest in our project.

Before diving deep into the writing tests for our project, learning about fixtures is essential. Fixture is a powerful feature of pytest. It provides a convenient way to prepare data or state before a test run. A fixture is any function designated by the pytest decorator fixtures. Fixtures have different scopes:

- Function: run once per test function. This is the default scope.
- Class: runs once per test class, regardless of how many test methods are in a class.
- Module: runs once per module, where a module is a file containing tests.
- Package: run once per package, a collection of test modules in a directory.
- Session: run once per session. A session is the entire test suite run from start to finish.

```
import pytest


@pytest.fixture(scope="function")

def sample_data():

    data = [1, 2, 3]

    return data


def test_data_length(sample_data):

    assert len(sample_data) == 3
```

In the preceding code, we first create a fixture **sample_data** with the scope function. This fixture simply returns a list of three numbers. In the test test_data_length, we use the sample_data fixture and verify the length of it.

Plugins are extensions to the framework that add additional functionality. Plugins in pytest can range from those handling test discovery, output formatting, and integration with other tools to plugins, enhancing testing capabilities for specific frameworks like Django.

Installing and setting up pytest for Django

For setting up our project. We must install pytest and its plugin for Django pytest-django (https://github.com/pytest-dev/pytest-django).

```
poetry add --dev pytest pytest-django
```

In the previous command, we used the **--dev** flag to specify that the dependency is only for the development environment.

pytest-django plugin provides useful tools and fixtures for testing Django applications.

Then we need to configure pytest to specify where the Django settings reside. Create a new file pytest.ini, at the root of your project with the following contents:

```
[pytest]

DJANGO_SETTINGS_MODULE = taskmanager.settings
```

The Pytest conftest.py file

The **conftest.py** file is a special file where fixtures can be shared across multiple test files. Unlike regular Python modules, **conftest.py** doesn't need to be imported explicitly by the test files. Pytest automatically recognizes this file and makes its contents available to test files.

Besides fixtures, **conftest.py** can implement plugin hook functions to modify pytest's default behavior or add new functionality.

Writing your first test with pytest

The first test we will write will be a simple unit test. In *Chapter 5, Django Views and URL Handling*, we created a view to get tasks by date. The URL view uses a converter DateConverter, which is perfect for writing our first unit test for the project.

Let's review the code of the class:

```
from datetime import datetime


class DateConverter:

    regex = "[0-9]{4}-[0-9]{2}-[0-9]{2}"


    def to_python(self, value):

        return datetime.strptime(value, "%Y-%m-%d")


    def to_url(self, object):

        return object.strftime("%Y-%m-%d")
```

The implementation is ideal for writing our first test since it doesn't require any fixture. Typically, when writing Django tests with pytest, a fixture is required to access the database or other resources.

Let's create a new file in **tasks/tests/test_converters.py** with the following code:

```
import pytest

from datetime import datetime

from tasks.converters import DateConverter


@pytest.fixture

def date_converter():

    return DateConverter()


def test_to_python(date_converter):

    # Test conversion from string to datetime

    assert date_converter.to_python("2023-10-05") == datetime(2023, 10,
    5)


def test_to_url(date_converter):

    # Test conversion from datetime to string

    date_obj = datetime(2023, 10, 5)

    assert date_converter.to_url(date_obj) == "2023-10-05"
```

Now, we can run the tests to verify the implementation of the DateConverter:

```
poetry shell

pytest

======================== test session starts ========================

platform darwin -- Python 3.10.11, pytest-7.4.3, pluggy-1.3.0

rootdir: /Users/mandarina/workspace/task_manager

plugins: django-4.5.2
```

```
collected 2 items

taskmanager/tasks/tests/test_converters.py ....                          [100%]

============================ 2 passed in 0.03s ============================
```

Congrats! Your project task manager has the first tests implemented and in the green state.

Understanding Django test database and pytest

Before writing more tests for our project, we need to understand how databases and tests are integrated.

Django creates a separate database for testing purposes. This ensures there is no interference with your development database. Each time you run tests, a new database is created and destroyed at the end of the test session.

Each test is wrapped in a transaction that is rolled back at the end of the test. Using transactions ensures that every test has a clean state.

pytest-django keeps the database usage at a minimum and when your tests need to access the database, you will need to use the decorator `@pytest.mark.django_db`. It will fail if your test accesses the database but lacks the decorator.

For testing transactions, you should use `@pytest.mark.django_db(transaction=True)`, which we will explore in subsequent sections.

Pytest-django fixtures

The plugin pytest-django comes with several useful fixtures that we will use in the next sections to write tests.

- **`db`**: Allows access to the database. This fixture ensures that the test is run with database access. When using the DB fixture, pytest understands that the test requires database access and automatically sets up and tears down the database for that test. Hence, there is no need to use the `@pytest.mark.django_db` decorator.
- **`db_transactional`**: similar to the DB fixture, this fixture permits transaction testing. It is more resource-intensive than its db counterpart.

- **`client`**: Provides a Django test client instance. The fixture allows the developer to make requests to simulate HTTP requests useful for testing views or APIs.
- **`admin_client`**: Provides a logged-in Django admin client. This fixture is similar to the client with the user already logged in with admin permissions.
- **`settings`**: Allows the modification of Django settings during tests. When using this fixture, any settings can be changed in the scope of the test. All changes are reverted when the test ends.
- **`django_user_model`**: allows tests to access the user model currently active in the Django project, facilitating the creation and manipulation of user instances for testing purposes.

Mocking and patching in tests

Mocks are objects that simulate the behavior of real objects. These mock objects are used in tests to control the returned values and record how they have been used. Some mocks could have some logic and raise exceptions to test particular scenarios.

Using mocks ensures that the test only tests the code in question, not its dependencies. It also makes the test more predictable and sometimes speeds up the tests.

Patching temporarily replaces real objects in a module with a mock object during a test.

Mocking and patching are powerful tools in a tester's arsenal, enabling effective unit testing by focusing on the unit of code itself rather than its dependencies. We will see how to use it in the follow-up sections.

Testing Django views

In *Chapter 5, Django Views and URL Handling*, we created a contact view that allows our users to claim a task. The view uses a service that will claim the task given a **`task_id`**. Create a new file in **tasks/unit/test_views.py** with the claim_task view test:

```
def test_claim_task_success(rf):

    user_id = 1

    task_id = 100
```

```
    request = rf.get(f"/claim_task/{task_id}")
    mock_user = MagicMock()
    mock_user.id = user_id
    mock_user.is_authenticated = True
    request.user = mock_user

    with patch("tasks.services.claim_task") as mock_claim_task:
        response = views.claim_task_view(request, task_id)

        mock_claim_task.assert_called_once_with(user_id, task_id)

        assert isinstance(response, JsonResponse)
        assert response.status_code == 200
        # Deserialize JSON response content
        response_data = json.loads(response.content.decode())
        assert response_data == {"message": "Task successfully claimed."}
```

In the unit test **test_claim_task_success**, the functionality of Django's **claim_task_view** is tested for a scenario where a task is successfully claimed. The test creates a simulated GET request using Django's **RequestFactory** and a **MagicMock** user set as authenticated. This setup replicates a typical user request in Django.

The tasks.services.claim_task function is mocked to focus the test solely on the view's behavior. The test checks that this function is called with correct parameters and verifies the view's response. It asserts that the response is a **JsonResponse** with a status code of 200 and that the JSON content of the response matches the expected success message. The test ensures that the **claim_task_view** behaves as expected in a successful task claim scenario.

The following test, **test_claim_task_not_exist**, is designed to verify the correct response of the **claim_task_view** when it encounters a non-existent task in a Django application.

```
def test_claim_task_not_exist(rf):
    user_id = 1
```

```
    task_id = 101
    request = rf.get(f"/claim_task/{task_id}")

    # Create a mock user with MagicMock
    mock_user = MagicMock()
    mock_user.id = user_id
    mock_user.is_authenticated = True
    request.user = mock_user

    with patch("tasks.services.claim_task", side_effect=services.Task.
    DoesNotExist) as mock_claim_task:
        response = views.claim_task_view(request, task_id)

        mock_claim_task.assert_called_once_with(user_id, task_id)
        assert isinstance(response, HttpResponse)
        assert response.status_code == 404
        assert response.content.decode() == "Task does not exist."
```

In the unit test **test_claim_task_not_exist**, the focus is on ensuring that Django's **claim_task_view** handles the case where a task does not exist. The test constructs a simulated GET request with Django's **RequestFactory** and a **MagicMock** user to simulate an authenticated user's request.

The **tasks.services.claim_task** function is mocked with a **side_effect** to raise a **Task.DoesNotExist** exception. This setup tests the view's error-handling capability. When **claim_task_view** is called with the mock request and a non-existent task ID, the test verifies that the mocked service is invoked with the right parameters. It then checks the response, ensuring it's an **HttpResponse** with a 404 status code and the content correctly indicates that the task does not exist. This test confirms the view's appropriate response to scenarios involving non-existent tasks.

We now examine a view interaction with the database. The following test will verify that the task creation works as expected. Create a new file in **tasks/tests/integration/test_views.py** with the following contents:

```
import pytest

from django.urls import reverse

from tasks.models import Task


@pytest.mark.django_db

def test_valid_form_submission_creates_task(client, django_user_model):

    url = reverse("tasks:task-create")

    user = django_user_model.objects.create_user(username="user",
    password="password", email="test@example.com")

    client.force_login(user)

    get_response = client.get(url)

    csrf_token = get_response.cookies['csrftoken'].value

    unique_title = str(uuid.uuid4())

    data = {

            "title": unique_title,

            "status": "UNASSIGNED",

            "csrfmiddlewaretoken": csrf_token,

    }

    assert Task.objects.count() == 0

    response = client.post(url, data)

    assert response.status_code == 302

    assert Task.objects.count() == 1

    created_task = Task.objects.get(title=unique_title)

    assert created_task.creator == user
```

The test starts by setting up the context. It creates a new user and uses the client to log in. Then, we calculate the URL and create a payload. We then execute the post request. The last test verifies that a 302 redirection is returned and confirms the task object's creation. Given that our view assigns the creator role to the authenticated user issuing the **POST** request, the test corroborates that the Task's creator aligns with expectations.

Testing Django forms

The form can be tested independently from the views. As an example, we will test the form **TaskFormWithRedis**. This form was introduced in *Chapter 7, Forms in Django* and has the functionality to prevent multiple submissions of the form using a UUID (Universally Unique Identifier). The form behaves so that the second time it gets submitted to the server, it will be rejected if the **UUID** was already processed.

Given the test's reliance on the database and Redis, it is classified as an integration test.

Let's create a new file in **tasks/tests/integration/test_forms.py** with the following test:

```
import pytest
from django.core.cache import cache
from tasks.forms import TaskFormWithRedis
import uuid


@pytest.mark.django_db
def test_task_form_with_redis_is_valid_fails_second_time():
    # Create unique UUIDs for testing
    uuid1 = uuid.uuid4()

    # Set up form data
    form_data = {
            "title": "Test Task",
            "description": "Test Description",
            "status": "UNASSIGNED",
            "watchers": "watcher1@example.com, watcher2@example.com",
            "uuid": uuid1
```

```
    }

    # First submission with uuid1
    form = TaskFormWithRedis(data=form_data)
    assert form.is_valid(), f"Form should be valid: {form.errors}"

    # Second submission with the same uuid1 should raise a ValidationError
    form_data["uuid"] = uuid1
    form = TaskFormWithRedis(data=form_data)
    assert not form.is_valid()
    assert form.errors == {"uuid": ["This form has already been submitted."]}
```

Initiation of the test occurs through generating a unique UUID and assembling form data, which involves fields such as title, description, status, and watchers. Initially, the form is submitted with this unique UUID, and the test checks to ensure the form is valid. The critical part of the test involves a second submission with the same UUID. It is expected that the form, upon a second submission, would fail its validity, raising a specific error **`This form has already been submitted.`** due to the UUID already used.

Test factories

Tests usually require setting up some data for the context of execution. The context often involves models and could lead to repetitive or long code when the relationship dependency is complex. Factory-boy (https://github.com/FactoryBoy/factory_boy) is a library that provides an efficient and flexible way to create test data.

A factory in factory-boy is a class that serves as a blueprint for creating instances of Django models. Each factory is linked to one model and has some configuration to specify how to generate new instances with default, custom or random values.

Attributes within a factory class align with the fields of a Django model. The library provides tools to create values that could be useful for test cases.

Let's create a factory for our main model, the task. First, we need to install factory-boy using poetry as a development dependency:

```
poetry add --dev factory-boy
```

Create a new file in tasks/tests/factories.py:

```
import factory

from accounts.models import Organization

from tasks.models import Task, TaskStatus

from django.contrib.auth import get_user_model

class OrganizationFactory(factory.django.DjangoModelFactory):

    class Meta:

        model = Organization


class UserFactory(factory.django.DjangoModelFactory):

    class Meta:

        model = get_user_model()


    username = factory.Faker("user_name")

    email = factory.Faker("email")

organization = factory.SubFactory(OrganizationFactory)
```

The UserFactory is a subclass of **`factory.django.DjangoModelFactory`** and is configured to create instances of the user model, which it retrieves using Django's **`get_user_model()`** method. The factory uses **`factory.Faker`** to generate realistic usernames and email addresses.

Let's add a **`TaskFactory`** to generate task instances. In the same file, add the new class:

```
class TaskFactory(factory.django.DjangoModelFactory):

    class Meta:

        model = Task


    title = factory.Faker("sentence", nb_words=4)

    description = factory.Faker("paragraph")
```

```
    status = factory.Iterator([status.value for status in TaskStatus])

    creator = factory.SubFactory(UserFactory)

    # The owner field can either be null or an instance of the User model.
    # This creates a User instance 50% of the time and sets the owner to None 50% of the time.
    owner = factory.Maybe(
            factory.Faker("pybool"),
            yes_declaration=factory.SubFactory(UserFactory),
            no_declaration=None
    )

    version = factory.Sequence(lambda n: n)
```

TaskFactory is a subclass of **`factory.django.DjangoModelFactory`**, designed to create instances of the Task model. It sets up an automatic generation of task titles, descriptions, and status fields. The title and description are generated using **`factory.Faker`**, producing realistic sentences and paragraphs. The status field iterates over the possible values defined in **`TaskStatus`**.

For the creator field, **`TaskFactory`** uses a **`factory.SubFactory`** to create related user instances. For the owner field, it uses **`factory.Maybe`** in conjunction with **`factory.Faker('pybool')`** to randomly decide whether to assign a user instance or set it to None, simulating scenarios where a task might not have an assigned owner.

Lastly, the version field uses a **`factory.Sequence`** to ensure a unique, incrementing number for each created task instance.

In the next section, we will use the TaskFactory for the API tests.

Testing the API

To show an example of TDD, we will develop a new feature for our API. We will create a new endpoint to claim a task. For this, we will start writing the test cases and iterate until green.

First, we need to start with the API design. Our new API endpoint will have the following specifications:

URL Path: /api/v1/tasks/{task_id}/claim

Method: PATCH

Body: Empty. The authenticated user will claim the task.

Response:

- Success: Status Code 200 Ok. empty response
- Failure cases:
    - o 404: Not found. The task_id was not found.
    - o 400: Bad Request. Task already claimed.
    - o 403: Forbidden. No authentication was provided.

Since claiming a task involves modifying its current attributes, such as status or owner, utilizing PATCH is more suitable. We used the claim in the path to differentiate from the CRUD operations we developed in the previous chapter.

We opt for `PATCH` instead of `POST` for our endpoint to adhere to RESTful principles. PATCH is intended to update an existing resource's state, while POST is typically used to create new resources.

The next step is to consider the test cases we want to verify. In *Table 10.1*, you can read all the test cases we will implement using TDD.

Name	Preconditions	Action	Expected Result
Test Successful Claim	A task exists with a status that allows claiming.	The authenticated user sends a `PATCH` request to claim the task.	The user claims the task, the status is updated to **In Progress**, and a 200 OK response is returned with the task details.
Test Task Not Found	No task exists with the given `task_id`.	The user sends a `PATCH` request to claim a non-existent task.	A 404 Not Found response is returned with an appropriate error message.
Test Task Already Claimed	A task exists but is already claimed by another user.	A user who tries to claim an already claimed task.	A 400 Bad Request response returned with an error message indicating the task was already claimed.

Name	Preconditions	Action	Expected Result
Test Unauthorized Claim Attempt	A task exists that can be claimed.	An unauthenticated or unauthorized user sends a POST request to claim the task.	A 403 Forbidden response is returned with an error message about lack of authorization.
Test Claim Without Authentication	A claimable task exists.	A PATCH request is sent to claim the task without any user authentication.	A 401 Unauthorized response is returned, indicating that authentication is required.

Table 10.1: *Test cases for task claim API*

We are almost ready to write our test cases using pytest. However, we need to create fixtures to authenticate our API client using one of the authentication methods we implemented in *Chapter 8, User Authentication and Authorization* in Django.

Let's define the fixture we will use for the test we will implement. Create the file **tasks/tests/conftest.py** with the fixtures:

```
from .factories import UserFactory

from accounts.services import issue_jwt_token


@pytest.fixture

def user() -> AbstractUser:

    user = UserFactory()

    # Ensure the user instance is saved if UserFactory doesn't save it

    user.save()


    # Fetch the content type for the Task model

    content_type = ContentType.objects.get_for_model(Task)


    # Fetch the 'change_task' permission

    change_task_permission = Permission.objects.get(

          codename="change_task",
```

```
            content_type=content_type,
    )
        add_task_permission = Permission.objects.get(
            codename="add_tasks",
            content_type=content_type,
    )

    # Assign the permission to the user
    user.user_permissions.add(change_task_permission)
    user.user_permissions.add(add_task_permission)
    return user

@pytest.fixture
def jwt_token(user: AbstractUser) -> dict[str, str]:
    token = issue_jwt_token(user)
    return {"Authorization": f"Bearer {token}"}
```

The user fixture employs a factory to instantiate a new user. The code fetches the permission object for the **change_task** and **add_tasks** permission to add it to the user. Lacking this permission should return a 403, as specified by one of our test cases in Table 10.1.

Thanks to our service layer in the accounts application, we can generate a valid JWT token in the **jwt_token** fixture. The **jwt_token** fixture is designated for tests requiring authentication.

We will use this Django client in every test since it will allow us to request the API. the **jwt_token** will be used when we need to authenticate.

Now, let's create a new file in **tasks/tests/integration/test_api.py** with the following contents:

```
import pytest
from ninja.testing import TestClient
```

The first test case will be test_successful_claim:

```
@pytest.mark.django_db

def test_successful_claim(client, user, jwt_token):

    task = TaskFactory(status=TaskStatus.UNASSIGNED.value, owner=None)

    response = client.patch(f"/api/tasks/{task.id}/claim", headers=jwt_
    token)

    assert response.status_code == 200

    task.refresh_from_db()

    assert task.status == TaskStatus.IN_PROGRESS.value

    assert task.owner == user
```

The test is marked with **`@pytest.mark.django_db`**, indicating that it requires access to the Django database. It first creates an unassigned task using **`TaskFactory`**. Next, the test simulates a patch request to the endpoint responsible for claiming tasks, passing the task's ID and the user's JWT token. The response's status code is checked to ensure 200, indicating a successful operation. Finally, the test verifies that the task's status is updated to **`IN PROGRESS`** and the task's owner is now set to the user who claimed it.

If we run the tests, we should get the following results:

```
poetry shell

cd taskmanager

pytest -vvv

FAILED tasks/tests/integration/test_api.py::test_successful_claim -
assert 404 == 200
```

Let's develop the new API endpoint to call our service layer to claim a task:

```
@router.patch("/{int:task_id}/claim")

def claim_task_api(request: HttpRequest, task_id: int):

    services.claim_task(request.user.pk, task_id)

    return HttpResponse(status=HTTPStatus.OK)
```

The new claim endpoint is lean thanks to our service layer function **`claim_task`** that accepts a **`user_id`** and a **`task_id`**. The endpoint returns The HTTP status 200 and an empty response.

Let's check if the test is now green:

```
pytest -vvv
```

This was just an example of using one test. Ideally, we should have all the tests before the code when following TDD. Let's add the rest of the test and check if we have green tests, open tasks**/tests/integration/test_api.py** and add the rest of the tests:

```
@pytest.mark.django_db

def test_task_not_found(client, user):

    response = client.patch("/9999999/claim/")  # Unlikely to exist ID

    assert response.status_code == 404


@pytest.mark.django_db

def test_task_already_claimed(client, user, jwt_token):

    other_user = UserFactory()

    task = TaskFactory(status=TaskStatus.IN_PROGRESS.value, owner=other_
    user)

    response = client.patch(f"/api/tasks/{task.id}/claim", headers=jwt_
    token)

    assert response.status_code == 400


@pytest.mark.django_db

def test_unauthorized_claim_attempt(client, user, jwt_token):

    content_type = ContentType.objects.get_for_model(Task)

    permission = Permission.objects.get(codename='change_task', content_
    type=content_type)

    user.user_permissions.remove(permission)

    user.refresh_from_db()

    task = TaskFactory(status=TaskStatus.UNASSIGNED.value, owner=None)

    response = client.patch(f"/api/tasks/{task.id}/claim", headers=jwt_
    token)
```

```
    assert response.status_code == 403


@pytest.mark.django_db
def test_claim_without_authentication(client):
    task = TaskFactory(status=TaskStatus.UNASSIGNED.value)
    response = client.patch(f"/api/tasks/{task.id}/claim")
    assert response.status_code == 401
```

Let's examine the specific conditions each test verifies:

- **`test_task_not_found`**: Checks the scenario where a user attempts to claim a task with an ID that does not exist in the database. A patch request is sent to an unlikely-to-exist task ID. The test asserts that the response's status code is 404.
- **`test_task_already_claimed`**: A task is created and assigned to another user after logging in. The test then attempts to claim this already-in-progress task for the logged-in user and checks if the response's status code is 400.
- **`test_unauthorized_claim_attempt`**: Despite the user being logged in and the task being unassigned, the test simulates a claim attempt with insufficient permissions. The tests remove the permission **`tasks.change_task`** to make sure the patch request will fail. The assertion checks for a 403 status code.
- **`test_claim_without_authentication`**: Without logging in any user, the test tries to claim an unassigned task. The assertion for a 401 status code checks that the system appropriately requires authentication for task claiming.

If we try to run the test with the current implementation, we will find that only two tests fail:

```
pytest
FAILED tasks/tests/integration/test_api.py::test_task_already_claimed - tasks.services.TaskAlreadyClaimedException: Task is already claimed or completed.
FAILED tasks/tests/integration/test_api.py::test_unauthorized_claim_attempt - assert 200 == 403
```

The test test_task_not_found is green since this service uses the query `Task.objects.select_for_update().get(id=task_id)` which raises an exception when the object is not found. The exception is the **`ObjectDoesNotExist`**, for which we created a custom handler in *Chapter 9: Django Ninja and* APIs, the **`on_object_does_not_exist`**.

The test **`test_claim_without_authentication`** is also green since we added authentication to all the endpoints using the auth when we created the NinjaAPI in the file **taskmanager/api.py**.

We need to update our code to make the test **`test_task_already_claimed`** green. For this, we need to catch in the view the exception from the service **`TaskAlreadyClaimedException`** and return the appropriate response.

Let's define a new ninja exception handler in the file **tasks/api/tasks.py**:

```
from ninja.errors import HttpError

from taskmanager.tasks.services import TaskAlreadyClaimedException


@router.patch("/{int:task_id}/claim")

def claim_task_api(request: HttpRequest, task_id: int):

    try:

        services.claim_task(request.user.pk, task_id)

        return HttpResponse(status=HTTPStatus.OK)

    except TaskAlreadyClaimedException:

        # Raise an HttpError with status code 400

        raise HttpError(status_code=HTTPStatus.BAD_REQUEST,
        message="Task already claimed")
```

By adding this custom exception handler for **`TaskAlreadyClaimedException`** the view will return the expected error 400. Let's re-execute the tests and check that the test is now green:

```
pytest

FAILED tasks/tests/integration/test_api.py::test_unauthorized_claim_
attempt - assert 200 == 403
```

We now have one test failing. Let's add the decorator to check for the permission **`tasks.change_tasks`**:

```
@router.patch("/{int:task_id}/claim")

@require_permission("tasks.change_task")

def claim_task_api(request: HttpRequest, task_id: int):

    try:

        ...
```

If we now run the test, we will see that all of them are green!

Behavior-driven development

Behavior-driven development (BDD) is a methodology that focuses on defining specifications of software behavior from the end-user's perspective. These specifications can be translated into automatic tests. Using BDD enhances the collaboration among developers, QA professionals, and non-technical stakeholders. BDD bridges the communication gap between technical and non-technical team members.

BDD has three key components:

- **Feature files**: These contain user stories composed in the Gherkin language, adopting the Given, When, Then format.
- **Scenarios:** There are concrete examples of how the software should behave in specific situations.
- **Step definitions:** For each step in a scenario, step definitions are written in code that executes these steps.

Note: Gherkin is a domain-specific language that enables you to describe business behavior without the need to go into detail about implementation. Gherkin language comprises a set of keywords, and among the most fundamental are **`Given`**, **`When`**, **`Then`**, **`And`**, and **`But`**. These keywords enable the structured writing of acceptance criteria for features.

- **`Given`** steps are used to describe the initial context of the system—the state of the world before the behavior of the feature begins.
- **`When`** steps are used to describe an event or an action. This is the behavior that triggers the subsequent outcome.

- **Then** steps describe the expected outcome or state of the world after the behavior specified in the When steps.
- **And** can be used to continue any type of step and is often used to add additional conditions or outcomes.
- **But** is used to define an action or outcome that should not happen.

We will start with the feature file. Create a new file in the directory **tasks/tests/bdd/api.feature** with the following scenario:

```
@django_db

Feature: Task Claiming

    Scenario: User creates and claims a task

   Given a user with necessary permissions

   When the user creates a task

   And the user claims the created task

   Then when the user lists tasks, the created task is shown as claimed
```

The scenario is self-explanatory. You can usually start with this when you need to create a new feature for your project. Anyone participating in the project can understand the scenario and discuss it correctly.

Subsequently, we must integrate pytest-bdd:

```
poetry add --dev pytest-bdd
```

Once **pytest-bdd** is configured, we shall create the steps. Some adjustments are needed to use **pytest-bdds** with **pytest-django**.

Open the file **tasks/test/conftest.py** and add the **pytest_bdd_apply_tag** hook. These pytest-bdd hooks allow us to use the tag **@django_db** in the feature file to mark it as a **django_db**, allowing the test to access the database.

```
def pytest_bdd_apply_tag(tag, function):

    if tag == "django_db":

            marker = pytest.mark.django_db(transaction=True)

            marker(function)

            return True
```

```
    else:
        # Fall back to pytest-bdd's default behavior
        return None
```

Next, we will create the step. Create a new file in **tasks/tests/bdd/test_api.py** with the following content:

```
import json
from pytest_bdd import scenario, given, when, then
from tasks.enums import TaskStatus
from django.urls import reverse

@scenario("api.feature", "User creates and claims a task")
def test_task_claiming():
    pass

@given("a user with necessary permissions")
def user_with_permissions(user):
    return user

@when("the user creates a task", target_fixture="create_task")
def create_task(client, jwt_token):
    # Code to create a task via the API client
    response = client.post(
        reverse("api-v1:create_task"),
        json.dumps({"title": "Sample Task", "description": "test
        description"}),
            content_type="application/json",
            headers=jwt_token
    )
```

```
    assert response.status_code == 201, response.json()

    return response.json()  # Assuming the response includes task details


@when("the user claims the created task")

def claim_task(client, create_task, jwt_token):

    task_id = create_task["id"]

    response = client.patch(reverse("api-v1:claim_task_api",
    kwargs={"task_id": task_id}), headers=jwt_token)

    assert response.status_code == 200  # Or whatever your API returns


@then("when the user lists tasks, the created task is shown as claimed")

def list_tasks(client, create_task, jwt_token):

    response = client.get("/api/v1/tasks/", headers=jwt_token)

    assert response.status_code == 200

    tasks = response.json()

    items = tasks["items"]

    assert any([task["id"] == create_task["id"] for task in items if
    task["status"] == TaskStatus.IN_PROGRESS])
```

Let's review what each function is doing.

- **`test_task_claiming`**: This function is a placeholder linked to the BDD scenario defined in the **api.feature** file. The **`@scenario`** decorator binds this test function to a specific narrative in the feature file.
- **`user_with_permissions`**: This function is also a placeholder, since our user fixture already contains all the permissions needed for the test.
- **`create_task`**: The task is created using an HTTP POST request. The client sends the request to the URL resolved by reverse("**`api-v1:create_task`**"). The request body contains JSON data representing the new task. The **`jwt_token`** fixture is included in the request headers for authentication. After sending the request, the function asserts that the HTTP status code is 201, indicating successful creation. This will be used as a fixture for posterior steps.

- **`claim_task`**: The step uses the task ID from the **`create_task`** fixture and sends an **`HTTP PATCH`** request to an endpoint designed to claim tasks. The URL for this request is dynamically constructed using the task's ID. The request includes the **`jwt_token`** for authentication. The function asserts that the response status is 200, indicating the successful claiming of the task.
- list_tasks: this function verifies that the created task is listed as **`IN_PROGRESS`** (or **`IN_PROGRESS`**). It requests an HTTP GET to fetch a list of tasks, including the **`jwt_token`** for authentication. After confirming the request's success (status code 200), it processes the JSON response to find the relevant task. The function checks if any task in the list matches the ID of the created task and has the status **`IN_PROGRESS`**.

The plugin **`pytest-bdd`** has lots of features for making more interesting BDD tests. Covering all the features could be a chapter by itself. It is recommended to read pytest-bdd documentation https://pytest-bdd.readthedocs.io/en/stable/.

To scale BDD tests as an application grows, tests should be modularized for reusability and organized with a tagging system for efficiency. Utilizing continuous integration to run targeted tests on commits and adopting parallel execution strategies can reduce test times. Maintaining tests through regular refactoring and involving all team members in test scenario development ensures tests stay current and manageable.

Advanced pytest features: Parametrization, plugins, and configuration

The advanced features of pytest can significantly elevate your testing strategy. Parametrization enables one test function to cover numerous scenarios by running it with various inputs. Plugins expand pytest's functionality, allowing for tailored integrations and enhanced output, while flexible configurations fine-tune test behavior to fit your specific requirements. These features make pytest a powerful asset for crafting sophisticated and efficient test suites.

Parametrization

Up to this point, we just covered the basic features needed to write normal test cases. Pytest is a versatile testing library offering numerous features to facilitate the writing and maintenance of tests. Among these features, parametrization stands out. It allows you to run a single test function multiple times with different sets of arguments, enabling more efficient and comprehensive testing without writing multiple test cases for similar scenarios.

We wrote our first unit tests for the converters in a previous section. One can consolidate the four test cases into a singular one using parametrize.

```
import pytest

from datetime import datetime


@pytest.mark.parametrize(

    "method, input_value, expected_output, expected_exception",

    [

        pytest.param("to_python", "2023-10-05", datetime(2023, 10, 5),
        None, id="valid_to_python"),

        pytest.param("to_python", "2023/10/05", None, ValueError,
        id="invalid_format_to_python"),

        pytest.param("to_url", datetime(2023, 10, 5), "2023-10-05", None,
        id="valid_to_url"),

        pytest.param("to_url", "2023-10-05", None, AttributeError,
        id="invalid_object_to_url"),

    ]

)

def test_date_conversion(date_converter, method, input_value, expected_
output, expected_exception):

    if expected_exception is None:

        assert getattr(date_converter, method)(input_value) == expected_
        output

    else:

        with pytest.raises(expected_exception):
```

```
        getattr(date_converter, method)(input_value)
```

The parametrize feature consolidates our test into a single one, by using four distinct arguments; within it, the if block inspects whether **expected_exception** is None. When the value is None, the test asserts that the result of calling a method on the date_converter object with **input_value** should equal **expected_output**. The method (to_python or to_url) is dynamically determined using **getattr()**. If, however, **expected_exception** is not None, the test enters the else block. The test uses the **pytest.raises** context manager to assert that the specified **expected_exception** is raised when the method is called with **input_value**.

Using parametrize allows us to extend to more cases easily. With the previous structure, we need to write a new test case function with additional code to maintain.

Plugin coverage

Pytest has a plugin to measure the code coverage of your Python projects. The plugin can be installed using poetry:

```
poetry add --dev pytest-cov
```

Following the plugin installation, you may execute the tests with coverage by appending the **--cov** flag:

```
pytest --cov=tasks
```

Once the execution of the tests is done, it will return a console report with the coverage of each file in the project.

The tests introduced in the preceding section have yielded a coverage metric of 77%.

Plugin xdist

pytest-xdist is a popular plugin for pytest that introduces several powerful capabilities, most notably the ability to run tests in parallel. TRunning tests in parallel can lead to significantly reduced test execution time, which is especially beneficial for large test suites or when running tests frequently as part of a development workflow. However, in the context of cost-effective CI worker instances, this approach may not yield significant benefits due to their limited processing capabilities.

You can install **pytest-xdist** with poetry:

```
poetry add --dev pytest-xdist
```

You can now execute the test with four workers using the flag **-n**:

```
pytest -n 4
```

Given the modest scale of our present test suite, employing xdist might introduce initial overhead, potentially decelerating test execution. If test suites are larger, executing the tests could save some time. If your tests cannot be run in parallel, this is a code smell and you should investigate the root cause of this problem. Each test should be isolated and independent – tests should not depend on the order they are run and not modify each other's state.

Using marks

The pytest mark constitutes a feature permitting the annotation of tests with various markers. These marks can be used for many purposes, such as categorizing, skipping, and so on. Categorizing tests can be helpful since they allow you to execute a subset of the tests, not the entire suite. For example, you can mark the test as slow and then run the tests that are not marked as slow.

Commonly Used Marks

- `@pytest.mark.skip`: Unconditionally skips the marked test.
- `@pytest.mark.skipif`: Conditionally skips a test based on a particular condition.
- `@pytest.mark.xfail`: Marks a test as an expected failure.
- `@pytest.mark.parametrize`: Used for parametrizing tests, letting them run with different arguments.

Here is an example of the skip usage:

```
@pytest.mark.skip(reason="not implemented yet")

def test_example():

    pass
```

If you want to execute all the tests except the ones marked as slow, you can use the not operator:

```
pytest -m "not slow"
```

In configuration tips we will see how to configure markers in the pytest.ini.

Configuration tips

The pytest.ini file is where you can specify various settings and preferences for how pytest runs your tests. It allows you to customize and control many aspects of your testing environment.

In the previous section, we created this file and set up the **`DJANGO_SETTINGS_MODULE`**. We will see other valuable options to add to this configuration file.

To define custom **`markers`** in **pytest.ini**, you would add a [pytest] section and then list your markers under a markers key. A short description typically accompanies each marker.

```
markers =

   slow: marks tests as slow

     integration: mark a test as an integration test
```

`addopts` stands for "additional options". This setting lets you specify command-line arguments that should be automatically used every time you run pytest.

```
addopts = -ra -vv -s
```

The given example, **`addopts = -ra -vv -s`**, combines several command-line flags.

- **vv**: This is a level of verbosity. In pytest, verbosity levels are controlled by the number of vs included in the command.
- **r**: It specifies what extra test summary information is reported.
- **a**: Includes information about all tests except those that pass, like tests that fail, are skipped.
- **s**: allows you to see the output while the tests are running, which can be useful for debugging or when you want to see the output of print statements or other logging.

```
testpaths =

   tests
```

`testpaths` specify the directories (and subdirectories) that pytest will look in to find test files.

Conclusion

Testing is a fundamental process to maintain and guarantee a certain level of quality in your project. By having a good test suite, your project will be robust and the team who maintains it will be able to refactor its code with more safety.

Pytest is a great framework, and we have reviewed its main features for writing tests for a Django project. By adopting Test-Driven Development (TDD), you will proactively think about and design your code to fulfill its intended use effectively.

Unit tests and integration tests serve complementary roles in a comprehensive testing strategy. Unit tests are focused, fast, and independent, targeting individual components to ensure that each part of the codebase performs as expected. In contrast, integration tests verify the interactions between modules or external systems, ensuring that combined components work as expected.

BDD has shown its power that not only allows us to verify scenarios automatically, but also helps in the collaboration of non-technical team members.

In the next chapter, we will prepare our project for real production scenarios using docker and Kubernetes to deploy our application for the first time.

Questions

1. What is the primary goal of software testing?
2. Define Test-Driven Development (TDD).
3. Why might test coverage metrics not always reflect the quality of testing?
4. Describe a scenario in which TDD might not be the best approach.
5. Explain the different scopes available for pytest fixtures.
6. Why does Django create a separate database for testing?
7. What is the difference between **`db`** and **`db_transactional`** fixtures in pytest-django?
8. Describe the purpose of mocking in unit tests.
9. How can integration tests differ from unit tests in Django forms testing?
10. In BDD, what language is used to write feature files?
11. Describe linking a BDD scenario to step definitions in code.
12. What is the role of pytest marks, and how do you run tests that exclude

a particular mark?

Exercises

1. Using a coverage tool, create a test suite that achieves at least 80% coverage on the Fibonacci function and verify the coverage.
2. Use TDD to develop a new function that calculates the factorial of a number. Start by writing tests for the factorial function before implementing the function itself.
3. Implement a new test case called **`test_claim_with_expired_token`** where you simulate the claim operation with an expired JWT token. The expected result should be a status code of 401.
4. Write a new test case called **`test_claim_with_insufficient_permissions`** where a user with only the **`add_tasks permission`** (and **`not change_task`**) tries to claim a task. Assert that the status code is 403.
5. Improve the coverage of the tasks Django application by 90%.

Chapter 11

Deploying Django Applications with Gunicorn and Docker

Introduction

In this chapter, we will go into the process of deploying Django applications using modern tools and practices. Our journey begins with Gunicorn, a robust WSGI server, and continues through creating a Docker image and understanding of Kubernetes architecture, highlighting their roles in Django deployment. We then explore how to add instrumentation to our Django application, focusing on optimizing database interactions. This chapter guide will give you the knowledge to deploy Django applications effectively, ensuring high performance and scalability.

Structure

In this chapter, we will cover the following topics:

- Introduction to Gunicorn
- Configuring Gunicorn for Django Deployment
- Understanding and Creating Dockerfiles for Django
- Using the image registry
- Introduction to Kubernetes

- Configuring a Kubernetes cluster for a Django application
- Adding liveness and readiness probes
- Adding Instrumentation for Django
- Prometheus Configuration
- Jaeger Configuration
- Database Optimization: Queries and Indexing

Introduction to Gunicorn

Python Web Server Gateway Interface (WSGI) is a specification that describes how a web server communicates with Python web applications. The standard is described in PEP 3333 (https://peps.python.org/pep-3333/). Gunicorn is a WSGI HTTP server for UNIX systems. It is compatible with many web frameworks, like Django and Flask. Gunicorn is commonly used in production environments and is known for its efficiency and speed.

In terms of architecture, WSGI acts as an intermediary interface between the Django application and the web server.

Info: A reverse proxy is a type of server that sits in front of web servers and forwards client requests to those web servers. Reverse proxy protects servers by hiding their identities from clients. When a client requests, the reverse proxy is the **face** of the back-end servers.

The request originates from the client or browser and is sent to the web server. The web server forwards this request to the appropriate WSGI server and finally reaches the Django project. The response does the same, but in the backward direction.

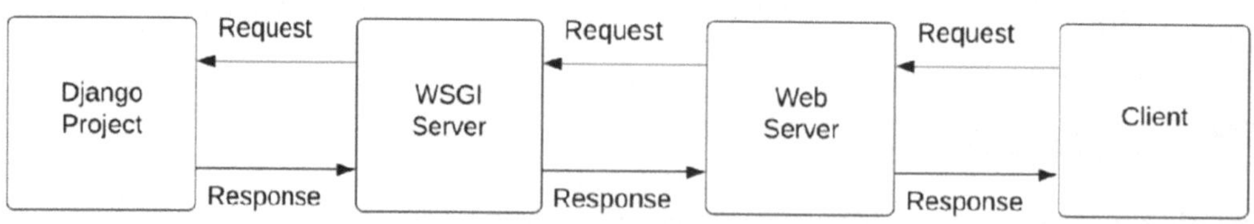

Figure 11.1: *How Gunicorn works*

Gunicorn forks multiple worker processes to handle requests. Each worker is a separate process with its own memory space and instance of the Python application. It supports synchronous workers based on traditional multi-threaded or multi-process web servers and asynchronous workers.

Configuring Gunicorn for Django Deployment

In this section, we will configure our Django project for using Gunicorn in production. Their configuration requires some changes in our settings to guarantee a safe environment and the installation of Gunicorn.

Our project's settings.py file, located in **taskmanager/settings.py**, contains development settings like `DEBUG = True`, which are not suitable for a production environment. We can use the environment variable `DJANGO_SETTINGS_MODULE` to specify which configuration to use in production. Using this environment variable, we will create a shared settings file called **taskmanager/base.py** and two more files **taskmanager/dev.py** and **taskmanager/production.py**.

Both dev.py and production.py will inherit shared configuration from base.py and the other two files will contain the corresponding values for each environment.

Rename the file from **taskmanager/settings.py** to **taskmanager/base.py**. Including the base.py in the book will be too extensive, you can check the **chapter_11 branch** to review its full content.

Now let's create the development **settings/dev.py** file with the following contents:

```
from .base import *  #noqa


DEBUG = True

ALLOWED_HOSTS = ["localhost", "127.0.0.1"]

SECRET_KEY = os.getenv("SECRET_KEY")

# Development-specific apps and middlewares

INSTALLED_APPS += [

    "debug_toolbar",

]

MIDDLEWARE += [

    "debug_toolbar.middleware.DebugToolbarMiddleware",

]
```

```
# Email backend for development

EMAIL_BACKEND = "django.core.mail.backends.console.EmailBackend:"
```

As you can see, we are adding configurations only related to the development environment that we do not want to have enabled in production. Let's review the **dev.py** settings:

- **DEBUG** is set to True. Having more verbosity when an error occurs is beneficial for the development environment. Using **DEBUG** will help troubleshoot problems while coding.
- **ALLOWED_HOSTS** is set to ['127.0.0.1', 'localhost'].
- **INSTALLED_APPS** The only Django application that we are using for development is the Django toolbar, which adds debug information about the execution of the request, including the queries to the database.
- **MIDDLEWARE** The only middleware we use for the development environment is the id toolbar middleware.
- **EMAIL_BACKEND** For the development environment, we set it up to the console printing. However, you can still use a server if you use Mailhog instead.

For production, we have the following settings in the **taskmanager/settings/production.py** file:

```
from .base import *


DEBUG = False

ALLOWED_HOSTS = os.getenv("ALLOWED_HOSTS", "localhost").split(",")

SECRET_KEY = os.getenv("SECRET_KEY")

# Email backend for production

EMAIL_BACKEND = "django.core.mail.backends.smtp.EmailBackend"

EMAIL_HOST = os.getenv("EMAIL_HOST", "mailhog")

EMAIL_PORT = int(os.getenv("EMAIL_PORT", "1025"))

EMAIL_USE_TLS = os.getenv("EMAIL_USE_TLS", "False") == "True"

EMAIL_HOST_USER = os.getenv("EMAIL_HOST_USER", "default@example.com")

EMAIL_HOST_PASSWORD = os.getenv("EMAIL_HOST_PASSWORD", "defaultpassword")
```

```
# Static files storage

# STATICFILES_STORAGE = 'your_production_static_files_storage'

# Media files storage

# DEFAULT_FILE_STORAGE = 'your_production_default_file_storage'


CACHES = {

    "default": {

        "BACKEND": "django_redis.cache.RedisCache",

        "LOCATION":  os.getenv("REDIS_LOCATION",
        "redis://127.0.0.1:6379/1"),

        "OPTIONS": {

            "CLIENT_CLASS": "django_redis.client.DefaultClient",

        },

    }

}
```

Let's review each of the settings:

- **DEBUG:** is set to False. These are the recommended settings for production. Having it enabled could lead to information leaks and a security incident.
- **ALLOWED_HOSTS:** This configuration ensures that Django will only allow requests sent to yourproductiondomain.com and reject requests to any other domain.
- **EMAIL_BACKEND:** The email backend uses the SMTP client, and it gets the information from environment variables.
- **STATICFILES_STORAGE** and **DEFAULT_FILE_STORAGE**: we will see in a later section how to configure a production environment using Amazon S3 buckets.

Since we made a refactoring, we must change all the references to **taskmanager.settings** to the new **taskmanager.dev** and **taskmanager.production**.

Open these files and change them accordingly:

- **manager.py**: Change the default value of **DJANGO_SETTINGS_MODULE** to **taskmanager.dev** in the line:

  - from **django.core.management** import **execute_from_command_line**
- **pytest.ini**: Change **DJANGO_SETTINGS_MODULE** to **taskmanager.dev**.
- **taskmanager/asgi.py**: Change the default value to **taskmanager.production** in the line:
  - **os.environ.setdefault("DJANGO_SETTINGS_MODULE", "taskmanager.settings")**
- **taskmanager/wsgi.py**: Change the default value to **taskmanager.production** in the line:
  - **os.environ.setdefault("DJANGO_SETTINGS_MODULE", "taskmanager.settings")**

Now, with our settings refactor, we are ready to install Gunicorn using poetry:

```
poetry add gunicorn
```

Before configuring Gunicorn for production, we need to test it with our project to ensure it works as expected:

```
export SECRET_KEY=test

gunicorn --workers 4 taskmanager.wsgi:application
```

By default, Gunicorn listen to port 8000, open on your browser the URL http://127.0.0.1:8000 and verify that the login page is shown. The **--workers** parameter specifies the number of worker processes to handle the requests.

Gunicorn can be configured by using a configuration file. Since we want to deploy the project to Kubernetes, we will extend this file with more settings. Let's start with some basic settings. Create a new file in the **taskmanager** directory at the same level as the **manager.py** file. Let's call it **gunicorn.conf.py**.

```
bind = "0.0.0.0:8000"

workers = 3

accesslog = "-"

errorlog = "-"
```

Binding to 0.0.0.0 means that Gunicorn can accept requests coming from any IP address that can reach the server. Running inside a Docker container on Kubernetes typically takes requests from any source.

The choice of 3 workers is a starting point. Determining the optimal number of workers depends on various factors, which will be discussed in the subsequent sections.

These settings configure where Gunicorn will write its access and error logs. The "-" setting tells Gunicorn to output the logs to **stdout** and **stderr**, respectively. These settings are typical because the Docker captures anything written to **stdout** and **stderr**.

Understanding and Creating Dockerfiles for Django

Containers are lightweight packages that contain everything needed to run a software application, including code, runtime, libraries and settings. Containers will run the software in a reproducible environment in different computing environments.

In *Chapter 2: Setting Up Your Development Environment*, we configured the docker to use it in a local environment. Now, we will use docker again, but for our production environment. To deploy our project into production, we will need a container image. To create a container image, we need to write a Dockerfile file. A Dockerfile contains instructions where most of them create a new layer, while others may only alter metadata. Docker images are made up of layers; each layer is read-only except for the last one.

Example of a Dockerfile with 5 instructions, resulting in 5 layers:

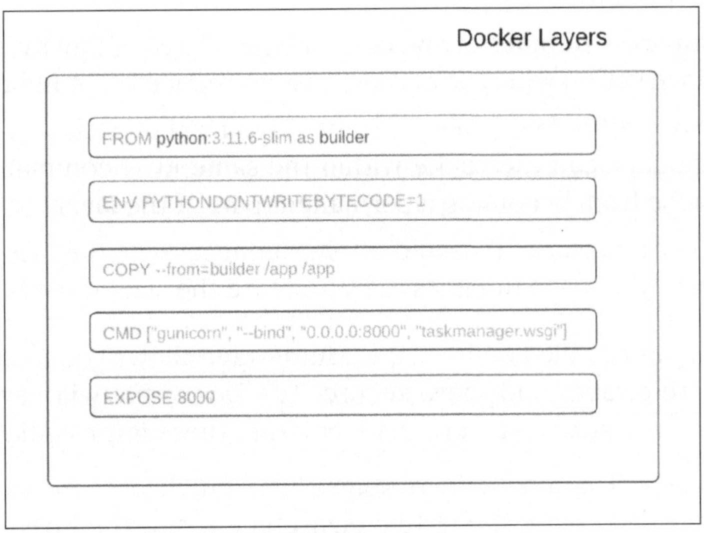

Figure 11.2: *Representation of Docker layers*

Here is a list of some useful Dockerfile instructions:

- `FROM`: Creates a base layer from an image.
- `ENV`: Sets an environment variable and creates a layer with this configuration.
- `RUN`: Executes commands and any files created during the process form a new layer.
- `COPY`: Copies files from the local file system into the container, creating a layer with these files.
- `WORKDIR`: Sets the current working directory for any subsequent Dockerfile instructions.
- `EXPOSE`: Informs Docker that the container listens to specific network ports at runtime.
- `CMD`: Provides the default command and arguments for an executing container.

Layers are stacked on top of each other. When you run a container, Docker takes all these read-only layers and adds a read-write layer. Any changes you make to the container file system, such as writing new files, modifying existing files, or deleting files, are made in this writable layer.

Info: Best Practices with Layers:

- **Minimize the number of layers**: Combine related commands into a single RUN instruction where it makes sense to reduce the number of layers.
- **Clean up within layers**: For example, if you install packages with apt-get, you should clean the cache within the same RUN command to prevent the cache from becoming a permanent part of the layer.
- **Use `.dockerignore`**: To avoid adding unnecessary files to your Docker context, which can unnecessarily increase the size of the built images.

Docker has a feature called multi-stage. Multi-stage allows you to create smaller images that are cleaner and more secure. The Dockerfile will have more than one stage and each stage can copy artifacts from these intermediate stages.

Our Dockerfile will comprise two stages: the build and the runtime stage. The build stage will create the virtual environment and the image will have all required dependencies. The build stage will also collect the static files.

The production stage will copy the virtual environment from the build stage and prepare the Gunicorn command.

Let's start with the build stage. At the root of the project directory, create a Dockerfile and populate it with the following content:

```
# --- Build Stage ---
FROM python:3.11.7-slim as builder

# Set environment variables
ENV PYTHONDONTWRITEBYTECODE=1 \
    PYTHONUNBUFFERED=1 \
    POETRY_VERSION=1.7.1 \
    POETRY_HOME="/opt/poetry" \
    PATH="$POETRY_HOME/bin:$PATH" \
    DJANGO_SETTINGS_MODULE=taskmanager.production

# Install Poetry - respects $POETRY_VERSION & $POETRY_HOME
RUN apt-get update \
    && apt-get install -y --no-install-recommends curl libpq-dev
RUN pip install "poetry==$POETRY_VERSION"

# Copy the project files into the builder stage
WORKDIR /app
COPY pyproject.toml poetry.lock* /app/

# Install project dependencies
RUN poetry config virtualenvs.create false \
    && poetry install --no-interaction --no-ansi --no-dev

# Copy the rest of the application's code
COPY taskmanager /app
```

```
# Collect static files

RUN poetry run python manage.py collectstatic --noinput
```

The Dockerfiles create a base layer from **python:3.11.7-slim**. We specify the minor version to make sure that building the image again will be more reproducible. The name of the stage is build.

Then, we set all the environment variables. We must note that we set all of them in one line, since having multiple lines will create multiple layers. Let's check what each environment variable does:

- **`PYTHONDONTWRITEBYTECODE=1`** tells Python to skip writing **.pyc** files, which are unnecessary in this context.
- **`PYTHONUNBUFFERED=1`** ensures that Python outputs are displayed in real-time, which is particularly useful for logging when running in containers.
- **`POETRY_VERSION=1.7.1`** specifies the exact version of Poetry to use, guaranteeing consistent builds.
- **`POETRY_HOME="/opt/poetry"`** designates a custom location for Poetry's installation.
- **`PATH="$POETRY_HOME/bin:$PATH"`** includes `$POETRY_HOME/bin` ensures that the shell and other programs can find the executables provided by Poetry without needing the full path.
- **`DJANGO_SETTINGS_MODULE=taskmanager.production`** sets the Django settings module to use, indicating that the container should run with the production settings of the Django application.

The subsequent two RUN commands employ apt-get to install essential dependencies needed for building and installing Python libraries. We include **libpq-dev**, since it is required for **`psycopg`**.

To install poetry, the second RUN command uses pip and the environment variable **`POETRY_VERSION`**.

With WORKDIR, we change the container's working directory to /app. we then copy the **pyproject.toml** and **poetry.lock**. Copying these two files will allow us to use poetry to install all the dependencies for production.

```
RUN poetry config virtualenvs.create false \

  && poetry install --no-interaction --no-ansi --no-dev
```

The command '**`poetry config virtualenvs.create false`**' is used for disabling **`virtualenv`** usage with poetry. We don't use **`virtualenv`** since the container already provides isolation. Following that poetry install, **`--no-interaction --no-ansi --no-dev`** installs the project's dependencies as defined in Poetry's lock file, doing so in a non-interactive mode that avoids the need for user input, without ANSI control characters for plain-text logs, and excluding development-specific dependencies to reduce the size and complexity of the production image.

Then we copy all the project source files with the instructions:

```
COPY taskmanager /app
```

The final instruction of the build stage is to collect static:

```
RUN poetry run python manage.py collectstatic --noinput
```

We use poetry run to make sure we use the poetry installed dependencies and no import error is raised due to missing dependencies.

If you opt to distribute the static files using a CDN, the collectstatic step is unnecessary and a different step should be followed.

Our build stage is ready. Our next step is to create the `Production` runtime stage. Just after the build stage, append the following instruction to the Dockerfile:

```
# --- Production Stage ---

# Define the base image for the production stage

FROM python:3.11.7-slim as production


# Copy virtual env and other necessary files from builder stage

# Copy installed packages and binaries from builder stage

COPY --from=builder /usr/local /usr/local

COPY --from=builder /app /app


# Set the working directory in the container

WORKDIR /app


# Set user to use when running the image

# UID 1000 is often the default user

RUN groupadd -r django && useradd --no-log-init -r -g django && \
```

```
    chown -R django:django /app

USER django


# Start Gunicorn with a configuration file

CMD ["gunicorn", "--bind", "0.0.0.0:8000", "taskmanager.wsgi"]


# Inform Docker that the container listens on the specified network ports
at runtime

EXPOSE 8000
```

The production stage creates a base layer from `python:3.11.7-slim`, the same as the build stage. Then we copy the virtual environment and the project source code:

```
COPY --from=builder /usr/local /usr/local
```

This **`COPY --from=builder /usr/local /usr/local`** command transfers files from the **/usr/local** directory of the builder stage to the same directory in the production stage.

The **/usr/local** directory in a Docker contains software and data that are installed locally from the source. In the Python ecosystem, when you install packages using poetry, they get installed into **/usr/local/lib/pythonX.X/site-packages/**, where X.X is the Python version number. When using `COPY --from=builder /usr/local /usr/local`, the intention is usually to copy Python packages installed in the builder stage.

```
COPY --from=builder /app /app

WORKDIR /app
```

These commands copy the project's source code into the **/app** directory and set **/app** as the working directory, where all our source code resides.

```
RUN groupadd -r django && useradd --no-log-init -r -g django && \

    chown -R django:django /app

USER django
```

The RUN command in the Dockerfile sets up a new system user and group named django, ensuring that the application runs with restricted permissions for enhanced security. It assigns this user ownership of the **/app** directory to maintain proper file permissions. The USER directive then switches the active user to Django so the container doesn't run processes as the root user, a recommended security practice. By not granting root access, the container is restricted from making certain changes to the host system, reducing the risk of privilege escalation attacks if the container were compromised.

```
# Start Gunicorn with a configuration file

CMD ["gunicorn", "--bind", "0.0.0.0:8000", "taskmanager.wsgi"]


# Inform Docker that the container listens on the specified network ports
at runtime

EXPOSE 8000
```

Finally, we have the command instruction that uses Gunicorn and then defines the container's listening port.

Using the image registry

A container registry allows you to store the container images with version control. Registries are also a way to distribute your container and a critical step in deploying a container application. When working with Kubernetes, the registry will be used to download the images in the deployment or the applications, as seen in the following section.

When working with a registry, docker provides commands to interact with it. You can download an image from the registry using the docker pull command.

```
docker pull ubuntu
```

There exist several container registries in the industry, and cloud providers usually offer a registry as a service. There exist public and private registries. The most popular public registry is docker hub, the default registry to pull images when using docker.

For uploading the image to the registry, docker provides the command push. Push will upload the image to the repository:

```
docker buildx create --use

docker buildx build --platform linux/amd64,linux/arm64 -t llazzaro/web_
applications_django:latest .

docker push llazzaro/web_applications_django:latest
```

For our example, since our GitHub repository is public, we will use the docker hub public repository to push and pull the image. However, for a production deployment, you must use a private repository. Exposing the docker image to the public will allow anyone to access your application code, which will be a security incident in most scenarios. Make sure your repository permissions are correctly configured.

Once our image has been uploaded to the registry, we can pull it with the docker command pull:

```
docker pull llazzaro/web_applications_django
```

Introduction to Kubernetes

A container orchestration system is software that automates the deployment, management, scaling and networking of containers. Kubernetes (K8s) is an open-source container orchestration system and is probably the most famous one. Kubernetes groups containers that make an application into logical units for easy management and discovery.

Before deploying our application to Kubernetes, we must cover some crucial components.

For deploying our application, it is not necessary to know how Kubernetes works internally. However, some knowledge will help us troubleshoot and understand how our application runs.

Cluster

The Kubernetes cluster is composed of nodes. All these nodes allow you to scale your application across different machines in terms of nodes. The cluster also has self-healing properties. When something fails, the scheduler will try to restart the failed container and reschedule it.

Node

Nodes are workers that run container applications. A node is a single machine in the Kubernetes cluster. This machine could be physical or virtual. There are two types of nodes: the master node and the worker node. The master node is responsible for scheduling and responding to cluster events. The other type of node is the worker node. These machines run your applications and are managed by the master node.

Each node has several components, but we just abstract everything as a node to keep it simple. The Kubernetes documentation (https://kubernetes.io/docs/home/) is an excellent source for learning more about node components.

Scheduler

The Kubernetes scheduler selects the most suitable node to run your application. The scheduler is a critical component and fundamental to workload management.

Pods

A pod is a set of one or more containers that share common resources like storage, network and a specification on how to run the containers. Kubernetes orchestrates containerized applications with a dynamic lifecycle, managing pods as non-permanent entities. Containers within a pod may be terminated by the scheduler to manage system resources, respond to application scaling directives, perform updates, or recover from failures.

While containers in Kubernetes can use local filesystems and memory, it's important for developers to recognize that such storage is ephemeral. Any data saved locally can be lost when the container is restarted or moved by the scheduler, therefore, for persistent storage, they should utilize Kubernetes volumes or external storage systems. While pods are commonly used for stateless services, they can also be part of stateful applications, particularly when managed through Kubernetes StatefulSet objects.

Deployments

Deployment is a way to specify to Kubernetes how to create or modify instances of the pods. Deployments are ideal for stateless applications and help roll out updates, roll back versions and scaling applications.

ReplicaSets

A ReplicaSet in Kubernetes is a mechanism that ensures a specific number of identical pod replicas are always running. It automatically replaces Pods that fail, get deleted or are terminated. ReplicaSets are crucial for ensuring high availability and resilience of applications.

Services

Services provide a persistent endpoint to access the pods distributed across one or more nodes. There are different types of services:

- **ClusterIP**: A **ClusterIP** service in Kubernetes provides a stable internal IP address for accessing a set of pods from within the cluster.
- **NodePort**: A **NodePort** service exposes a service on the same port of each selected node in the cluster, making it accessible from outside the cluster using **<NodeIP>:<NodePort>**.
- **LoadBalancer**: A **LoadBalancer** service in Kubernetes automatically integrates with the cloud provider's load balancer, allowing external traffic to be evenly distributed to the pods.

Configmaps and Secrets

A **ConfigMap** is a store for non-confidential data as key-value pairs. The store can be used to save configuration files, environment variables, and command line arguments.

Secrets is similar to **ConfigMap**, but it provides an extra layer of security, and its purpose is storing secrets.

Ingress

Ingress in Kubernetes is a key component for managing incoming traffic to services within a cluster. Acting as the entry point for external access, it routes external requests to the appropriate services. Ingress often includes capabilities like load balancing and SSL termination, effectively directing and securing communication with services inside the cluster.

StatefulSets

The pod component is ideal for stateless applications. However, some applications require persistent storage or stable network identifiers. Typically, this is used for databases or caching services. In this chapter, we will use **statefulsets**, but we recommend using managed services whenever possible. Most cloud providers offer managed database services that will reduce maintenance and management overhead. Managed services also provide robust security features and high reliability. Using **StatefulSet** is still possible, but your team or company must manage these essential and critical resources.

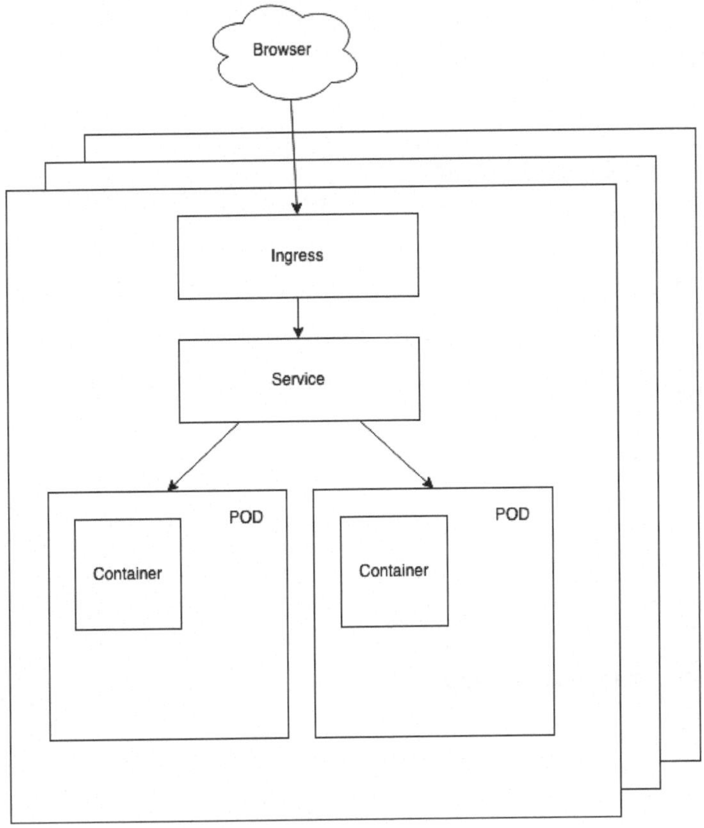

Figure 11.3: *Kubernetes Architecture Overview*

The Kubernetes architecture diagram represents the core components of a Kubernetes cluster. At the forefront is the Ingress, which acts as the entry point for external traffic, directing requests to the appropriate services. Service serves as an abstraction layer that efficiently manages access to the Pods. Pods are the smallest deployable units in Kubernetes. Each Pod encapsulates one or more containers, which are running instances of applications. This arrangement illustrates the flow from external access to internal process management.

Configuring a Kubernetes cluster for a Django application

The most basic Kubernetes configuration requires a deployment and a service. Let's start with a deployment, create a new file in the new directory k8s at the root of the repository, then create a new file in this directory with the name **deployment.yaml** and populate it with the following contents:

```
apiVersion: apps/v1
kind: Deployment
metadata:
  name: taskmanager-deployment
spec:
  replicas: 3
  selector:
    matchLabels:
      app: taskmanagerapp
  template:
   metadata:
     labels:
          app: taskmanagerapp
   spec:
     containers:
     - name: taskmanagerapp
          image: llazzaro/web_applications_django
          ports:
          - containerPort: 8000
```

Every Kubernetes configuration file needs to specify the API version. In this particular file, we defined it to use **app/v1**. The kind indicates the type of resource we will configure, which in this case is deployment.

We use the metadata field to set a unique name. As a convention, we use the postfix -deployment. Using this name will be helpful when troubleshooting problems.

The spec (specification) sections set the replicas to 3. The replicas allow Kubernetes to have three instances of the pod for the deployment. This is a way to have high availability and load distribution for our project.

Then we use the select to instruct Kubernetes which application the specification has to be applied, which is the **`taskmanagerapp`**.

Under the template, the spec for the containers within the Pods is defined. It specifies that each Pod should run a single container, named **`taskmanagerapp`** and that this container should use the Docker image **`llazzaro/web_applications_django`**.

In this configuration, we use **`llazzaro/web_applications_django`**, pulling the image from the **`dockerhub`** public registry. You must change this to point to the appropriate registry when using a private registry.

The ports section under the container spec exposes port 8000 of the container, suggesting that the Django application listens on this port for incoming HTTP traffic. In this case, our port was set to the same one our docker file exposes since it is the port where our Gunicorn is listening to serve the Django application.

Next, we create a new file for the service configuration in the k8s directory. Let's call it **services.yaml** and populate it with the following contents:

```
apiVersion: v1

kind: Service

metadata:

  name: taskmanagerapp-service

spec:

  type: NodePort

  selector:

    app: taskmanagerapp

  ports:

    - protocol: TCP

      port: 80

      targetPort: 8000
```

The file starts with an **`apiVersion`** set to v1 and metadata to form the unique name **`taskmanagerapp-service`** using the postfix **`-service`**. This name will be handy for identifying the resource in the Kubernetes cluster for troubleshooting.

This file creates a service using **NodePort**. The selector uses the same application name, **taskmanagerapp**, to apply this service specification. **NodePort** will expose the service on each cluster node's IP and use the static port 80 protocol TCP that HTTP uses. The **targetPort** settings indicated to which port in the Pod the service will forward the traffic.

With these two files, we are ready to try our first deployment. There are several ways to configure the Kubernetes cluster. We will use the official **kubectl** command.

Note: To install **Kubectl**, follow the official installation instructions on the Kubernetes website: https://kubernetes.io/docs/tasks/tools/.

Installing **kubectl** should be straightforward.

You can also have a local Kubernetes cluster using **Minikube** or the official docker.

We recommend following the official **Minikube** installation at the website: https://minikube.sigs.k8s.io/docs/start/

If you are willing to use official docker, you can follow these steps: https://www.docker.com/products/kubernetes/

Our first step will be to create a new kubernetes namespace. A Kubernetes namespace is a way to divide a cluster of resources between multiple applications logically.

```
kubectl create namespace taskmanager

>namespace/taskmanager created
```

To apply the deploy and service config to the cluster, we need to execute two commands:

```
kubectl apply -f k8s/deployment.yaml

deployment.apps/taskmanager-deployment created

kubectl apply -f k8s/services.yaml

service/taskmanagerapp-service created
```

To see the pods created by the deployment, let's execute the following command:

```
$ kubectl --namespace taskmanager get pods -l app=taskmanagerapp

NAME                                  READY   STATUS    RESTARTS   AGE
```

```
taskmanager-deployment-667bd87b6-gxv7c   1/1   Running   0          31s
taskmanager-deployment-667bd87b6-lsgch   1/1   Running   0          31s
taskmanager-deployment-667bd87b6-mgjs9   1/1   Running   0          31s
```

You can check the logs of each container with the command:

```
$ kubectl --namespace taskmanager logs taskmanager-deployment-667bd87b6-
gxv7c
[2023-11-14 18:46:38 +0000] [1] [INFO] Starting gunicorn 21.2.0
[2023-11-14 18:46:38 +0000] [1] [INFO] Listening at: http://0.0.0.0:8000
(1)
[2023-11-14 18:46:38 +0000] [1] [INFO] Using worker: sync
[2023-11-14 18:46:38 +0000] [7] [INFO] Booting worker with pid: 7
[2023-11-14 18:46:38 +0000] [8] [INFO] Booting worker with pid: 8
[2023-11-14 18:46:38 +0000] [9] [INFO] Booting worker with pid: 9
```

Now you can access your service using the node IP address and with the exposed service port. You can get the service port with the kubectl command:

```
$ kubectl get services --namespace taskmanager
NAME                    TYPE       CLUSTER-IP      EXTERNAL-IP   PORT(S)
AGE
taskmanagerapp-service   NodePort   10.107.151.88   <none>
80:30893/TCP   8m52s
```

In my environment, the node port is 30893, but Kubernetes can assign any number in the range of 30000-32767 by default. You can get the node IP address with the command:

```
kubectl get nodes -o wide
```

If you are using macOS and docker desktop, you can use localhost and the node port.

We still need to set the environment variables for a proper configuration of our Django application. In the same k8s directory, let's create a new file with **ConfigMaps** called **configs.yaml** with the following content:

```
apiVersion: v1
```

```
kind: ConfigMap
metadata:
  name: taskmanager-settings
data:
  DEBUG: "False"
  ALLOWED_HOSTS: "localhost"
  DB_NAME: "mydatabase"
  DB_USER: "postgres"
  DB_HOST: "postgres"
  DB_PORT: "5432"
```

In this configuration file, we define a `ConfigMap` with the same `taskmanager-settings`. In the data section, we set the values of the environment variables for our containers. `DEBUG` mode is set to **False,** which indicates a production environment. The `ALLOWED_HOSTS` is configured for `localhost`, in a natural production environment. This setting should be set to your domain. Database configurations such as `DB_NAME`, `DB_USER`, `DB_HOST`, and `DB_PORT` set the values to connect to a PostgreSQL database named `mydatabase` running on localhost with the default port `5432`.

Let's apply the ConfigMap to the cluster:

```
kubectl --namespace taskmanager apply -f k8s/configs.yaml
```

Using `statefulset` for a `Postgresql` database is a common approach to deploying an application that requires persistent storage and stable network identity. Using a `statefulset` for a production environment has several drawbacks and will increase your projects' maintenance costs. For practical reasons, we will use `statefulsets` in this chapter. However, always consider using managed cloud solutions.

The first step is to set up a persistence storage for PostgreSQL. We need to understand two concepts when setting up persistent volumes (PV).

- **PersistentVolume**: Storage in the cluster that has been provided by and administrator or dynamically provided using a storage class.
- **PersistentVolumeClaim**: this is a way to request the usage of the storage by a project. this is usually specified in the `statefulset` configuration file.

You don't have to manually create a persistent volume when using the docker desktop for Kubernetes. The storage class will automatically create a persistent volume that meets the requirements of the volume claim. If you use **`statefulsets`** in Kubernetes, you may need to request the persistent volume to your cluster administrator.

Let's create a new file in the k8s directory called **statefulset-postgresql.yaml** with the following contents:

```
apiVersion: apps/v1

kind: StatefulSet

metadata:

  name: postgres

spec:

  serviceName: "postgres"

  replicas: 1

  selector:

   matchLabels:

   app: postgres

  template:

   metadata:

   labels:

      app: postgres

   spec:

   containers:

      - name: postgres

        image: postgres:16

        ports:

          - containerPort: 5432

         env:
```

```
        - name: POSTGRES_DB
              valueFrom:
                configMapKeyRef:
               name: taskmanager-settings
               key: DB_NAME
        - name: POSTGRES_USER
              valueFrom:
                configMapKeyRef:
               name: taskmanager-settings
               key: DB_USER
        - name: POSTGRES_PASSWORD
              valueFrom:
                secretKeyRef:
               name: taskmanager-secrets
               key: DB_PASSWORD
        - name: PGDATA
              value: /var/lib/postgresql/data/pgdata
    volumeMounts:
        - name: postgres-storage
              mountPath: /var/lib/postgresql/data
volumeClaimTemplates:
  - metadata:
          name: postgres-storage
    spec:
          accessModes: ["ReadWriteOnce"]
          resources:
         requests:
```

```
          storage: 10Gi
```

The **`statefulset`** name is PostgreSQL and uses a single replica. The container uses the Postgresql image 16. Configuration of the environment variables is defined in the previous **`ConfigMap`**, and the **`POSTGRES_PASSWORD`** will be defined in the Kubernetes secret to ensure it is secured appropriately. A volume mount (**/var/lib/postgresql/data**) is defined for data persistence, which is linked to a PersistentVolumeClaim named postgres-storage. This claim requests 10Gi of storage and will be dynamically provisioned with the **`ReadWriteOnce`** access mode, indicating that a single node can mount the volume as read-write. The other PostgreSQL settings use the **`ConfigMap`** values from the **`taskmanager-settings`**.

Let's apply the new **`statefulset`** to the cluster:

```
kubectl --namespace taskmanager apply -f k8s/statefulset-postgresql.yaml
```

Verify its status with the get **`StatefulSet`** command of **`kubectl`**:

```
$ kubectl get statefulset --namespace taskmanager

NAME      READY   AGE

postgres   1/1   63s
```

We still need to set the **DB_PASSWORD**, **SECRET_KEY** and **JWT** secrets, since those are secret values we need to store them in the secrets API of Kubernetes.

The PostgreSQL **`StatefulSet`** requires a service:

```
apiVersion: v1

kind: Service

metadata:

  name: postgres

spec:

  type: ClusterIP

  ports:

  - port: 5432

    targetPort: 5432

    protocol: TCP

  selector:
```

```
  app: postgres
```

Apply the new config:

```
kubectl --namespace taskmanager apply -f k8s/statefulset-postgresql.yaml
```

The next step is to create the file with the secrets, but since this file will contain secrets in plain, we need to encrypt this file before committing it to the repository.

The sops (Secrets OPerations) is an open-source tool (https://github.com/getsops/sops) used to encrypt, decrypt, and edit sensitive data files. Sops support key management services like AWS Key Management Service (KMS), Google Cloud KMS, Azure Key Vault and PGP. Sops is format agnostic and it could be used for JSON, YAML and other types of files.

Info: you can install sops in macOS with brew:

```
brew install sops
```

in linux:

```
apt install sops
```

We are going to use sops with PGP, the first step after installing PGP is to generate a key:

```
gpg --full-generate-key
```

After generating your key, list your GnuPG keys to get your key ID.

```
gpg --list-secret-keys --keyid-format LONG
```

Save the **pgp-key-id** of the newly generated key since we are going to use it for encrypting the secrets file we are going to create in the k8s directory with the following contents a file named **secrets.yaml**:

```
apiVersion: v1

kind: Secret

metadata:

  name: taskmanager-secrets

type: Opaque

stringData:
```

```
  SECRET_KEY: "your-secret-key"

  DB_PASSWORD: "your-db-password"

  JWT_SECRET_KEY: "jwt_secret"

  JWT_SECRET_KEY: "jwt_refresh_secret"
```

This configuration file creates a secret with the name **taskmanager-secrets** with the secrets **SECRET_KEY**, **DB_PASSWORD**, **JWT_SECRET_KEY** and **JWT_SECRET_KEY**.

```
GPG_TTY=$(tty)

export GPG_TTY

sops --pgp <pgp-key-id> -e -i k8s/secrets.yaml
```

Sops will open a text editor with the decrypted contents. Once you quit the editor, it will encrypt the file if you try to open the file **k8s/secrets.yaml** directly with a text editor. You see that the values of the **DB_PASSWORD** and **SECRET_KEY** are encrypted.

Using sops will allow us to commit the file to the repository safely.

Info: When using sops, it is required to decrypt the file to apply it to the Kubernetes cluster. If the pgp secret is only owned by one team member, that could be a problem since it will be the only one with this power. When using a cloud key manager, you can share the key among team members or even with a CI/CD pipeline.

To apply the secrets to the cluster, we first need to decrypt it and apply the decrypted secrets. You can do it with the following command:

```
sops -d k8s/secrets.yaml | kubectl apply -f -
```

Having the **ConfigMaps** and Secrets is not enough to have the environment variables set in our containers, we need to change our **deployment.yaml** file to instruct this:

```
apiVersion: apps/v1

kind: Deployment

metadata:

  name: django-app-deployment

spec:
```

```
replicas: 1
...
template:
 ...
 spec:
   containers:
   - name: taskmanagerapp
       …
         envFrom:
           - configMapRef:
               name: taskmanager-settings
           - secretRef:
               name: taskmanager-secrets
```

With the new change in the deployment configuration file, we describe how to set the environment variables using a **ConfigMap** and secrets referenced by the name.

Re-apply the deployment configuration to the cluster:

```
kubectl apply -f k8s/deployment.yaml
```

Note: if you need to force a new deployment to refresh secrets or config, you can rollout restart the deployment with the command.

```
kubectl rollout restart deployment taskmanager-deployment
```

For troubleshooting is helpful to tail the logs of all the containers by application label, the command is:

```
kubectl get pods -l app=taskmanagerapp -o name | xargs -I {} kubectl logs
--tail=10 -f {}
```

Our application is almost ready to be used. However, we need a way to run the migrations. There are many alternatives to execute the migrations. We will opt to create a Kubernetes job that will use the **ConfigMaps** and secrets to perform the migration.

```
apiVersion: batch/v1
kind: Job
metadata:
  name: taskmanager-migrate
spec:
  template:
   spec:
     containers:
       - name: taskmanagerapp
           image: llazzaro/web_applications_django
           command: ["python", "manage.py", "migrate"]
           env:
           - name: DJANGO_SETTINGS_MODULE
           value: "taskmanager.production"
          envFrom:
         - configMapRef:
             name: taskmanager-settings
            - secretRef:
             name: taskmanager-secrets
    restartPolicy: Never
  backoffLimit: 4
```

This Kubernetes configuration file defines a job resource named **taskmanager-migrate**, which will execute database migrations for our project. It specifies a container named **taskmanagerapp** using the image **llazzaro/web_applications_django**. The primary command executed in this container is **python manage.py migrate**, which applies database migrations as defined in the Django project. The environment variable **DJANGO_SETTINGS_MODULE** is set to **taskmanager.production**, ensuring the correct Django settings are used. The **restartPolicy** is set to **Never**, indicating that the job should not be restarted automatically if it fails or completes. The **backoffLimit** is set to 4, which limits the number of retries for the job to four attempts in case of failure. This job resource effectively automates the process of database migration.

Now apply the new jobs configuration:

```
kubectl --namespace taskmanager apply -f k8s/jobs.yaml
```

Once the configuration is applied, Kubernetes will execute it and our database will be migrated.

You can check the status of the execution when getting the pods:

```
$ kubectl get po --namespace taskmanager

NAME                                     READY   STATUS      RESTARTS   AGE

postgres-0                               1/1     Running     0
4h33m

taskmanager-deployment-8569bd7646-nvhgg   1/1        Running      0
16m

taskmanager-migrate-hvm8t                0/1     Completed   0          17m
```

The status should be Completed. If you want to re-execute the migrations again, you will need to replace the current migration job with force:

```
kubectl replace --force -f k8s/jobs.yaml --namespace taskmanager
```

If you now browse to the **nodeIP:nodePort** you should see the login page.

If you want to create the superuser using the management command. We can create an interactive bash shell with the command:

```
kubectl exec -it taskmanager-deployment-8569bd7646-nvhgg --namespace taskmanager -- bash

django@taskmanager-deployment-8569bd7646-nvhgg:/app$ python manage.py createsuperuser
```

The last step to finish the cluster configuration is to deploy a redis service using 1Set. For this, we need to create the **StatefulSet** and the service.

Create a new configuration file in the k8s directory called **redis-statefulset.yaml** and populate it with the following configuration:

```
apiVersion: apps/v1
```

```
kind: StatefulSet
metadata:
  name: redis
spec:
  serviceName: "redis"
  replicas: 1
  selector:
   matchLabels:
   app: redis
  template:
   metadata:
     labels:
          app: redis
   spec:
     containers:
     - name: redis
          image: redis:7.0
          ports:
          - containerPort: 6379
          volumeMounts:
          - name: redis-data
            mountPath: /data
  volumeClaimTemplates:
  - metadata:
     name: redis-data
    spec:
   accessModes: ["ReadWriteOnce"]
```

```
  resources:
        requests:
          storage: 1Gi
```

This configuration file defines a **StatefulSet** named **redis**, which is used to deploy a Redis server within the cluster. The **StatefulSet** ensures stable and unique network identifiers and persistent storage for the Redis instance. It specifies a single replica, meaning one instance of the Redis server will be running.

The **selector** and **template** sections define the label **app: redis**, which is used to match the created pods with the StatefulSet. The **redis** container uses the image **redis:7.0** and opens port **6379**, the default port for Redis.

The **volumeMounts** section attaches a volume for persistent data storage to the **/data** directory inside the container, ensuring that Redis data persists across pod restarts.

The **volumeClaimTemplates** provide a template for creating a **PersistentVolumeClaim** named **redis-data**. This claim requests a storage volume of **1Gi** with **ReadWriteOnce** access mode, meaning the volume can be mounted as read-write by a single node. This volume is used by the Redis container to store data persistently.

We now have a single-node Redis instance in the Kubernetes cluster, with persistent storage to maintain data across restarts and deployments.

For the service to provide access to our **redis** instance, create a new file in **k8s/redis-service.yaml** with the following contents:

```
apiVersion: v1
kind: Service
metadata:
  name: redis
spec:
  type: ClusterIP
  ports:
   - port: 6379
    targetPort: 6379
```

```
  selector:
    app: redis
```

This configuration provides a stable network endpoint to access the Redis instance. It defines a **ClusterIP** service named **redis**.

The service exposes port **6379**, both as its port and targetPort. The selector with **app: redis** ensures this service routes network traffic to the correct pods, specifically those labeled as part of the Redis application.

By using a **ClusterIP** service, this configuration ensures that the Redis instance is consistently reachable at a known IP address within the cluster

We will need to update the **ConfigMap** to use the new **StatefulSet**, edit the file **k8s/configs.yaml** and add the new environment variable with the **redis** hostname:

```
REDIS_LOCATION: "redis://redis-0.redis.taskmanager.svc.cluster.local/1"
```

Apply the new configuration to the cluster:

```
kubectl --namespace taskmanager apply -f k8s/configs.yaml
kubectl --namespace taskmanager apply -f k8s/redis-service.yaml
kubectl --namespace taskmanager apply -f k8s/redis-statefulset.yaml
# rollout restart the taskmanager application
kubectl rollout restart deployment taskmanager-deployment --namespace taskmanager
```

If you want to test if the **redis** connection works, you can log in and create a new task or open an interactive shell to connect to **redis** using the **kubectl exec** command.

Adding liveness and readiness probes

Probes are a way for Kubernetes to understand when the container is ready to start accepting traffic (readiness) and when it needs to be restarted (liveness).

Liveness probes are used to determine if the application within a container is running. When the liveness probe fails, Kubernetes will kill the container and restart it according to the restart policy. Be careful with adding external dependency checks like Redis or a database check to the liveness probes. If these services are temporarily unavailable, Kubernetes will keep restarting your containers.

Readiness determines if the application within the container is ready to service requests. When the readiness probe fails, Kubernetes will not send traffic to the pod, but it doesn't restart it. Some applications could take some time to load and this could be a useful use case.

We will implement the probes in a new Django application called Health. In this application, we will add two views, one for liveness and the other for readiness.

Create the new app with the **startapp** management command:

```
python manage.py startapp health
```

Open the taskmanager/base.py and add the health application:

```
INSTALLED_APPS = [
    # ...
    "health",
    # ...
]
```

In **health/views.py**, implement your health check logic:

```
from django.core.cache import cache
from django.db import connections
from django.http import JsonResponse

def liveness(request):
    # Perform checks to determine if the app is alive
    return JsonResponse({"status": "alive"})

def readiness(request):
    try:
            # Check database connectivity
            connections["default"].cursor()

            # Check cache (e.g., Redis) connectivity
```

```
        cache.set("health_check", "ok", timeout=10)

        if cache.get("health_check") != "ok":

              raise ValueError("Failed to communicate with cache
              backend")


        return JsonResponse({"status": "healthy"}, status=200)

  except Exception as e:

        return JsonResponse({"status": "unhealthy", "error": str(e)},
        status=500)
```

The liveness probe returns a simple json, while the readiness check verifies database and cache (Redis) connectivity in this example. If any check fails, it returns an unhealthy status.

In **health/urls.py**:

```
from django.urls import path

from . import views


urlpatterns = [

   path("liveness/", views.liveness_check, name="liveness_check"),

   path("readiness/", views.readiness_check, name="readiness_check"),

]
```

In the projects **taskmanager/urls.py** add the health application URLs:

```
...

urlpatterns = [

   ...

   path("health/", include("health.urls")),

      ...

]
```

Finally, we need to update our **k8s/deployment.yaml** to configure Kubernetes to use the new probes:

```
apiVersion: apps/v1
kind: Deployment
...
spec:
  ...
  template:
   ...
   spec:
   containers:
   - name: your-app-container
      ...
      readinessProbe:
         httpGet:
              path: /health/readiness/
              port: 8000
              httpHeaders:
              - name: Host
                value: "localhost"
         initialDelaySeconds: 10
         periodSeconds: 5
      livenessProbe:
         httpGet:
              path: /health/liveness
              port: 8000
              httpHeaders:
              - name: Host
                value: "localhost"
```

```
        initialDelaySeconds: 15

        periodSeconds: 10
```

In this configuration, both the readiness and liveness probes are set up to use the /health/readiness and /health/liveness endpoint accordingly. The **`initialDelaySeconds`** and **`periodSeconds`** are configurable based on how quickly your application starts and how often you want to check its health. We set the Host headers to localhost or any other host in the **`ALLOWED_HOSTS`**. Otherwise, django will reject the request and the probe will fail.

The implementation of these endpoints must be correctly done. If you implement a liveness probe that checks for readiness, it could produce unwanted restarts. The configuration of the probes is also necessary. A high frequency and low timeout could restart the containers prematurely, not allowing the application to recover. You can shoot yourself in the foot with the wrong configuration or probes that don't check what they should do.

Adding Instrumentation for Django

Instrumentation enhances a system with monitoring and observability capabilities. Instrumentation involves the collection of metrics, logs and traces. With all the collected data, instrumentation provides insights into our system and helps us understand the performance and behavior of the system.

There are different ways to do instrumentation:

- **Code**: You can embed code in your application, such as logging or metrics collections.
- **Library**: Use libraries or frameworks that automatically collect data, such as request counts, response times, error rates and more.
- **Agent-Based**: You can have an agent running along with the application that collects metrics and traces without changing the application.

In system observability, there are two pivotal concepts: metrics and traces.

Metrics are numerical representations of data measures over intervals of time. These data allow system administrators to monitor trends, detect anomalies and make informed decisions about resource allocation and performance optimization.

On the other hand, traces contain detailed information about a single request from our system until its culmination. Traces will provide information about system interactions and invaluable information when diagnosing problems.

OpenTelemetry is an open-source observability framework. The framework offers APIs and libraries to collect distributed traces and metrics from your system. We will follow the library approach by using open telemetry to enable instrumentation in our Django project.

For monitoring and alerts, we will use the open-source solution Prometheus. Prometheus provides collects and stores metrics as time series data. The project also provides a powerful query language called PromQL that allows the user to select and aggregate data from the collected metrics. Prometheus primarily uses a pull model for metrics collection. It scrapes metrics from configured endpoints at regular intervals.

Info: Prometheus is a monitoring system and time series database. It is used to record the metrics and provides a way to query the data. Prometheus has an alerting feature that can be triggered based on the collected data. We will use Prometheus to collect Django metrics.

As a tracing system, we will use Jaeger, another open-source solution. Jaeger provides real-time visualization and monitoring and it is designed for high scalability and supports cloud-native environments like Kubernetes.

Here is an overview of how our observability will be in our Kubernetes deployment.

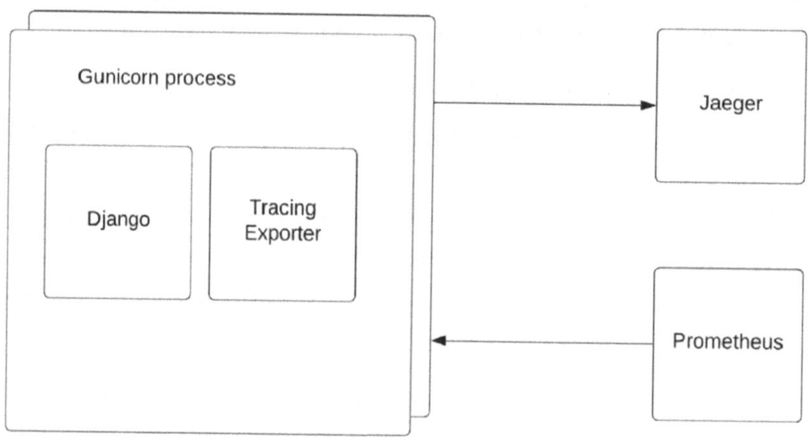

Figure 11.4: *Overview of observability architecture*

Prometheus configuration

For connecting our Django project to Prometheus, we need to expose the metrics of our application via a URL that Prometheus will scrape periodically. A third-party application exists that will extend our project with a new metrics endpoint. Django-Prometheus (https://github.com/korfuri/django-prometheus) exports the metrics of the ORM and caching, besides requests and response metrics.

Let's install **django-prometheus**:

```
poetry add  django-prometheus
```

Once added, we need to change our setting **taskmanager/base.py** to add Django Prometheus to the **INSTALLED_APPS** and then add two **middlewares**:

```
INSTALLED_APPS = [

   ...

   'django_prometheus',

   ...

]
```

Make sure to add the **PrometheusBeforeMiddleware** as the first element and the **PrometheusAfterMiddleware** as the last element of the **MIDDLEWARE**. All other middlewares should go in the middle.

```
MIDDLEWARE = [

    'django_prometheus.middleware.PrometheusBeforeMiddleware',

    ...

    'django_prometheus.middleware.PrometheusAfterMiddleware',

]
```

Next, add to the taskmanager/urls.py the prometheus urls:

```
urlpatterns = [

    ...

    path('', include('django_prometheus.urls')),

]
```

You can now browse to http://localhost:8000/metrics and verify that **django-prometheus** was properly configured.

PROMETHEUS_LATENCY_BUCKETS is a configuration setting where you define the buckets for a latency histogram. Selecting different bucket ranges affects the granularity, and thus, the precision of observed latency measurements.

While Prometheus histograms do not directly calculate percentiles, the bucket configuration indirectly impacts how you can estimate percentiles. Each bucket in a Prometheus histogram accumulates the count of events that fall into its range. By examining these counts, you can estimate your data's distribution and approximate percentiles.

Info: Percentiles are a statistical measure used to understand data distribution in a dataset. They are instrumental in performance monitoring.

Percentiles are often used to analyze response times, latency, or other metrics. For example, the 95th percentile of response times might be used to understand the upper limits of user experience on a web application.

Percentiles help in understanding the distribution of data.

Since we are deploying our application to a Kubernetes cluster, we need to install Prometheus and configure it to scrape our task manager service. Helm is a package manager for Kubernetes. Helm simplifies the process of installing complex Kubernetes applications.

You can download Helm from the official GitHub repository https://github.com/helm/helm/releases.

First, add the Prometheus community chart repository to Helm:

```
helm repo add prometheus-community https://prometheus-community.github.io/helm-charts

helm repo update
```

Prometheus can now be installed using Helm:

```
helm install prometheus prometheus-community/prometheus --namespace taskmanager
```

Verify that the Prometheus pods are running with the command:

```
kubectl get po --namespace taskmanager

NAME                                                   READY   STATUS
RESTARTS        AGE

…

prometheus-alertmanager-0                              1/1       Running
1 (8m27s ago)   133m
```

```
prometheus-kube-state-metrics-6b464f5b88-lghfj          1/1          Running
2 (7m12s ago)   133m

prometheus-prometheus-node-exporter-zv6vv               1/1          Running
1 (8m26s ago)  133m

prometheus-prometheus-pushgateway-7857c44f49-cg9js   1/1     Running     1
(8m27s ago)   133m

prometheus-server-8ffdb69d-t7bsr                        2/2          Running
2 (8m26s ago)   133m
```

Next, we must configure Prometheus to scrape metrics from our Task Manager project, to do this we need to change the **k8s/services.yaml** file and add some annotations.

```
apiVersion: v1

kind: Service

metadata:

  name: taskmanagerapp-service

  annotations:

    prometheus.io/scrape: 'true'

    prometheus.io/path: '/metrics'

    prometheus.io/port: '8000'

spec:

  …
```

Re-apply the settings to the cluster:

```
kubectl apply -f k8s/services.yaml --namespace taskmanager
```

Now Prometheus will have the `taskmanager` service as a target. Prometheus will start to scrape the metrics endpoint using the cluster IP.

In a Kubernetes cluster, our service could have any IP address and it could change on resource allocation. To solve the `ALLOWED_HOSTS` issue for IP addresses, we can install a third-party application that allows us to allow by CIDR (Classless Inter-Domain Routing), which extends the functionality of `ALLOWED_HOSTS` but for ip addresses.

The project is called **`django-allow-cidr`** (https://github.com/mozmeao/django-allow-cidr). It can be installed with poetry:

```
poetry add django-allow-cidr
```

Open the taskmanager/base.py and add the new middleware:

```
MIDDLEWARE = (
    'allow_cidr.middleware.AllowCIDRMiddleware',
    ...
)
```

Once installed, open the **taskmanager/production.py** and append the new configuration:

```
...
ALLOWED_CIDR_NETS = ['10.1.0.0/16']
```

This new setting will allow requests using the IP address in the range 10.1.0.1 to 10.1.255.255.

You can open Prometheus UI using port-forward:

```
kubectl port-forward service/prometheus-server 8001:80 --namespace taskmanager
```

Openwithyourbrowserhttp://localhost:8001/targets?search=taskmanagerapp-service and verify that the **`taskmanager`** is listed with state UP (green). You can also open the logs of the **`taskmanager`** pod and search for a request to the metrics endpoint.

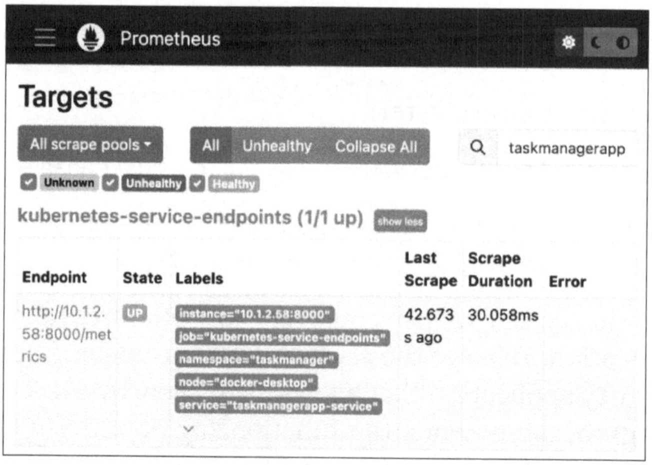

Figure 11.5: *Prometheus Targets showing task manager status*

Jaeger configuration

The OpenTelemetry Protocol (OTLP) is a part of the **`OpenTelemetry`** project. The protocol is designed to standardize the collection and reporting of telemetry data for cloud-native software. Starting version v1.35, Jaeger supports OTLP in the collector, so our integration with Jaeger will be easier since it will not require a specific open-telemetry collector. We can now use the native one.

We need to install an open-telemetry library to add instrumentation to our project.

```
poetry add opentelemetry-sdk opentelemetry-instrumentation-django
opentelemetry-exporter-otlp opentelemetry-api
```

We just installed the following libraries:

- opentelemetry-instrumentation-django (https://github.com/open-telemetry/opentelemetry-python-contrib/tree/main) The official OpenTelemetry instrumentation for Python module for Django. This library provides automatic instrumentation for Django applications.
- opentelemetry-sdk and opentelemetry-api (https://github.com/open-telemetry/opentelemetry-python) the API provides the interfaces and structures for telemetry, the SDK provides the actual implementation for how traces and metrics are collected, processed, and managed.
- opentelemetry-exporter-otlp (https://github.com/open-telemetry/opentelemetry-python) The OpenTelemetry Protocol (OTLP) exporter. Exporters in OpenTelemetry transmit collected telemetry data to backend analytics tools.

Create a new file **taskmanager/tracing.py** and populate the file with the following contents:

```
import os

from opentelemetry import trace

from opentelemetry.instrumentation.django import DjangoInstrumentor

from opentelemetry.sdk.resources import Resource

from opentelemetry.sdk.trace import TracerProvider

from opentelemetry.sdk.trace.export import BatchSpanProcessor

from opentelemetry.exporter.otlp.proto.grpc.trace_exporter import
```

```
OTLPSpanExporter


def init_tracing():
    jaeger_host = os.getenv('JAEGER_AGENT_HOST', 'localhost')
    jaeger_port = int(os.getenv('JAEGER_AGENT_PORT', '4317'))
    jaeger_insecure = os.getenv('JAEGER_INSECURE', False)
    service_name = os.getenv('SERVICE_NAME', 'taskmanager')

    resource = Resource(attributes={
    "service.name": service_name
    })

    trace.set_tracer_provider(TracerProvider(resource=resource))

    otlp_exporter = OTLPSpanExporter(endpoint=f"http://{jaeger_
    host}:{jaeger_port}", insecure=jaeger_insecure)

    span_processor = BatchSpanProcessor(otlp_exporter)

    trace.get_tracer_provider().add_span_processor(span_processor)

    DjangoInstrumentor().instrument()
```

Since our Django application uses Gunicorn in production, we will use a post-fork to send the metrics to Jaeger. When Gunicorn starts, it forks multiple worker processes from a master process to handle the incoming requests. The post-fork phase refers to the system's actions after forking the process. Using post-fork will add tracing to each work process separately and the post-fork phase is used to initialize resources specific to the worker.

Open the file **Gunicorn.conf.py** and add the `post-fork` at the end of the file:

```
def post_fork(server, worker):

    from taskmanager.tracing import init_tracing

    init_tracing()
```

Our Django project is ready to export telemetry to a Jaeger collector using OTLP. We need to install Jaeger in our cluster. Since we are using a local Kubernetes cluster, we will deploy Jaeger all-in-one using an in-memory database. Usually, you will want to install Jaeger with persistent storage like `ElasticSearch` or Cassandra in production, but for our local Kubernetes cluster, we will opt for in-memory storage.

We will use the all-in-one collector since it has the OTLP collector, but in a production environment, it will be more efficient to have a collector that only accepts OTLP. The all-in-one accepts all supported formats.

To install Jaeger, we will use the helm again:

```
helm install jaeger-in-memory jaegertracing/jaeger \

  --set provisionDataStore.cassandra=false \

  --set provisionDataStore.elasticsearch=false \

  --set storage.type=memory \

  --set storage.memory.maxTraces=100000 \

--set allInOne.enabled=true
```

Finally, we need to set the environment variables for our Django containers:

```
apiVersion: apps/v1

kind: Deployment

metadata:

  name: taskmanager-deployment


spec:

  replicas: 1

  selector:
```

```
    matchLabels:
      app: taskmanagerapp
  template:
    …
        env:
        - name: JAEGER_AGENT_HOST
          value: "jaeger-in-memory-collector.taskmanager.svc.cluster.local"
        - name: JAEGER_AGENT_PORT
          value: "4317"
        - name: JAEGER_INSECURE
          value: "True"
```

We are using the hostname of the Jaeger collector. The hostname is composed of first the name of a collector service, which in this case is jaeger-in-memory-collector, followed by the namespace and finally with svc to indicate that the resource is a service and the last part is the default domain name for Kubernetes clusters.

JAEGER_AGENT_PORT is set to the **grpc port 4317** and we are using an insecure connection since we never deployed certificates in our local cluster. For a production environment, it is recommended to use a secure connection. This chapter focuses on configuring the components to send traces to Jaeger.

Apply the new configuration changes to the cluster:

```
kubectl apply -f k8s/deployment.yaml --namespace taskmanager
```

kubectl rollout restart deployment taskmanager-deployment

It is possible to open Jaeger UI by doing a port-forward:

```
kubectl port-forward service/jaeger-in-memory-query 16686:16686
```

You can open the `http://localhost:16686` to see the Jaeger UI:

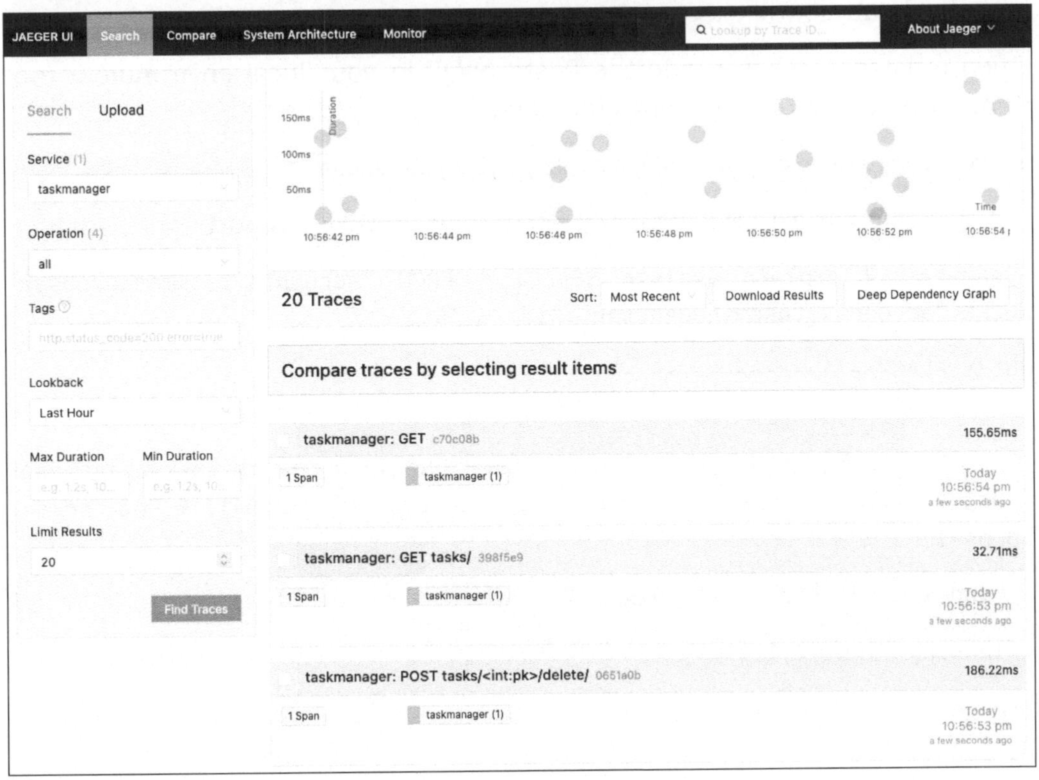

Figure 11.6: *Jaeger showing tracing information*

Database Optimization: Queries and Indexing

As we have seen before, scaling the Django application is easy with kubernetes since we can increase the replicas in our Kubernetes configuration and the cluster will create more pods that can handle more traffic. When you are in this situation where your cluster is scaling with multiple pods, sooner or later, you will hit too much of the database and it will become your bottleneck.

Databases are very fast, and they have a very complex architecture behind them that is very extensive to explain, but I highly recommend studying them.

That said, you will find that your project has slow queries. After all the instrumentation is added, you can find a slow endpoint and with the tracking information, you can find the slow-performing queries.

PostgreSQL has a statement `explain analyze`, which will generate a report on how the database will execute your query.

Open a database shell inside the PostgreSQL in your local environment (not Kubernetes), with the following command:

```
docker-compose exec -u postgres db psql mydatabase
```

Now you can use `explain analyze` to see the PostgreSQL report:

```
mydatabase=# explain analyze SELECT * FROM "accounts_taskmanageruser"
WHERE "accounts_taskmanageruser"."id" = '5';

QUERY PLAN-----------------------------------------------------------
---------

 Index Scan using accounts_taskmanageruser_pkey on accounts_taskmanageruser
(cost=0.14..8.16 rows=1 width=1977) (actual time=0.041..0.046 rows=1
loops=1)

   Index Cond: (id = '5'::bigint)

 Planning Time: 2.128 ms

 Execution Time: 0.244 ms

(4 rows)
```

In the **`EXPLAIN ANALYZE`** output from a SQL query, we observe a detailed breakdown of the query's execution plan. The process utilizes an Index Scan on the **`accounts_taskmanageruser`** table, explicitly leveraging the **`accounts_taskmanageruser_pkey`** primary key index, indicating an efficient search strategy based on indexed columns.

The example is the scratching surface of the vast knowledge required for query optimization. However, knowing this tool could help you improve the performance of queries.

When analyzing the results of an **`EXPLAIN ANALYZE`**, there are several key aspects to consider for understanding and optimizing query performance:

- **Scan Type**: Look at whether the query uses a Sequential Scan (scanning the entire table) or an Index Scan/Index Only Scan (using an index to find rows). Index Scans are generally faster, especially for large tables.
- **Cost Estimates**: The cost values (like cost=0.14..8.16) are estimates of the query's execution cost, given in arbitrary units. The first number is the

startup cost before the first row is returned, and the second is the total cost to return all rows.

- **Rows and Width**: The estimated number of rows (rows=) and the average row width (width=) are crucial. Significant discrepancies between estimated and actual row counts can indicate that the database's statistics must be updated, leading to suboptimal query plans.

It's important to understand that adding indexes is not always the solution to performance improvement. You need to understand your application usage. Is your application read-intensive? or is it write-intensive?

Adding indexes to a database can significantly speed up read operations, especially for large datasets, as they allow the database to locate data without scanning the entire table. However, excessive indexing can be counterproductive in write-intensive applications, where data is frequently inserted, updated, or deleted.

Every time a record is inserted, updated, or deleted, all indexes on that table need to be updated accordingly. This update in the index data structure can substantially increase the time it takes to write data, as each index update involves additional disk I/O operations and processing.

Index maintenance requires additional CPU and memory resources. In a write-intensive environment, this can increase strain on the database server, potentially impacting overall system performance.

Although indexes significantly optimize read queries, they introduce compromises in environments with heavy write operations. The challenge lies in striking a balance by creating indexes that substantially enhance critical read operations without disproportionately affecting write performance.

Conclusion

Throughout this chapter, we have navigated the complexities of deploying Django applications in a production environment. By employing Gunicorn, Docker, and Kubernetes, we have demonstrated how to create robust, scalable, and efficient deployments. Our discussion on database optimization and static file management has further emphasized the importance of performance tuning in web applications. You are now better prepared to tackle the challenges of deploying Django applications, ensuring they are well-optimized, secure, and ready to scale according to the demands of modern web traffic.

Questions

1. Explain the concept of a Kubernetes Pod.
2. How does Gunicorn interact with Django applications?
3. Explain the difference between **`StatefulSets`** and Deployments in Kubernetes.
4. How does instrumentation aid in Django application deployment?
5. Discuss the trade-offs of using indexes in database optimization for Django.
6. Analyze the benefits and limitations of using Redis as a caching and session store in a Django application deployed on Kubernetes.

CHAPTER 12

Final Thoughts and Future Directions

Introduction

This chapter summarizes our journey and guides your ongoing exploration and growth within the Django universe. We'll revisit important learnings from building a Task Management App, evaluate the Django ecosystem, and explore additional tools and libraries that complement Django's capabilities. Further, we'll explore the potential enhancements for our Task Management App, discuss staying updated with Django through resources and communities, explore Django's career opportunities, contemplate Django's future, and provide tips for continuous learning and improvement. This chapter will consolidate your understanding and inspire you to further your Django expertise.

Structure

In this chapter, we will cover the following topics:

- Summary of learnings: Building a task management app
- Evaluating the Django ecosystem: Strengths and weaknesses
- Exploring additional Django tools and libraries
- Potential enhancements for the task management app

- Staying updated with Django: Resources and communities
- Career opportunities with Django skills
- Thoughts on Django's future: Upcoming features and trends
- Tips for continued learning and improvement

Summary of learnings: Building a task management app

This book guides us from starting the task management project from scratch to deploying it to a Kubernetes cluster. We began by building an appropriate development environment that helped us make a homogeneous development environment when working in a team. We then configured the initial skeleton for our project and learned important architecture patterns like MVT that are important to understand when working with Django.

By developing the models, we laid the foundation of our project. Every Django project orbits around a model. We also learned the importance of having a service layer representing a proper interface between different Django applications. The service layer will promote loose coupling and high cohesion, which opens the path to future easy changes.

We also learned how to deal with essential framework features, like URL patterns, the template engine, and the forms. With this toolset, you will have a robust set of features that will help you tackle most of the problems you will face while building web applications.

Once we added authentication to our task management project, we started to have an actual web application with the possibility of using groups and permissions. Thanks to the great community of Django, the project can be easily extended to use OAuth using libraries like **`django-auth`** (https://github.com/pennersr/django-allauth).

Building an API using the API first approach is necessary to understand and following it will save you time and frustration. The API first approach lets you quickly iterate without writing or changing code.

Opting for Django Ninja over Django Rest Framework (https://github.com/encode/django-rest-framework) enabled us to develop a modern API, utilizing burgeoning libraries like Pydantic, known for their superior serialization capabilities.

The famous framework for testing pytest shows that it integrates perfectly with Django, providing an excellent development experience when writing tests. TDD is a process that will help you think about using your classes and functions instead of going directly to the code and writing complex code.

Understanding the distinctions between various types of tests is crucial. Using BDD will help you improve the quality of your project and your team's communication since writing the scenarios is a team activity and should be discussed to ensure they are what you need to build.

Finally, we learn how to build docker images following best practices and how to use those images to deploy them into a Kubernetes cluster that allows us to scale the application. We also learned how to add instrumentation to our application to have better insights into the behavior of the application and use traces to troubleshoot production issues. We also briefly covered improving slow queries by following specific database queries.

Evaluating the Django ecosystem: Strengths and weaknesses

Django proves it has become the top choice framework when building web applications. It facilitates rapid development, provides a secure environment, and offers scalability.

It's important to acknowledge that it has a steep learning curve for someone without experience with any technology, since it requires learning several concepts that could be hard to master all at once. The framework also has some limitations in handling asynchronous requests.

Still, there are some debates on using a service layer or not. Some people are more pragmatic and prefer not to have a service layer. However, when the project needs to grow and the number of developers in the development team exceeds a certain threshold, not having a service layer could create a big ball of mud.

Exploring additional Django tools and libraries

In this book, we tried to cover the most important and most used Django tools and libraries. However, there is a vast number of great libraries that we could not cover.

Django Channels is a project that takes Django and extends its abilities beyond HTTP - to handle WebSockets, chat protocols, IoT protocols, and more.

- **Django Haystack**: Modular search for Django, offering a way to add search functionality with multiple backends like Solr, Elasticsearch, and so on.
- **Django Filter**: A reusable application for Django that provides a simple way to filter down a query set based on user-supplied parameters.
- **Django Storages**: A collection of custom storage backends for Django, supporting services like Amazon S3, Google Cloud Storage, and more.
- **Django Anymail**: Integrates Django with transactional email services like Mailgun, SendGrid, Amazon SES, and so on for handling email sending.

We also never covered how to work with background workers, which is a significant problem to solve in many web applications. Celery is an open-source, distributed task queue system in Python, designed to handle asynchronous tasks and scheduling by efficiently distributing work across threads or machines. Celery with frameworks like Django allows for scalable, efficient task management, essential for maintaining a seamless user experience.

Potential enhancements for the task management app

Our task management application is in its baby steps. There are several enhancements that we can add to the project.

Regarding our Kubernetes deployment, we didn't cover deploying the static files over a CDN. For applications with high traffic, this is a must for serving the static files. It will improve your application performance and save costs since your backend will not need to serve the files.

We added excellent instrumentation to our project. However, we didn't cover any monitoring tools like Grafana or Kibana, which can be used with Kubernetes for log monitoring and analysis, providing insights into the application's behavior and performance.

Implementing Two-Factor Authentication (2FA) in web applications significantly enhances security by requiring users to provide two distinct forms of identification before granting access. In addition to securing user accounts, 2FA delivers an added layer of trust and safety for the entire system, making it a critical feature for applications handling sensitive data or requiring elevated security measures.

Building a Continuous Integration and Continuous Deployment (CI/CD) pipeline is a transformative process that automates the stages of software development, from code integration to deployment. In a CI/CD pipeline, developers frequently merge their code changes into a central repository, where automated builds and tests are run. This continuous integration helps identify and fix integration issues early, maintaining a high code quality.

Staying updated with Django: Resources and communities

Keeping pace with technological advancements takes time and effort. Even today, you can easily get lost and follow the wrong trend with the Internet.

The most critical resource for Django is the official GitHub repo and checking the change log of the alpha or beta versions. Clone and install a Django development version to try and test the new features. If you have enough courage, you can report or fix a bug.

Following Django developers on X (previously Twitter) is important since you will get the latest information:

https://twitter.com/djangoproject

https://twitter.com/loic84

https://twitter.com/MariuszFelisiak

https://twitter.com/simonw

https://twitter.com/carltongibson

https://twitter.com/evildmp

The Twitter links are just some of the people to follow, but there are many more to follow related to Python and Django.

The Reddit community (https://www.reddit.com/r/django/) could be a place to discover new libraries.

And, of course, reading books!

Career opportunities with Django skills

Django is one of the most popular web frameworks for Python. Many companies are using it and its demand is growing strong. Finding a Django developer with several years of experience is also problematic. Finding specific candidates is hard, so learning Django will improve your probability of getting a well-paid job.

Python has also become a programming language in high demand. Learning Django will also make you learn Python; thus, this is a win-win scenario. If you don't get a job because of Django, most likely, you will get it to know Python. It is also vital that you not only focus on the framework features, but also on architecture patterns that will help teams to scale to an unknown size.

Thoughts on Django's future: Upcoming features and trends

Django's future is moving towards more seamless integrations with front-end frameworks, enhanced asynchronous support, and more profound AI and machine learning integration. Django is increasingly adopting asynchronous features, drawing inspiration from frameworks like FastAPI. This shift allows Django to handle a large number of simultaneous connections, making it more suitable for real-time web applications, such as chat applications or live notifications. These developments will probably shape Django's role in the web development landscape, keeping it relevant and influential in the face of evolving technological trends. With the recent release of Django 5.0, many projects will need to migrate over the following years to utilize the latest features and improvements offered by this primary version of Django.

Tips for continued learning and improvement

In the ever-evolving world of technology, continuous learning is critical. For Django developers, this means mastering the framework and adapting to new tools and practices. Building personal projects, contributing to open-source Django projects, and staying engaged with the community are effective ways to continue growing and staying relevant in the field.

Conclusion

As we conclude this book, we reflect on Django's rich and diverse landscape. We navigated the practicalities of building a Task Management App, explored Django's strengths and weaknesses, and discussed various tools and libraries that enhance Django's functionality. We also pondered the potential future developments in Django, keeping an eye on upcoming trends and features. The journey with Django continues. The field of web development is dynamic, and Django, with its robust community and consistent updates, remains a relevant and powerful framework. I encourage you to continue learning, experimenting, and growing. Contribute to open-source projects, stay connected with the community, and keep yourself updated with the latest in Django. Remember, the learning journey is continuous, and each step you take further enriches your skills and understanding. Django is not just a framework; it's a gateway to a world of opportunities in web development. Let's keep exploring, keep learning, and keep building.

Index

Symbols